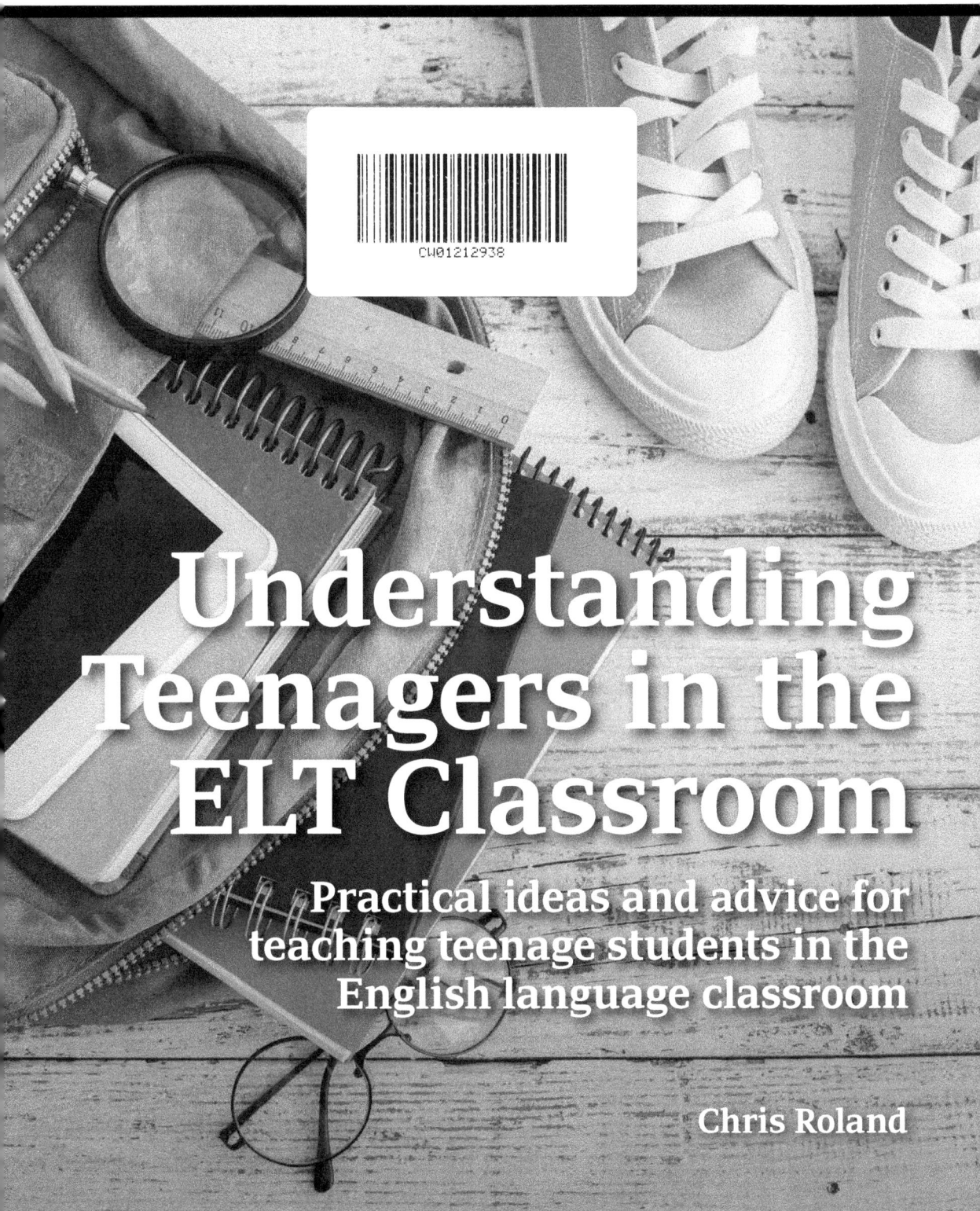

Teaching English

Understanding Teenagers in the ELT Classroom

Practical ideas and advice for teaching teenage students in the English language classroom

Chris Roland

Understanding Teenagers in the ELT Classroom

© Chris Roland

The author has asserted his rights in accordance with the Copyright, Designs and Patents Act (1988) to be identified as the author of this work.

Published by:
Pavilion Publishing and Media Ltd
Rayford House
School Road
Hove, East Sussex
BN3 5HX

Tel: 01273 434 943
Fax: 01273 227 308
Email: info@pavpub.com

First published 2018.

All rights reserved. No part of this publication may be reproduced, stored in a retrieval system, or transmitted in any form or by any means, electronic, mechanical, photocopying, recording or otherwise, without prior permission in writing of the publisher and the copyright owners.

A catalogue record for this book is available from the British Library.

Print: 978-1-912755-00-4
PDF: 978-1-912755-01-1
Epub: 978-1-912755-10-3
Mobi: 978-1-912755-11-0

Pavilion is the leading training and development provider and publisher in the health, social care and allied fields, providing a range of innovative training solutions underpinned by sound research and professional values. We aim to put our customers first, through excellent customer service and value.

Author: Chris Roland
Production editor: Mike Benge, Pavilion Publishing and Media Ltd
Cover design: Emma Dawe, Pavilion Publishing and Media Ltd
Page layout and typesetting: Phil Morash, Pavilion Publishing and Media Ltd
Printer: CPI Anthony Rowe

Understanding Teenagers in the ELT Classroom

Also available from English Teaching professional at Pavilion Publishing and Media

Become an Online English Teacher	ISBN 978-1-910366-77-6
Teaching English One to One	ISBN 978-1-898789-12-3
Teaching English with Drama	ISBN 978-1-898789-11-6
Teaching Grammar: From Rules to Reasons	ISBN 978-1-911028-22-2
Teaching English: Best Practices for Blended Learning	ISBN 978-1-911028-84-0
A Practical Introduction to Teacher Training in ELT	ISBN 978-1-910366-99-8
ETpedia	ISBN 978-1-910366-13-4
ETpedia Business English	ISBN 978-1-911028-20-8
ETpedia Young Learners	ISBN 978-1-911028-21-5
ETpedia Materials Writing	ISBN 978-1-911028-62-8
ETpedia Technology	ISBN 978-1-911028-58-1

For full details of all our books, *English Teaching professional* and *Modern English Teacher* magazines, go to: www.pavpub.com/english-language/

visit: **www.etprofessional.com**
www.modernenglishteacher.com

Contents

About the author 6
Introduction 7
1. A closer look at classes, teachers and students 17
2. Planning lessons with teenagers 29
3. Classroom micromechanics 39
4. Task design and instructions 55
5. Group dynamics and order 67
6. Affect: speaking positively to our students with care 77
7. Logistical questions: homework, L1 and seating 91
8. Tidy learning, messy learning and simple clutter 101
9. Autonomy and student-fronted classes 113
10. Teenagers and technology 123
11. Differentiation 133
12. Repetition, assimilation, memorisation 145
13. Remembering irregular verbs 157
14. Movement and space 167
15. Getting them talking 179
16. Listening and reading 193
17. Grammar and writing 203
18. Using video clips in the classroom 217
19. Personalisation 229
20. Testing, exams and report writing 241
21. Techniques for teaching low-level teens 255
22. Awareness and reasoning with teenagers 265
23. Control of the class 275
24. Classroom management strategies 287
Why teach teens? 301

About the author

Chris is a teacher, trainer and 'ideas man', well-known for his lively but practical sessions on the international conference circuit. He has taught in both the private academy sector and mainstream education system in Spain as well as holding posts with the British Council in Damascus and Barcelona. He works with teachers across a wide range of contexts. These include in-house training for ELI, the language school where he is based in Seville; intensive courses on methodology; tutoring on Trinity Certificate and Diploma courses for Active Language, Cádiz and Oxford TEFL, Barcelona and as a trainer of state school teachers in both Catalonia and previously in Aleppo. He is a regular speaker at events organised by TESOL Spain, has a close working relationship with APPI, the association for teachers of English in Portugal, and has contributed many articles to *English Teaching professional* magazine.

Introduction

My first ever class with teenagers took place in a language academy in a small village in Andalusia. I had decided that the best way to start the year off with my 15 and 16 year olds would be to make the opening lesson as fun and dynamic as possible. To this end, I settled on drama as it had served me well in my short teaching career with adults up to that point. There was a copy of a book called *Off Stage!* (Case & Wilson, 1979) in the teachers' room which contained sketches for students to act out and had really taken my fancy. So, armed with a short piece about somebody trying to follow yoga instructions from a cassette, I went into class, introduced myself and explained to my new students what I wanted them to do.

> *"In this play, there are two actors, so you work in pairs. One of you is going to be the voice on the cassette. The other is going to be a person learning to do yoga. You listen to the cassette and try to follow its instructions by doing the moves that it tells you to do."*

> *"Do we have to pretend to do yoga?"*

> *"Yes, you start off on the floor… cross legged I think…no, er… just sit normally on the floor."*

> *"Both of us?"*

> *"No, just the partner playing the role of the person but you'll swap roles after so you both get a go at doing the yoga."*

I handed out the scripts, put them in pairs and waited.

Nobody moved.

"Come on then," I said cheerfully.

Nothing.

The realisation hit me hard. They were refusing to do it. It had not occurred to me that this was even possible. The international adult classes I taught back in Nottingham had never refused to do anything. My universe became just a little bit brighter, a little more vivid but also a little fuzzier round the edges. The moment had come alive but was imbued with a sense of slightly giddying uncertainty. It felt as if everything was to play for and that the class going well or the class going badly hung in the balance (a characteristic of all the teens classes I have taught since and my first important lesson).

"You do it," said a blond short-haired lad.

"Yeah," his friend, a dark short-haired lad, backed him up.

Sensing an opportunity, I entered into negotiations with them.

"If I do it, will you do it afterwards?"

"Yes."

So I did it. I acted out the yoga practitioner's role on the floor in front of 12 Spanish teenagers. They watched keenly and even gave me a round of applause at the end.

"Now it's your turn."

Nobody moved. I thought the two boys had been speaking on behalf of the whole group. I was wrong (another useful lesson).

"Why don't we just read it to each other from our chairs?" asked one of the girls.

A number of internal dialogues ran at loggerheads to each other through my mind. Do I go full psycho on them or do I just give in? Is drama under extreme coercion going to be the fun way to start the year that I'd envisaged? No, it isn't, Christopher (said the voice closest to reason). Just give in.

"Yeah… okay. Read it to each other from your chairs."

That is what they did – apart from the above-mentioned boys who made good on their word and performed the moves to the sketch as well. Those boys are now in their 30s – older than I was then. I saw one of them recently at a local fete held in the very same village and we had a laugh about the class and about that whole year, which went quite well in the end (they even asked for some more sketches by the end of the year!). For me, it was the start of my journey teaching teens, which seems to have flown by and to be flying by still; sometimes highly frustrating, sometimes highly rewarding, nearly always intense and very seldom dull. It has given me hundreds more stories, some of which I wish to share with you in the pages that follow. In these pages, I would like to offer what I feel to be the most valuable insights I have gained over the last two decades. I am working on the premise that, try as we might, we all make mistakes every day but that we can learn from those mistakes. I have not included all my mistakes – as there would not be room – just the lessons learned.

Many of the manuals and articles I have read on how to teach teens consist of bullet-pointed advice reeled out in the imperative. While that kind of information has its place, I am not so interested in telling you *how* to do the job. I want to talk to you *about* doing it, and to explore the underlying principles and factors which might make or break an activity or a lesson. That is the sort of discussion that I feel truly widens teachers' repertoires. It is the sort of discussion that will be of value when you are sitting at home thinking over why one of your classes is not going the way that you want or when you have seen a really good teaching idea at a conference but are wondering how to make it work in your own class with your own students.

Who the book is for

This book is for anyone and everyone who has the job of teaching English to teenagers, including those older students who might be classed as young adults, and pre-teens, who actually might still be 11 or 12. I currently teach classes of a dozen or so but I have taught larger classes of 30 in a regular school and all the ideas discussed here will apply there too.

This book is also for teacher trainers (present and future), be they working at a local in-house level, regional or national levels, and for teachers wishing to make advances in their own professional development either by undertaking small scale classroom research or pursuing formal teaching qualifications.

Those professionals involved in a supporting role to teachers such as directors of study, materials writers or publishers – people who were perhaps teachers before but who are starting to feel their time away from the classroom – might also find the book a useful reminder of some of the more important considerations for teaching this age group.

If you are preparing to teach teenagers but have not done so yet, I hope that the depth of context provided by way of anecdotes and explanation will be helpful. Ultimately, it is the reader's own experience that any writer's words need to resonate with, and as that experience grows, as you experience the issues in your own classes in real time, so will the level of resonance. It might then be worth revisiting certain chapters once you have been actively teaching for some time. For now, I am assuming that the reader is familiar with basic concepts and ELT terminology such as "pairwork", "gap-fills" and "concept-checking questions". If not, there are some excellent general manuals for new and pre-service teachers available (for example Scrivener (2005) or Harmer (2007)).

How the book is organised

In putting this book together, I have chosen areas in which teachers have most often asked for guidance (in in-house training settings) and ones that teachers have fed back on as being most useful (from my workshops on the international conference circuit).

Each chapter follows the same pattern:

- The first part begins with a **Discussion** of a certain facet of teaching teens. Here I will identify key issues and tease out conflicting factors that may pull us in different directions in the classroom. To do so, I shall outline situations I have experienced in my own teaching and also draw upon writers and trainers who have played a role in my own development. As nothing happens in a vacuum, especially not teaching, I shall also draw on a number of related disciplines such as psychology, philosophy, anthropology and even primatology.

- In the second part of each chapter, **Practical applications**, the discussion will take a more practical turn and I will outline some classroom applications and techniques.

- Each chapter will then end with three summary sections. The **Questions for reflection** box may serve as summary to the chapter or as prompts for exchanging ideas where the chapter is being used in a training setting. By way of example, such a section based upon my opening anecdote might read:

- A number of resources are available for download at www.pavpub.com/understanding-teenagers-resources/. You will be directed by the text when appropriate to access these.

Questions for reflection
- What assumptions did Chris make about his teenage class on their first day?
- How might he have encouraged his students to participate more fully in the sketch?
- Would you be able to do a theatre type sketch with your students? Why or why not?
- Did Chris' students need to get down on the floor to benefit from the activity?
- What value do you think theatre might have in class?

The **Things to try** list gives practical suggestions about next steps to take and the **Things to share** section is meant to help orientate anyone wishing to undertake a small classroom project and report back to colleagues via a workshop, or simply wishing to run a discussion group. My rationale here is that the people who can help teachers the most are other teachers, and that the ultimate value in knowing something is sharing it.

Finally, I have provided a **References** section at the end of each chapter if you wish to follow up on any of the concepts referred to. You will notice I have regularly referenced myself. This is not out of vanity, I promise, but by way of appreciation for the numerous magazines, small publications and associations that have helped bring my work to the teaching profession up to now.

References
Case D & Wilson K (1979) *Off Stage!* London: Heinemann.

Harmer J (2007) *The Practice of English Language Teaching*. Essex: Pearson.

Scrivener J (2005) *Learning Teaching*. Oxford: Macmillan.

Acknowledgements

This is a book about teaching teenagers and I am a teacher of teenagers. That means I make mistakes and I need support on a daily, weekly and monthly basis. I would like to thank my current centre director, Jude McGovern, for providing that support. The ideas that follow are very much grounded in my core teaching practice and her patience and cooperation make that activity so much easier.

I would also like to thank the institution where I teach, English Language Institute (ELI) in Seville, for their flexibility with respect to dates and work schedules, and for their general encouragement when it comes to getting me to ELT events. Their helpful attitude and co-operation, especially that of Elspeth Pollock, Catt Boardman, Bridget Buckley and Richard Johnson, has allowed me to enjoy a continued presence on the conference circuit and to deliver training courses in an ever-widening sphere.

Finally, at ELI, I would like to thank Caroline Miles for giving me my first crack at teaching teenagers, all those years ago.

Thanks also to Sue Cleveland and Lesley Denham at the British Council Barcelona for the help I received from them during my time there – both in terms of backing my own professional development on courses and for putting me together with regional and national teaching associations in Spain and Portugal.

In the world of ELT, doors seldom open by themselves. In this respect I would particularly like to thank Paul Seligson and Hugh Dellar – between them they have very kindly put me in touch with numerous event organisers and associations in recent years, leading to the opportunity to speak at new venues and to visit new countries.

Similarly I would like to thank Ceri Jones and Daniel Barber for so often thinking of me with when it comes to new projects such as materials writing and online work.

I would like to thank Simon Pearlman and Danielle Jones for inviting me to form part of their team of Trinity Certificate trainers and to Nicola Meldrum for having me on board as a Trinity Diploma tutor.

Thanks also to Robin Walker and Ronnie Lendrum for introducing me to the world of residential immersion teaching, with a focus on CLIL and collaborative learning. Robin's sage and grounding advice in recent years has also been appreciated.

In terms of my own development, I have been lucky to have had some great tutors and would like to thank Adrian Tennant for providing inspiration on my CELTA course. My DELTA tutors, David Clark, Neil Forest, Vicki Anderson and Gerard McLoughlin at IH Barcelona were fantastic, and Julian Edge, course tutor on the distance MA in TESOL at Manchester University, was the person who most helped me become aware of the small moves and options open to us as writers when describing our practice – though I have never met the man in person!

I would like to thank Mark Levy at the British Council in Spain for the two-day course he ran on classroom management all the way back in 2001. Seeing the topic treated in such depth there, I believe, set me off on the path that ultimately led to the title you are holding.

Special thanks to Alberto Gaspar, Manuela Pinto, Sónia Ferreirinha, Nídia Cunha, Isabel Brites, Rómulo Neves and everybody else on the APPI team for inviting me over to Portugal various times a year, year after year, and looking after me so well while providing such a wonderful platform to share many of the ideas found here, with live audiences.

Helena Gomm, editor of *English Teaching professional* magazine, played a key role in this book happening. For the last ten years she has provided a forum for my ideas by accepting articles for the magazine and last year at the ETP Live! event in Brighton put me in touch with Emma Grisewood at Pavilion Publishing. Thank you to Helena, Emma and to Danny Norrington-Davis for inspiring me to propose the project.

Thank you also to Mike Benge, Ruth Chalmers and Karen Cameron for making the editorial process of my first book such a pleasant one.

Finally, I'm indebted to my parents in law, Rosario Villalobos González and the late Marcos Gorosito for welcoming me into their family and for their endless help and support.

Dedication

I would like to dedicate this book to three very important people in my life:

Raquel Lía Gorosito Villalobos. You have seen this work grow from its beginnings and have always encouraged me. The thousands of conversations we have had, spanning two decades, have left me a smarter, more human, human being.

Susan and George Roland. The unfaltering love I have received from you every day from the very first breath I took has been like a rock. It means I never have, nor ever will, feel truly alone. Thanks Mum. Thanks Dad.

Key tenets for teaching teens

You will notice a number of underlying principles repeated throughout the course of this book. To give you an idea of what is to come, here are the basic principles I try to follow:

1. Have my own rationale for each and every class activity clear and certain in my head.
2. Be willing and able to explain this to students.
3. Allow each student to do as much as possible, as often as possible.
4. Provide a sense of consequence to each classroom activity.
5. Include one-to-one student-teacher interaction, even in busy classes.
6. Embed articulations of positive regard into my spoken exchanges with students.
7. When it comes to (mis)behaviour, state even the obvious.
8. Address classroom management issues at the start of lessons.
9. Be constant, cheerful and a little bit annoying with my recycling of vocabulary and verbs.
10. When a student is seriously stuck, just tell them the answers.
11. Provide students with an escape valve for their restlessness and feeling trapped.
12. Try to leave students' sense of dignity intact.
13. Exploit students' L1 productively and fearlessly.
14. Allow student movement, self-expression and personality into my classes.
15. Emphasise the positive value of errors, corrections and rewrites or re-recordings.
16. Use exams and testing as the springboard for further learning.
17. Give misbehaving students a way out – space and opportunity to make better decisions.
18. Do my most effective classroom management work between lessons.
19. Make full use of my institution, director and supporting admin staff.
20. Take the time to enjoy my students' progress in English.

1. A closer look at classes, teachers and students

Discussion

What teenage classes are like

I hope you will agree that the aim of your life is not to get to the end as quickly as possible. I hope you will agree that we are on this planet to live. Similarly, the aim of teaching a class of teens is not simply to get to the end. The aim of teaching a class of teens is to do it well and to enjoy that class.

Many lesson plan templates and pro formas have boxes for teachers to fill in the aims of the lesson they are about to teach – target language, intended procedures, interaction patterns, stages and timings. Something I would like to see on every lesson plan and on every observation form, be it at pre-service, in-house or diploma level, is an additional box with the question: *"What do you think you are going to enjoy about the class you are about to teach?"* This question helps put the teacher back in the room and the 'you' back into the teacher.

Nonetheless, the experience of being in a room with teenagers can be intense. Teenagers are not monsters. They are simply young people between the ages of 13 and 19. Nonetheless there are significant differences between teaching this age range and teaching primary or adult classes. The sensation I referred to in the introduction that everything is riding on the outcome of *this* moment, from moment to moment and in every moment, never really goes away. Everything might be going well and, suddenly, it is not. There is an ever-present tension between what you want to get pushed through, in teaching terms, and what you will manage. Throughout this book you will encounter sets of tensions – opposing forces and conflicting factors. Teaching teens is all about balancing these tensions to find a workable position. Identifying them, acknowledging them and appreciating them is the aim of the chapters that follow.

Being questioned

A prominent characteristic of teenage classes – one I have come to even appreciate over the years – is that whatever you are doing might suddenly be called into question. At any time in class a student might ask you: *"Teacher, why are we doing this? What's it for? What's the point of it?"*

Having an answer and being able to couch it in terms, concepts and language that your teenagers can understand is a massive addition to your teacher toolkit. For example:

An intermediate class of teenagers have read a text explaining how various household objects were invented. They have then each chosen one of the objects and copied ten keywords onto a Post-it note. Using the Post-it note alone they are now trying to retell how their chosen object was invented to a partner.

> Student: *"Teacher, why do we have to repeat our presentation to another partner?"*
>
> Teacher: *"How many times have you done it?"*
>
> Student: *"Two times, teacher."*
>
> Teacher: *"Twice. Which was easier?"*
>
> Student: *"The second time."*
>
> Teacher: *"And you looked at your Post-it less the second time?"*
>
> Student: *"Yes."*
>
> Teacher: *"Okay, so that means the words are going from the paper, into your head, which is where we want them. So you walk out of this classroom with English words in your head. That is a good use of your time here, yes?"*
>
> Student: *"Yes."*
>
> Teacher: *"But this time when you practise it, see if you can look at the Post-it just two or three or four times. Then tell me how many."*
>
> Student: *"Okay."*

Here the teacher has not used terms like *target language*, *reconstruction*, *assimilation*, *automatisation*, or *memorisation* but the concepts are still underpinning their explanation.

What you want to achieve with your teens will *regularly* be questioned. One very important aim of teacher training is for the teacher to be able to provide credible answers. On a training course, those articulations are addressed to the trainer in the rationale sections of plans as well as pre- or post-observation discussion. In our day-to-day teaching, it is our students we must win over. If you can reach the point where a teenage group understands the reasoning behind the activity types they complete, where they have actually taken on board those language learning principles and share some of their teacher's conviction for them, then you are setting yourself up for an extremely rewarding term or year. To this end, Barber and Foord (2014) suggests stopping a class over the first few lessons and for each new activity asking them: *"Why are we doing this?"*

Teacher mindset

Your classes happen in your head. You are the one that makes sense of what goes on in each of those 60 or 90 minute sessions – at least for yourself. The conceptual structures you arrive with and how you mentally frame developments in the room will ultimately determine whether or not you walk away feeling the lesson was an overall success.

Event versus learning

One conceptual distinction to make here is between thinking about the class as an event on the one hand, and thinking about the learning that is going on in the class on the other. The class as an event involves how we manage a group of youngsters on a practical and logistical level for a determined period of time in a determined physical setting. It is how we maintain order, promote positive attitudes and encourage participation. It is how we arrange seating, organise groups and distribute our attention. It is also how we may have to control noise and fend off objections, complaints or requests to play games rather than covering course material. It is everything to do with the physical and social dynamics of bringing together and supervising our teenagers till the lesson is over.

Most of your stress and anxiety probably comes from thinking about the class as an event. The class as an event, however, is secondary. It exists solely to serve the learning that is going on. When we start thinking about our classes in terms of the latter, a lot of apprehension simply melts away as we shift focus.

The learning experience is how we help our students take on core vocabulary. It involves creating opportunities for repetition and pointing out that the same word that came up in our teacher anecdote appears in the course book. It involves helping students with verb forms and tenses. Can they write them? Can they say them? Can they use them? Are they still trying to pronounce the *gh* in *bought* and *caught*, for example? It involves the teacher checking to see if students have grasped from a sentence in a text – *"She was taught to cook by her sister"* – who it was that actually did the teaching. It involves replaying key stretches of speech on audios so that students can hear and understand why the answers to listening comprehension questions are what they are. It involves learners knowing the difference between 'colleague' and 'college' and 'custom' and 'costume' in terms of pronunciation and meaning. It involves them being able to speak by themselves about themselves for long enough to be able to convey something of substance, and to be able to say what they want, when they want.

Being drawn to extremes

We all try to pay attention to our students, to see them as best we can and to understand them, but what draws our attention most can vary from day-to-day, class-to-class and moment-to-moment in our teaching career.

Please imagine you have given your teenage class an exercise. At a given point in time it is most probable that there are:

a. One or two students on task, doing exactly what you asked and doing it well.

b. A majority that are reasonably focused and performing to the best of their abilities.

c. Some students who have yet to start or who have started then stopped and need a nudge.

d. One or two students who are not on task at all and may even be distracting others.

It is the final category that we tend to notice first, which may give us the impression that a class is going badly when only a few individuals are not co-operating. The next category we tend to notice is the first one, which might prompt us to try to move the class on to another task before the majority of students are ready. We could create similar categories for willingness, ability or students that stand out in terms of character and personality. My point here is that our tendency as teachers to notice extremes often means that, objectively, our classes are going neither as badly nor as well as we think. We may need to retrain our eye to take in the middle ground, the whole picture, and to resist being drawn to salient features.

Experiencing stress

Another useful point to note is that stressful thoughts tend to come in pairs and can result in what I have called 'stress sandwiches' (Roland, 2015). The psychologist Albert Ellis explained how we tend to think in words (1965). If we look at a typical snippet of a teacher's internal verbalisations or self-talk during a span of 20 or so seconds in class, it might go something like this:

"The window's shut. Looks grey but muggy outside."

"It's 4.24. Is the clock slow? No."

"Lucia and Mariano are working well together. I'll put them together again."

"Paco still hasn't started the exercise and just seems to be messing about."

"He's seen me and put his head down."

"Sergio's clicking his pen top. Sergio needs some help."

"Need to pop out and buy coriander in the break."

"Luis isn't here. If he were coming he'd probably have arrived by now."

"Is Maria stuck?...no."

"We're going a bit slowly."

"Cristina's helping Marta."

"It's 4.25."

"Where's the air con remote?"

"Rafa's working well. He's got some weird new trainers on."

"Elena's finished. Lucia and Mariano have finished."

"Paco's mum came in yesterday to say he's failing English at school."

"Is my phone off?"

It is the existence of the two antagonistic thoughts (in bold) which set up a stressful situation for the teacher, mutually exacerbate one another and squeeze out the richness of anything in between – resulting in the teacher being less able to appreciate the positive things happening in the class.

Stressful situations are by their very nature tricky and there is often no quick fix solution, but being able to recognise all the factors involved in an uncomfortable situation helps us identify where we can most effectively direct our action. In this case, it might be to try to focus on creating a closer dialogue between Paco and his mum.

Student mindset

In my experience, teenagers do generally enjoy and benefit from English instruction in a group. However, most will struggle at some time or other with being in the class, or simply being in their seats.

How students experience the moment

Macro-maxims such as *"English will be good for your future"* or *"This language will come in useful if you are ever on an exchange visit abroad"* can often feel a very long way off for teenagers compared to the vividness of the present moment. Understandably, they are concerned with here and now questions such as: *"What do I have to do to get through this lesson?"* *"What's the easiest way to complete this exercise and please the teacher?"* *"What happens if I don't do the exercise?"*

A reduced sphere of action and passivity as a form of protest

By the end of a day, our teenagers will have sat through more lessons than us. Teenagers spend all day being told what to do by adults with a very limited scope of freedom – often not being allowed to speak freely or to move from their places. Additionally, they are asked to collaborate and cooperate on a succession of tasks of their teachers' choosing. Under such circumstances doing nothing or saying nothing can be a very powerful response. Paul Newman's character in the 1967 film *Cool Hand Luke* tells us *"Sometimes nothin' can be a real cool hand"*. Our teenagers certainly have to learn to negotiate with very little. When you ask a teenage student to do something and they shrug, huff or proceed sluggishly, it might be as close as they feel they can go to refusing. If you ask a teenager a question, and if they clam up, it could be that they do not feel like talking about that topic and are unable to discern that your main motive is not to probe but to give them the opportunity to practise speaking about themselves in English.

Feeling bigger than the moment

Sometimes our teenage students feel bigger than the exercise we have asked them to do. They feel bigger than every other person in the room and bigger than the room, too. Sometimes they want to explode out of this instant as if there were a cosmos inside of them. Meanwhile the teacher says: *"Sit down. Sit still. Sit straight. Stop talking. Stop shaking your leg. Stop looking around and get on with Exercise 2C on page 38."*

Feeling bigger than the moment is a metaphor I use to talk about the struggle students sometimes have to contain themselves in the space and the freedom we have apportioned them. It means having more energy in you than you can get out in this moment with all its accompanying limitations and constraints[1]. For our students struggling against restlessness, anything that helps make that moment a little bit bigger, richer, varied, a little bit less suffocating, can be considered a lifeline for them.

---

[1] I believe this is where involuntary motor tics come from as well (such as eye blinking or facial twitches) – surplus energy needing to escape and doing so through habitualised, slightly misplaced but nonetheless highly regulated channels (for more on tics see Ganos *et al*, 2014).

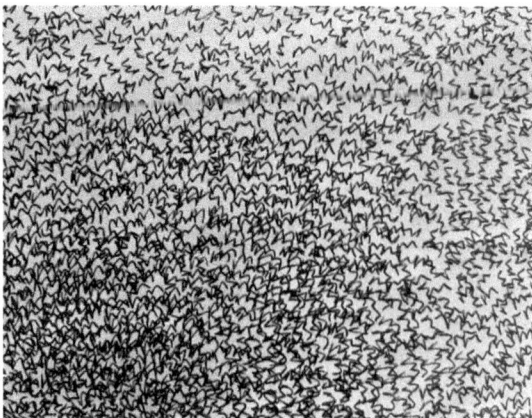

Figure 1: The product of a student who might be feeling trapped in the moment – reconstruction of something I discovered circa 2015. This student had written the first letter of her name hundreds of times.

Practical applications

For the reasons just discussed, one of the results of putting teachers and teenage students together in a room is the creation of tension. Diffusing that tension is one of our ongoing goals.

Offering either X or Y

In a critique on liberalism, political and social philosopher Slavoj Zizek (2001) points out that the choice between two pre-determined alternatives gives the person choosing only the illusion of freedom. When presented with two ready-made options, there is a human tendency to go for one or the other, rather than reject the whole system, which Zizek calls the "radical choice".

We can borrow this in a slightly sneaky way (and perhaps in exactly the opposite manner to which Zizek intended).

Clara and Mary are hardworking students who bring a lot to the class but today they are too busy chatting to practice the dialogue they are working on.

Teacher: *"Okay, girls. You've got two options. First option: You change partners for just five minutes. Clara you work with Ana. Mary you work with Alex. You practice the dialogue then come back together."*

Mary: *"And the second option, teacher?"*

Teacher: *"The second option is you stay where you are but practice the dialogue three times now and you read it to me at the end of the class – but it has to be good."*

Clara: *"Second option, teacher."*

In fact, the teacher did all the choosing as they created both options, but still the girls are back on task and they feel a stronger sense of ownership over their renewed activity. This is all part of what I have described as working 'cleverly' with teens (Roland, 2012, where I first mentioned this strategy). Each day of teaching involves hundreds of such small manoeuvres and micro-negotiations. The accumulation of these can be massive and mean the difference between a class feeling right or feeling wrong.

Strategic use of the toilet

We often think of students needing the toilet as something that interrupts class but external fixtures can be our allies too. Albert is jumping around and cannot get settled. He is even annoying himself.

Teacher: *"Albert, go to the toilet."*

Albert: *"Sorry, teacher?"*

Teacher: *"Go to the toilet."*

Albert: *"But are you throwing me out?"*

Teacher: *"Not at all. Have a quick walk about. Put a bit of water on your face. Then come and do the exercise."*

He goes, comes back and gets on. Albert needed a break from a certain version of Albert trapped in a particular situation. We have given him a nudge onto the next bit, like we might a record or a CD that has got stuck.

Juan is struggling to stay in his chair.

> Teacher: *"Juan, go and have a look at the class photos from last year in the corridor. I want you to count how many students I had last year. Then come and tell me."*

Again, we have made the moment slightly bigger and more bearable for Juan and we have given the students he is sitting next to a little rest as well. Having small errands at the ready can be useful. There may be memos or admin slips that need to go to the secretary or materials borrowed from another teacher to be returned. Students might be sent to select a film or reader from the bookshelf in reception or the library.

Students as a mirror

Now and then I look at a class and think to myself: *"Why are they all so loopy today?"* Then I catch a reflection of myself leaping about in an equally loopy way. Teachers and their students often mirror each other.

In the private language academy sector, I have spent various years in classrooms without external windows. I have noticed time and again that the behaviour of students (and their teachers) seems to be more erratic before heavy rains or a storm, often having been puzzled by it until coming out of class and seeing the darkened sky[2].

At other times, teachers and students can set one another off. For this reason, I recommend that teachers try not to blast away with their volume or energy settings up to ten. Using your normal speaking voice whenever possible and standing or sitting but not pacing or prowling will help avoid your own energies unsettling your students. If you are operating on maximum from the start, you have nowhere to go if you do later need to up your level of animation or assertiveness in response to what your class is doing. Running on the 'small' you rather than the 'big' you – being your everyday self rather than trying to be the teacher all of the time will also leave you less drained at the end of the day, week or term.

---

[2] Thanks to Dr Michael Persinger at Laurentian University for confirming in personal correspondence that this may be so.

Similarly, in order to calm a class down, the teacher has to go to a calm place in their heads first and lead by example. The teacher that says *"Relax"* in a relaxed voice, *"Calm down"* in a calm voice or *"Quiet please"* in a quiet voice is doing just that.

One final observation on the matter of feeling tired might prove useful. You may well feel tired the morning after a full or heavy teaching day that went badly. However, the most tired that I ever feel is the morning after a teaching day that went *really well*. If you have been teaching into the afternoon or the evening and you come out of classes buzzing because you feel you nailed the last few lessons, as it were, you can expect to flag a little the next day and perhaps make allowances for that.

Questions for reflection

- Does the distinction between class as an event and learning experience make sense?
- If so, which do you spend more time thinking about yourself?
- Do you ever offer students X or Y type alternatives?
- Could you use spaces outside of your classroom to give restless students a break?
- When your students are loud or restless, do you mirror them?

Things to try

1. For each lesson you teach next week, try to identify one thing you hope to enjoy.
2. Think back to a stressful moment in class. Write out your internal thoughts at the time. Was there a pair of stressful thoughts creating a 'sandwich'?
3. Think back to a recent class activity that you were happy with. Write a paragraph-length description. What was it about the activity that you liked? Can you draw out and build on these elements in future lessons?

Things to share

Exchange lesson plans with a colleague. For each stage of each other's plan, roleplay a teenage student asking the teacher: *"Why are we doing this? What's the point of this?"*

- Try to come up with credible answers each time.
- Try to grade the language for the target level.
- Try to couch the answers in concepts the students will understand.

References

Barber D & Foord D (2014) *From English Teacher to Learner Coach* [online]. E-book. The Round Available at http://the-round.com/resource/from-english-teacher-to-learner-coach/ (accessed July 2018).

Ellis A in Shostrom EL (1965) *Three Approaches to Psychotherapy*, film. Available from Psychological and Educational Films, 3334 East Coast highway, Suite 252, Corona del Mar, California 92625, USA.

Ganos C, Münchau A & Bhatia K (2014) The semiology of tics, Tourette's, and their associations [online]. *Movement Disorders, Clinical Practice*. Available at: https://onlinelibrary.wiley.com/doi/full/10.1002/mdc3.12043 (accessed July 2018).

Roland C (2012) Tailoring tasks for teens. *APAC ELT Journal*. October **76**.

Roland C (2015) Stress sandwiches. *English Teaching professional* **99**.

Zizek S (2001) *On Belief*. New York: Routledge.

2. Planning lessons with teenagers

Discussion

Planning vs preparing

People sometimes ask how long I take to plan a lesson. My answer is anywhere from 30 seconds to 15 minutes to *plan* the lesson, which involves decisions about the content, looking at coursebook pages and getting everything straight in my head. Having done that, I still have to *prepare* the lesson, which may involve making additional photocopies, ensuring there is blank paper if it will be needed and checking audios. It may involve tidying my teacher's table, cutting things out, locating highlighters or Post-its, preparing visual prompts, locating video clips and making simple worksheets, templates or grids. Finally, for me, preparing the lesson involves putting the books and materials to be used in a pile and in the correct order, especially if I will be teaching various classes with little turnaround time.

Planning results in clarity of vision. Preparation is when that clarity translates into the smooth and efficient use of the classroom, its facilities and the materials therein. At the very least we want to make sure that the objects in the classroom, our pedagogic props, are not acting as obstacles to our teaching and that we are not bumbling about looking for a missing DVD, misplaced register or homework record, leaving our teenage students to fill up dead time with their own L1 discussions.

It is possible to have planned thoroughly at home but still not be fully ready to start when students walk in. This will often result in the lesson losing impetus right at the start, especially if we have to leave our class unattended as we dash back to the teachers' room for materials.

With experience, planning becomes more compressed and important steps become automatic. I generally leave myself 30 minutes total per class for both planning and preparing – though I regularly spend additional time working on supplementary materials, preparing projects or conducting my own classroom research.

On the other hand, I also know first rate teachers, some of whose first language is English and some whose first language is not, who like to spend longer familiarising themselves with reading texts, audios and exercises, considering alternate answers and predicting possible explanations to student queries.

A closer look at planning

"What am I going to do with them?" This is the killer question to avoid. Whenever we start to plan in response to this question, we take ourselves to a place where we are thinking about the lesson in terms of filling up time and keeping people busy. *"What can I teach them?"* is a much better alternative. I suggest we unpack that a little further to give us the following:

1. What words and sentences are the students going to see, hear, practise and learn?
2. How can that best be done in terms of logistics and practicalities?
3. What should they be able to do by the end of the lesson and how will we be able to see that?

The first and third points are concerned with our students' learning experience. I think it is reasonable to say that all lessons should include some new language, some opportunity for the students to practise that language and some guidance from the teacher on their language production via correction or feedback. The second point is about how managing the classroom as an event facilitates those two. It is a means to an end but it is still very important.

Avoiding a shaky start

There are various points at which the dynamics of a teenage class can break down or pressure from the students can overwhelm the teacher. At the start of the lesson students may swamp you with requests for clips, games, songs or activities you have done before that they want to do again. This is a good time to make it known that you have a plan by holding it up or writing it out in one corner of the board – even if it is just a simple list. Once students are aware that the plan existed before the start of the class, you can then distance yourself from it, making the plan responsible for proceedings rather than yourself. My typical responses here are:

"Sorry, look there's a list. This stuff is decided beforehand."

Or:

"We've got to get through this first, but if we do then maybe – just maybe."

Avoiding later breakdowns

Another potential breakdown often comes about two-thirds of the way through a class when students feel they have already worked hard and deserve a rest. Similarly, when a teacher looks undecided about what activity to do next their students will often try to help them decide. It can be useful, firstly, to publicly cross off lesson goals as they are achieved, secondly not to appear to consider requests, and thirdly to have included a game, clip, song, communication or mingle activity or whole class discussion at the planning stage. Doing so means you can incorporate these activities on your own terms and in a way that that compliments your lesson aims.

Demonising the coursebook

Sometimes teachers feel that their planning has to involve something that is not from their coursebook for it to be acceptable to their students. We might express mild guilt to colleagues over coffee or in the staffroom:

"It's just going to be all book today for mine."

We may even go as far as apologising sympathetically to our students:

"Yeah sorry guys, I know it's boring but …"

I wonder how many times our teenage students start out feeling positive or neutral towards their new coursebook and are subconsciously influenced by their teacher's ambivalence or apathy towards it. My advice, especially with your teenage groups, is not to openly slate your coursebook in class. That undermines your own position. I would suggest the following as a standard affirmation:

> *"It's a good book. These are good authors. A lot of work went into this. It's good material. Let's learn it and if it's not enough, we can learn something else."*

However, planning from a book does not necessarily mean doing everything exactly as the book states, as we shall see below.

Practical applications

Doing the book better

At the start of most units or double page spreads there are some lead-in questions. Rather than asking students to turn to a certain page and discussing these, make a note of them and start off a whole class conversation before they have opened their books, giving the beginning of the lesson a more spontaneous and natural feel.

Similarly, if there is a listening exercise included in the lesson you are going to teach, you might consider playing students the audio, or part of it, before they look at anything in their books, with the very general primer: *"Listen to this then tell me something afterwards"*. I have found this encourages a more holistic type of listening and gives everyone the chance to contribute something. Well-known teacher trainer and coursebook writer Paul Seligson (drawing on Revell & Norman, 1997) often makes the point that whenever we accompany audios with visual text, the eye takes over. Just listening to audio, with books closed, cuts out such distraction.

If there are grammar exercises in the lesson you are going to teach, you may wish to hand over responsibility for going over the correct answers to one of the students, letting them be the teacher and providing them with the correct answers and a few supporting scripts on the board such as:

> *"_____, could you tell me the answer to number ___ please?"*

✔"That's right."

"Can you repeat that again for everyone please?"

✘"Are you sure?"

"Anyone else?"

"Has everyone got that?"

Again, with grammar exercises, and also vocabulary exercises, it is worth asking yourself at the planning phase:

*"What can we do with this exercise **after** it has been completed and corrected that will help the material stick?"*

Planning for each student

These are some lines from *O Fortuna* and *Fortune Plango Vulnera*, medieval poems from the 13th century set to music by Carl Orff in the 1930s as part of his *Carmina Burana*.

"Fortune rota volvitur:	*"The wheel of Fortune turns;*
descendo minoratus;	*I go down, demeaned;*
alter in altum tollitur;	*another is raised up;*
nimis exaltatus	*far too high up*
rex sedet in vertice	*sits the king at the summit –*
caveat ruinam!"	*let him fear ruin!"*

My favorite online version of this is Jean Pierre Ponelle's TV adaptation. The centrepiece of the set for these two songs is a large wheel with various characters as its spokes. As the wheel of fortune turns, sometimes you are at the top as king or queen, sometimes on the decline as previous ruler, at the bottom as dead ruler or on the assent as future ruler. The relevance of this will be explained below.

When you think about a teenage class you are about to teach, especially a difficult one, whose are the faces that spring to mind? Following on from Chapter 1, I predict that the first students who pop into your head are the most challenging ones (followed, perhaps by the most co-operative ones), and consequently our thinking can be influenced by them even at this early stage. What we do might become subconsciously geared towards satisfying, appeasing or entertaining *them*.

To remedy this bias, I decided to make my own wheel of fortune. Using a splitter pin I mounted a plastic plate (as the wheel) on a piece of card and around the edges of the plate I stuck passport-sized photos of each of the students in a class (their names, initials or other representative photos as 'avatars' would do).

Figure 2: Wheel of fortune

The wheel goes on my classroom wall and each day, as I plan their lesson, I turn it round by one increment, so that a new student is at the top. If Samuel is at the top today, it is his lesson. Whatever we do is pitched to a learner of his level, profile and needs. I also try to make sure I spend a couple of minutes talking to Samuel specifically or checking his work. I will partner up with him if we are doing a speaking activity in pairs and there is an uneven number of students, rather than making a three. The others will get their turn but today it is Samuel's day.

I have been using wheels of this sort for the last two years and currently have four on my classroom wall for different classes. Not only are they a highly visual aid to sharing your attention fairly at the planning stage, but they can also be used to allocate roles such as class monitor or who is going to "be the teacher". In my academy classroom, in winter, I also have a large blanket and whoever is at the top of the wheel gets to cover themselves with that, along with the students sitting either side of them, should they wish to share it.

First day of the year

A time when you see teachers of teenage groups especially jittery and apprehensive is in the hours preceding their first classes of the academic year. Having not yet worked with or maybe even met the groups they are preparing for, they try to plan comprehensively, covering all bases and eventualities.

This is a time when photocopying machines get the heaviest and most unnecessary use, with teachers printing off get-to-know-you worksheets, info about the course, refresher quizzes to see what students remember from last year, class contract templates, treasure hunt activities to help students get to know their way around the coursebook, pages from the first unit in case some students do not yet have the coursebook, needs analysis questionnaires and more.

In recent years, I have cut my first lesson planning and preparation down to the bare bones. My objectives for the first class with a teenage group are now:

1. Listen to each student speaking, briefly, and give them some feedback.
2. Get a short sample of each student's writing, marking it on the spot if possible.
3. See what each student can hear from a few lines of audio.

This type of lesson is about evaluation. It is a 'teacher-busy', hands on, in-the-moment evaluation to give you an idea about each student as the lesson progresses, rather than an entry test that needs to be taken away and marked. This approach turns what otherwise might be a patchwork first day into a purposeful data gathering exercise for the teacher.

For a more in-depth description of one of my typical first days please see **Downloadable resource 1**.

Planning for the past

We normally plan for our next class but we can try planning for our previous class too. It may sound a little counter-intuitive but by this I mean taking the last lesson you taught a group and asking: *"What can I do with them today that will make sense of what we did last time? What can we do that will be a continuation of the objectives we didn't quite reach or a celebration of the ones we did?"*

What we do today or even tomorrow affects how we think about what we did yesterday, and, in that restricted sense, last week's lesson is never quite over.

Simple worksheets, structure and appearances

I want to talk about appearances for a moment.

Compare giving a class a blank piece of paper and asking them to write about their plans for next weekend on it to giving them a piece of paper with the title *My plans for the weekend* already printed at the top. There may not be much difference, but there is some indication of premeditation on the part of the teacher, a sense that this is the way things were meant to go. Now look at the difference a box makes:

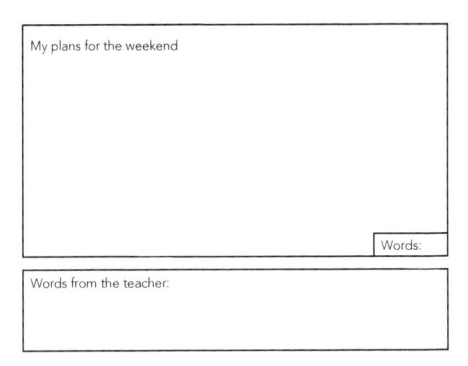

[Form template: "My plans for the weekend" box with "Words:" field, and "Words from the teacher:" box below]

Figure 3: The inclusion of boxes provides a sense of purpose

It feels like it was meant to be written in. We have also included a box for when students come up to your desk and ask: *"How do you spell…?" "How do you say…?"* You can scribble the word in there and they can integrate it into their text at leisure. There is a little box for students to write in the word count. Finally, in the version below, we have played two little Jedi mind tricks (for those readers familiar with the *Star Wars* saga).

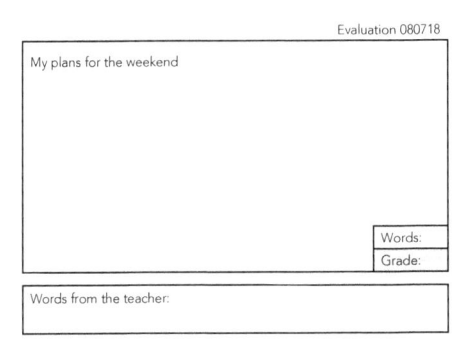

[Form template: "Evaluation 080718" at top, "My plans for the weekend" box with "Words:" and "Grade:" fields, and "Words from the teacher:" box below]

Figure 4: Additional features enhance the form

There is a shaded "for official use only" style box to remind students this is going to be looked at later and also an official looking number. This number does not have to mean much more than the date. Both features are designed to create a sense of distance and bestow upon the form a sense of otherness – a strategy that teacher trainer and materials writer Ceri Jones refers to as "making the familiar unfamiliar" (2012).

"Is it evaluated, teacher?"

"Everything you do is evaluated."

"What's this number, teacher?"

"Don't worry about that number."

I think that every teacher looking at this instinctively knows it would give us more success than the plain piece of paper, and that is before the students have even written a word.

Questions for reflection

- Are you able to draw a distinction between planning and preparing?
- If so, which is your stronger skill?
- Could the first five minutes of your classes be streamlined for efficiency? How?

Things to try

1. Try planning your lessons with a different class member in mind each time.
2. Employ a wheel of fortune or a similar system for sharing out your attention.
3. When planning your next classes, make conscious links back to your previous ones.
4. When designing worksheets and templates, experiment with varying degrees of structure. Where does it help? Where is it prescriptive?

Things to share

Before starting with new groups during this or the next academic course, discuss with colleagues:

- What is that we really want out of the first lesson?
- How can we reduce materials for that lesson but increase purposefulness?

Follow up by experimenting with lesson format and style.

References

Jones C (2012) *Giving Tired Topics a New Twist*. Talk given in Seville at the ACEIA conference.

Orff C (2017) Carmina Burana Vocal/Piano Score. Shott Music.

Revell J & Norman S (1997) *In Your Hands: NLP in ELT*. London: Saffire Press.

3. Classroom micromechanics

Discussion

The analogy

To get at the nuts and bolts of what happens in a teenage class, I use an analogy to the scientific discipline of micromechanics. Micromechanics involves taking a compound substance and then looking at one of its elements very closely or looking at its elements one-by-one, to determine how the whole will behave (Qu & Cherkaoui, 2006). Real micromechanical engineers use electron microscopes. For our purposes, I suggest the question: *What is each student doing at a given moment in the class?* Freeze framing the action like this, as an act of recall, allows us to deconstruct tasks and interactions retrospectively – or to hypothesise at the planning stage what an imagined activity might look and feel like.

3.33% of a conversation

Many of the examples in this chapter, and discussions throughout the book in general, use the above focus question as a point of departure or return. The first I have called "3.33% of a conversation". This is the mistaken supposition that if there are 30 students in a class, and one of those students is having a conversation with the teacher, then somehow that conversation gets divided up equally and all the students get a share of it, as illustrated below.

3. Classroom micromechanics

$S_{3.33\%}\ S_{3.33\%}\ S_{3.33\%}\ S_{3.33\%}\ S_{3.33\%}\ S_{3.33\%}$
$S_{3.33\%}\ S_{3.33\%}\ S_{3.33\%}\ S_{3.33\%}\ S_{3.33\%}\ S_{3.33\%}$
$S_{3.33\%}\ S_{3.33\%}\ S_{3.33\%}\ S_{3.33\%}\ S_{3.33\%}\ S_{3.33\%}$
$S_{3.33\%}\ S_{3.33\%}\ S_{3.33\%}\ S_{3.33\%}\ S_{3.33\%}\ S_{3.33\%}$
$S_{3.33\%}\ S_{3.33\%}\ S_{3.33\%}\ S_{3.33\%}\ S_{3.33\%}\ S_{3.33\%}$

3.33%

(conversation ÷ 30 = 3.33%)   T

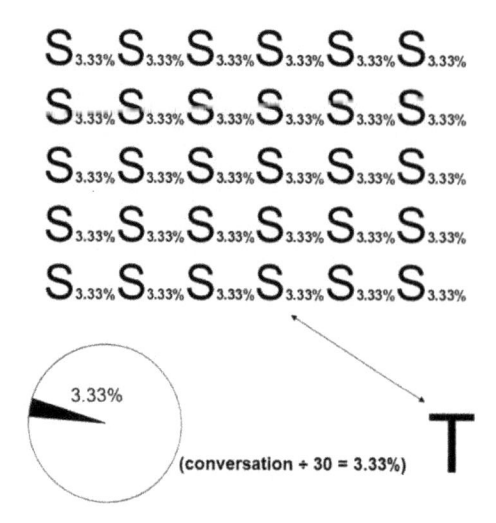

Figure 5: How we imagine a conversation gets divided

We can adjust the figures for smaller classes of 15 or 12 to 6.66% and 8.33% accordingly. It makes little difference because this is not what actually happens. In terms of real activity and interactivity, the teacher and the student they are talking to at that moment get nearly all of it.

S S S S S S
S S S S S S
S S S S S S
S S S S S S
S S S S S S

50%

(conversation ÷ 2 = 50%)   50% T

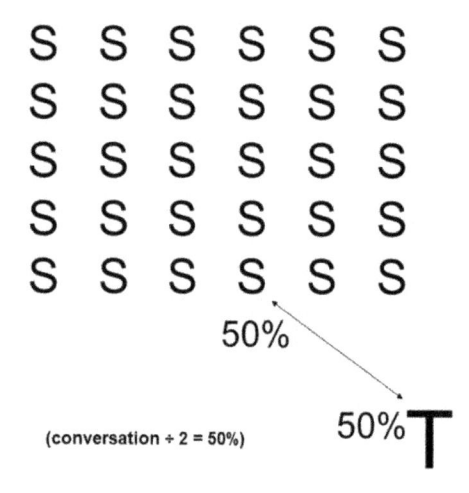

Figure 6: What really happens

If it is not your conversation you are not in play, unless you try to become one of the speakers, which might be seen as attempting to contribute but which might also be easily construed as interrupting. So what is each student doing at this point in the class? In order for this conversation to work as if the teacher was talking to one person, all the other students have to repress themselves to some extent – listening attentively as if it were their conversation. This is why such 'conversations' with the class simply do not work – or at least cannot be maintained for very long. It is a point that we systematically overlook because as the teacher we always get 50% of the action. Therefore what seems to the teacher like 'doing speaking' might feel very different from where their students are sitting.

Imaging the class

In the world of 3D illustrations, a technique called 'cut away' is often used to provide a look into the interior of an object, such as the working parts of a machine, by slicing away the exterior layers. Another technique, known as 'ghosting', leaves those exterior layers intact but renders them semi-transparent. This allows the viewer to focus on a single part of a system while bearing the whole in mind or to see the whole but with all the individual parts visible. A third type of illustration is the 'exploded view' where the parts of a machine are moved away from each other so that everything is visible but kept in the same order and proportion in terms of position and distance. If you are not aware of these different techniques, I would encourage you to look online to appreciate the difference between them and how each facilitates the understanding of something very complex.

We need to develop the same sort of view – at least in our minds – of what goes on in our classes. It involves both fragmenting our mental schema of the class, ignoring some parts, concentrating on others and moving things away from each other conceptually (things that in reality are very close) in order to think about them better *but* simultaneously keeping the inter-relatedness of them all in mind.

At any given moment we might see a single student across a number of superimposed dimensions. A central concern is how they are engaging with the linguistic content of an activity (such as the exercise in front of them) and how it connects with what language they already know. Then, on top of that, there is how they are picking up on clues from their surroundings:

the board, help from classmates and the teacher's additional support. Underlying all of this is how well they understand the intrinsic workings and rationale of the task itself coupled with our initial instructions when setting it. Going deeper, we need to consider how they relate to the rest of the group in terms of integration – or distraction. On a similar level, how do they relate to the teacher in terms of compliance, respect, regard and recognition? These two – group and teacher – will probably jostle for alternating top position. Then, at the deepest level, we might consider a student's relationship to themselves in terms of more primal energies. Are they twitchy and unsettled? Are they able to rein that in to make decisions that benefit themselves and the group?

That is just one student. We would have to multiply it by 8, 12, 15, 20 or 30 to give us a cut away ghosted shot of a whole class – which in any case will be constantly shifting as we progress through various stages of an activity, through various groupings and multiple interactions. I am not sure how an exploded view of all the psycho-linguistic social cognitive elements of an English class could be represented but I do know that the glimpses we get of the complexity of the whole can be both fascinating and overloading. Fortunately, at any moment of the lesson, we can switch from the macro to the micro, and along any given dimension, ask ourselves: *"What is each student doing right now?"* Or: *"What is this particular student doing right now?"*

Using questions as a punishment

I would like to take a brief trip back into our recent past to look at one of the darker sides of education. Please bear with me if you find the tangent a strain as I do believe this analogy has value.

The cane is a light flexible rod made from rattan – palm vines that can grow up to 100 metres tall – and was extensively used as punishment in British schools during the 19th and 20th centuries to whack naughty students across the buttocks or open hands. Despite a number of earlier government commissioned enquiries (for example Highfield & Pinsent, 1952), corporal punishment was only finally phased out in Britain towards the end of the last century.

The question, on the other hand, is a wonderful tool. Asking questions about the world is a precursor to knowledge and discovery. As pointed out by progressive educationalists Charles Weingartner and Neil Postman (1969), the question is the building block to everything in education.

As communicative language teachers, we start out with good intentions. We have lots of questions at the ready and we try to engage our students with them. Occasionally though, as the class goes on, it becomes apparent that some students are not as interested in the meaningful conversation or exchange of information as we had envisaged and we start to wield our questions more like we might do a cane. We start to use those questions to startle any students who are not paying enough attention, to cut in on and cut out their own private conversations. *"Listen to what I'm saying because it could be you next, yes, I might ask you … a question!"*

That is not the best reason to be asking questions. Ideally, our students should want us to ask them questions. I am driving towards split second introspection on the part of the teacher. It involves us asking: *Why am I about to ask this student this question at this time? If it's for classroom management, then maybe I'm not making the best choice of student in terms of class dynamic and the flow of language content across the lesson.*

If you ever find yourself standing in front of a class asking questions to students because they are not paying attention, perhaps the best thing to do is save your breath, sit down and set them a task to be getting on with. Meanwhile you can try to figure out how to encourage them to ask you questions or to ask each other.

You are next

Imagine everyone is listening to you except Juan (and the student he is talking to). You may be tempted to direct your next question towards him, but whatever type of question it is, Juan has not been following and he is not going to know the answer. The class, as a conversation, is going to stall. In fact, Juan is probably the worst person you could ask next. In order to re-engage him, however, a quick aside will work wonders: *"Juan, listen because I'm going to ask you in a minute"*. That will not affect the flow of the class and it will give Juan the necessary heads-up in order to check which question you are on or where in the text he should be and to formulate some sort of a response. In most cases, it will also bring his own private conversation to an end.

The micromechanics of dialogue

Let us imagine the class as one long script. That script is what everyone says and the class dynamic is how that script unfurls. It is the terrain of spoken text between teacher and students, and between students and students. At any point we can revisit parts of the script, study, abridge or annotate them. In many ways, the lesson (and especially the language lesson) *is* what is said between the people in the room. When reflecting upon a lesson, as well as recalling what students were doing it is useful to think about what they were saying, in what language, to whom and why.

Practical applications

What is the likely answer to the following question:

What will a given student be doing at a given moment in the class?

As often as not, I'm afraid the answer will probably be that he or she will be waiting. This is not because we are innately inefficient as teachers. Rather, it is a natural consequence of the ratios of one teacher to 10, 20, 30 or more students we work with. The ratio of a single teacher to numerous students is one of the many default blueprints we have inherited from classrooms of former times. It is particularly problematic in classes with teens who, like younger learners, want to engage with their teacher and receive his or her attention, but unlike primary-aged children are less happy to share that attention by doing whole class activities. The ratio puts a ceiling on what we can do in terms of listening to and speaking to individual students, on the quality of support we can provide on a one-to-one basis, and the interactivity of our whole class explanations. In short, it affects nearly every facet of instruction. ELT instruction in groups does have its good points (affording mutual support, socialisation and the fact that from a communicative perspective the students have a large number of different people to talk to) but the teacher to student ratio is something we normally have to work round.

The micromechanics of going over exercises

Polina is a student in a pre-intermediate class of teens. She is doing an exercise that involves matching verb phrases such as 'get up' and 'have breakfast' with thumbnail pictures of somebody going about their daily routine. Polina finishes the exercise first and is waiting for her classmates. Once everyone has finished they begin going over the exercise with the teacher. Polina is waiting for her turn to answer.

Teacher: *"Dima, number four."*

Dima: *"Get dressed."*

Teacher: *"That's right. Alex?"*

Alex: *"Get dressed."*

Teacher: *"Number five."*

Alex: *"Sorry. Have breakfast."*

Teacher: *"That's great. Thank you. Next, anyone?"*
[Here it comes]

Polina: *"Yes, me teacher."*

Teacher: *"Okay, Polina?"*

Polina: *"Go to work."*

Teacher: *"Correct."*

That was it. That was the interaction. That was Polina's spoken language practice for the first 25 minutes of class.

I am going to make the daring assertion here that there may in fact be as much learning potential in the *going over* of an exercise from the book as there is in the language content of that exercise itself. This is perhaps especially true for anything up to intermediate level where students lack a lot of transactional language.

We can put the following scripts on the board, using a different colour for each speaker. This is similar to the script suggested in Chapter 1, but here the students work in pairs.

    A: *"What did you think number 1 was?"*

    B: *"I thought it was _____."*

    A: ✔ *"Yes, me too."* OR
       ✘ *"Oh. I didn't. I thought it was _____."*

    B: *"Mmm. Okay yeah. I see what you mean."* OR
       "Mmm. Let's ask the teacher."

Now Polina and her classmates can discuss their answers together, occasionally checking with the teacher. At points of the dialogue they have options to agree or disagree. Suddenly we have a roomful of people engaged in meaningful exchange.

For lower level classes especially, it is important to get language moving. Language that has stopped moving becomes stale and stagnant. Language that is never given an airing goes to private places in students' heads and buries itself as half memory. In contrast, this transactional language is not only out there but it is also the stuff of real life. It is what makes up much of our daily chit chat. I introduced a couple of new elements to the above script, underlined below, and we have a completely different conversation, applicable to a completely different setting.

    A: *"What did you think of the film?"*

    B: *"I thought it was rubbish / fantastic."*

    A: ✔ *"Yes, me too."* OR
       ✘ *"Oh. I didn't. I thought it was rubbish / fantastic."*

    B: *"Mmm. Okay yeah. I see what you mean."* OR
       "Mmm. Let's go home / grab a drink."

There are innumerable variations on dialogues like these. They can be used as a vehicle for a wide variety of structures. By the end of each exercise students are often able to complete an exchange from memory. The dynamic can be tweaked as well. If your students are having problems staying on script as equal partners in the conversation then one of them can be given the answers and put in charge of the other as 'teacher'.

A: *"What did you put for number 1?"*

B: *"I thought it was _____."*

A: ✔ *"That's right. Well done, my friend. You're a rock star."* OR
✘ *"Sorry. That's not what I've got here. It says _____."*

B: *"Okay, I've corrected that. Shall we move on? "*

A: *"Sure thing."*

Bottlenecking

This is the term I use to describe classroom situations where progress on the part of the many is contingent upon actions completed by the few. It is where one or more students are waiting for their peers to complete something before they can have their turn.

As a teacher, some bottleneck situations occur before you realise. Here I shall outline four such possible situations, which may resonate with you from some point in your teaching career, offering solutions for each.

Potential bottleneck situation #1

In an attempt to increase interactivity and participation in a large class of 30, the teacher is asking his students to come up to the board one-by-one and write one of the answers to a sentence transformation exercise. At any given moment there are 29 students waiting for one student to finish writing their sentence.

Solution to problem #1

Multiple writing surfaces would be one answer here. These could be additional wall mounted boards (see Chapter 14 p171) or mini-boards.

Another solution would be to increase the number of students writing at the board at any one time. While teaching classes of 25-30 students in a regular school I used to put all the exercises and question numbers from each end of unit revision page on the blackboard, dividing it into boxed sections which corresponded to the page itself. While students were completing the page in their books, I would walk round assigning each one an exercise and question number and giving them a piece of chalk: Alex 1a), David 1b), Sara 1c) etc. They would then come up to the board en masse. We would regularly have as many as 15 students there at the same time, passing their pieces of chalk to a classmate when they had finished.

Occasionally teachers object that this would be too chaotic and too noisy. The odd teacher has reacted in horror. Each teacher, group and setting is different, but I myself have only ever found this type of movement to have a calming, almost therapeutic effect.

Potential bottleneck situation #2

In a class of 13 year olds who are sat in horseshoe formation (around the outsides of the class) and who are all very eager to put their hands up and answer a question, the teacher has started asking the students on her left and is working slowly around the room. The students on the far right have temporarily disengaged from the activity because they know there is no chance of them being asked for another few minutes. The students on the left who have already been asked know that they will have to wait now until everyone has had a turn before being asked again and so have similarly disengaged.

Solution to problem #2

One solution, covered on pre-service teacher training courses, is to ask students randomly. Although this does not mean that the total wait time is actually any less, it makes it less predictable and the bottleneck therefore less obvious. Similarly, allowing the student who has just provided an answer to nominate the next student grants the group just a smidgen more agency and opportunity for playfulness.

In both these scenarios, however, we still have one student answering and the remainder waiting for their turn. Putting the class in groups and appointing 'teachers' who have the answers, perhaps with scripts as discussed above, will get language moving much more readily. To remove the bottleneck altogether, we could simply copy up or project the answers to the exercise for everyone to see at once – perhaps asking students to correct each other's work. This last option may seem counter-intuitive as one of the default practices of classrooms is that the teacher retains control by having the answers and feeding them to the class one-by-one. While this allows us to control pace and to be able to explain answers that students might have got wrong before moving on, it does not always necessarily improve productivity or dynamic, so alternatives are worth exploring.

Potential bottleneck situation #3

A teacher has asked his students to write a roleplay in pairs. First, they are to write a draft version, then they are to have it checked by the teacher before redrafting, practising, and – if there is time – performing the roleplay for the class. Again, this is a large class with over a dozen pairs and several groups of three all writing their sketches.

Five pairs finish their rough versions at the same time and bring them to the teacher who now has a line of students queueing at the teacher's table. A couple of students are becoming restless in the queue and have started shoving each other in a harmless but distracting manner. As two more groups finish, the queue is growing faster than the teacher can check the work.

Solution to problem #3

One workaround here is to use a 'creeping corrections' technique. Right from the word go, as students are working on their dialogues, the teacher starts to circulate or to call them over and corrects as much as they have done. This way, as groups finish and bring the whole of their scripts to the teacher, a portion of each will already be corrected. This will lighten the load later on and reduce bottlenecking. While this technique does involve interrupting pairs of students while they are creating, I have found that they recover very quickly.

Another option is to allow groups to move on to practising their rough versions of the roleplays, perhaps sending them off to different locations (just outside the door, a spare room or the playground) and recalling them one-by-one to look at any corrections to the script. This may feel a little back-to-front and means that students are rehearsing a script that may not be their final one, but it may help them notice their errors and help them self-correct.

A third very simple logistical solution is to have pairs who have finished the roleplay move on to exercises from their workbooks until the teacher is free. If the page and exercise numbers have already been specified, the students will know what to expect and this transition will run more smoothly.

Another variation on this last solution is to split the class from the beginning of the lesson and have half the students working on exercises and half writing roleplays. Once the first group of actors have finished their scripts and are practising, the second group can begin writing. The lesson ends with those who started off on the roleplays doing the exercises and those who started off on the exercises rehearsing.

Potential bottleneck situation #4

The teacher has asked an intermediate group of students to do some in-class writing about an upcoming local festival. It is not covered in the book but is important for the community and all of the students are involved in some way and have been either preparing or looking forward to it for weeks. A minute or so into the task it becomes clear that in order to write, the students need a lot of terminology specific to the festival and to their L1, much of which has no straight translation or obvious equivalent in English. The students either do not have mobiles or have not brought them to class. Progress becomes slow and the teacher begins to feel overwhelmed by the number of requests for vocabulary that they are receiving.

Solution to problem #4

Somehow we need to anticipate vocabulary here. The first strategy I use for such situations is to create my own picture dictionary consisting of internet images of the most prominent aspects of the festival we are going to describe. I accompany each image with the most accurate translation or explanation in English possible and leave a space below for students to write in their own familiar L1 term. By looking at this before the writing task, we arm students with the language they will need and take considerable strain off the teacher during the task itself.

A second strategy is to locate a description of the festival to be studied on a culture or tourism webpage or in an online encyclopaedia and have the English version of the description visible to the students as they write. You may need to copy, paste and edit the material in order to clear up inaccuracies and shorten or simplify long or complicated sections. Using this strategy, it makes little sense to then ask students to describe the festival – as they might as well simply copy the description you have provided. Rather, here they can be asked to write about *their* experience of the festival the previous year and to say what they are looking forward to from the same festival this year, as well as how it might be different or how it might be similar.

Rolling referrals

Imagine the following classroom exchange:

Ebba: *"Teacher, what does 'arrangement' mean?"*

Teacher: *"It's when you make a plan with somebody else, when you agree to do something with them at a future time."*

Ebba: *"What? Sorry?"*

Teacher: *"I think you say* ['arrangement' in student's L1]*."*

Ebba: *"Thank you."*

Edvin: *"Teacher?"*

Teacher: *"Yes Edvin?"*

Edvin: *"What is 'arrangement'?"*

Teacher: *"Ask Ebba."*

Ebba looks up and Edvin asks her. Now Ebba might not be the strongest student in the group but she has suddenly become the owner of new knowledge that is valuable. And the next student to ask about the word 'arrangement' gets referred to Edvin. I call this technique *rolling vocabulary referrals*. It constitutes a small but useful tweak to the ongoing dialogue of the class.

Loose connections

In each group, on each row or table, there is normally a 'loose connection' that is not quite hooked up to the rest. The challenge is how to keep those individuals in the loop and not isolated from the activity of the rest. Imagine we are playing a whole class game with students in three teams of five.

In one group, Toni is the loose connection. He does not know any of the answers and is not following the game. Patricia knows the next answer but she gave us the last answer.

> Teacher: *"I want the answer to come from Toni this time."*
>
> Patricia: *"But he doesn't know it."*
>
> Teacher: *"You tell Toni. Toni tells me."*

So Patricia whispers the answer quite emphatically into Toni's ear and Toni tells the teacher. He was not the originator of the answer and probably only half understands what he has said, but the answer has gone through him nonetheless. He is involved on some level and is back in the loop.

Student tannoy

Max is stood next to our table as students come to the end of an activity. We lean over to Max and say quietly: *"Max, can you ask everyone to sit down and look this way please"*. Max rises to the task of spokesperson.

> Max to the class: *"Sit down everyone and look this way!"*
>
> Teacher to Max: *"Please."*
>
> Max to the class: *"Please!"*
>
> Teacher to Max: *"Now ask everyone to turn to page 51 and do exercise A."*
>
> Max to the class: *"Turn to page 51…"*

Yes, there is an element of pantomime. Max knows that too, but it is a new interaction pattern in terms of the diffusion of power and mandate. It is one more micro-manoeuvre to our toolbox.

Questions for reflection

- Do you tend to speak to your whole class as if they were one person?
- If so, can you see any alternatives to this dynamic?
- How often do you use questions as a classroom management tool?
- How much time do your students spend waiting for the next thing to happen?
- When was the last time you experienced bottlenecking in class?

Things to try

1. Next time you are planning a classroom task in which there are various stages for students to complete, test your plan by asking:
   "What will each student be doing at each point of the task?"
2. Try providing students with scripts that they can use to discuss the answers to exercises together. Experiment by loading these scripts with functional language and structures suitable for their level.

Things to share

Start to note down exchanges of language between students that serve as examples of good communication, that demonstrate learning or that represent the sort of student-to-student dynamic you consider desirable.

- When talking to colleagues or leading workshops, these will help others get a feel for the activity you are describing.
- In write ups such as articles or formal self-evaluation, examples of real utterances are more credible evidence of learning than statements such as, *"The activity went well"*.

References

Highfield ME & Pinsent A (1952) *A Survey Of Rewards and Punishments in Schools*. London: Newnes Educational Publishing Co. Ltd.

Postman N & Weingartner C (1969) *Teaching as a Subversive Activity*. New York: Delta Publishing Co.

Qu J & Cherkaoui M (2006) *Fundamentals of Micromechanics of Solids*. New Jersey: Wiley.

4. Task design and instructions

Discussion

Task design is how you anchor your students' engagement with English language in the moment. Instructions are how you convey the particulars of that design to your class.

Our students understand that doing what their teacher asks is the surest way to a happy life in the here and now, but if doing so requires more exertion, focus or technical ability than they are able to give in the moment then they will most likely delay starting or stall later on. Consciously or subconsciously a type of internal reckoning occurs, and it goes something like this: *"What is the easiest way for me to get this task done and how will the teacher know that I'm doing, or that I have done, what they asked?"*

Tweaking criteria

To ensure students engage with language, we can manipulate a huge range of factors. We can choose the medium of delivery (spoken or written texts) and whether the students have something to refer to as they complete the task (versus books closed). We can tailor the language content of a task and we can introduce an element of play or an element of tension. We can stipulate groupings, what type of responses are required, and primarily whether there is pressure to perform or pressure to produce. In terms of performance, we can decide to monitor peer-to-peer interaction or to evaluate a live public rendition or student recordings. In terms of production, we can decide on the layout and length of a project and how the left-over evidence of a student's endeavours is to be processed and interpreted.

Measurability

The key lies in measurability. It is worth looking over your lesson plan and asking at each and every point:

"How am I going to know if a student is on task and engaging with language here? What will the class sound like and look like at this stage of the lesson? What will they be saying to each other? What will they have down on paper at this point? What will I be doing: spot checks, one-to-one support or sitting with different groups?"

As a trainer observing lessons, I can tell when the dynamic of an activity looks, sounds or feels different to how the teacher giving the class had imagined it. The teacher's voice is the giveaway. It becomes flatter and strained – rather than the more shaky, tinny sound of actually being nervous.

A teenage class will tell you indirectly if the task you have set is measurable. On an extremely astute but instinctive level they will ascertain more quickly than you can if your plan has left you control points by which to monitor, regulate and evaluate their activity. If it has not, you will not be in a position to recognise or reward hard work either.

Shopping receipt analogy

When a written response is required, I use the following analogy as primer. First, I show the class a supermarket receipt and say: *"This is a receipt. It shows that you have spent your money on something. It is **proof** that you have spent your money on something."*

Then I hold up a paragraph or an essay.

*"This is a piece of writing. It shows that you have spent your English lessons listening and looking and learning. When you go home at the end of the day, **this** is what I am left with as proof of your hard work. Make it as good as you can!"*

This is an example of sharing our teacher logic with students using clear mental images they can grasp and is something we shall look at in more detail in Chapter 22.

Timing each other

We can change the complexity of a task with a few simple adjustments. Over the years I have accumulated a number of low-cost digital watches, namely the Casio F91W and W59 1V models. When the plastic strap breaks on one, I replace it with another, resulting in a collection of three or four strapless watches which all have a stopwatch function on them. After having done a vocabulary exercise in the coursebook that involves matching lexis to thumbnail pictures, I distribute the watches and in groups students cover the words and time each other to see who can name all the pictures the fastest or who can reduce their personal best by the most seconds. The same can be done by allowing students to use the timer on their mobile phones, borrowing stopwatches from the PE department in a school or deploying a class set of sand clocks. Here we have manipulated task conditions to introduce an element of play and a certain facilitative tension that encourages further engagement with the target language content once the initial exercise has been completed.

Input language

For any given task we need to ask: *"Will students actually have the language they need? If not, where will that input come from?"* Ideally a language task should stretch a student's capacity, but if we have not thought about where support will come from in a structured and systematic way, then most likely the teacher will be called upon to provide it in a more random on-the-spot fashion. Whenever we ask our learners to do something with nothing, we are setting up a potential stalling point where we may have to jump in and save the activity.

In a domino-style game where higher-level teens have to match the first and second sentence halves of idioms, for example, what happens to gameplay if nobody knows the idioms at all? By providing players with a full set of complete and correct sentences as a reference sheet, we allow them to play the game but with recourse to the information they need to make informed decisions while still being exposed to correct language.

Track switches

Track switches, or points, are the mechanisms by which a train changes the set of rails that it is on. In classes where students share a common first language (L1), or subgroups of them do, the reality is that they will at some point revert to that language. In some classes L1 might even be the norm with English the exception. In others, English may successfully have been established as the dominant language of the lesson with students slipping back into L1 just occasionally. Where we predict heavy L1 use, we can build a number of track switches into the staging of our tasks. These track switches are points at which students need to change code from L1 to English in order to perform a transaction that fulfils the task requirements.

If students are going to report back to the class on a discussion they are having with a partner, then even if the initial conversation ends in L1, we have reinstalled English by the end of the stage. If students are conducting a survey, we might stipulate that the responses need to be entered into the corresponding boxes on their form by the questioner in full English sentences – again, pushing the activity back towards English as interviewer and interviewee together try to work out how to best convey the latter's contributions. During board games in groups, we can include the rule that if a player doesn't complete their turn in English then it doesn't count, even appointing a referee to police players and dock points where necessary, providing multiple prompts to track switch back to English.

Task design for tweens and teens

Tweenagers, *tweens* or *tweenies* are expressions sometimes used for children aged ten to twelve – those in between their primary and secondary years. Classes of this age or with a mix of tweens and teens can feel very different to those of true teenagers. Unsurprisingly they often share, characteristics of both primary and secondary. As with younger groups, it can feel as if you have been dropped onto a moving conveyor belt. Without wishing to drift into unhelpful generalisations, 10, 11 and 12-year-olds tend to display much more of a continuous mode of activity – as if they are 'on' right from the word go to the very end of the lesson – chattering, fidgeting and vying for the teacher's attention. Unlike older adolescents who might not want to appear too eager in front of their peers, some tweens will try to answer every question, often with variations on "Me! Me! Me!", their hands straining in the air without caring much what the others think of them. Students of this age can sometimes be so busy trying to impress their teacher they do not realise their enthusiasm is actually putting a strain on that very same person. Rather than appreciate the learning aims underpinning a lesson, they will tend to gravitate towards a points, praise and play paradigm.

Task design for older teens

Some years back I was charged with teaching intermediate English to a group of first and second year undergraduates in a private university. For three weeks my attempts to set up any type of pair work failed. It then dawned upon me that I was probably teaching a class of teenagers. I checked their ages and indeed they were all either 18 or 19. Older teens do not stop being teens because they are at university or in higher level classes. The setting may encourage a shift in attitude towards greater responsibility but they still need structure at a task level.

Practical applications

Getting students to listen to each other

As human beings we do things for a reason. If there is not a good enough reason to do something, we will not do it. Teenagers are no exception.

Imagine we put two students, Raquel and Sara, together as a pair for a speaking exercise. What motive does Raquel have to listen to Sara struggle to tell her something in English that she has already told her three times before in their shared L1? Moreover, Raquel and Sara have been going to the same school since they were seven. They share the same subjects, neighbourhood and friends. Raquel could answer most of the discussion questions in the coursebook for Sara without even asking. Raquel therefore stops listening. Sara sees there is no point in going on and their practice task in English grinds to a halt.

If we can actually give Raquel something to do – some rationale for her role as a listener – then we are halfway there. While she is asking Sara questions, we can equip her with a little responsibility. She can rate her classmate's answers out of ten – with a score of ten being a reply that is at least three times longer than the question itself including a difficult word and no mistakes. Raquel can pencil in the scores she has given next to each question. These new performance related criteria will ensure fuller engagement with the activity.

We can go further. Having established Raquel's role, we can also make her accountable for her scores. Here the nuts and bolts of getting teenagers to listen to each other equates to a sort of rolling consequence. Receiving a score gives a sense of consequence to speaking. Awarding a score gives a sense of consequence to listening. At the end of Sara's turn, Raquel totals up the points she has given and works out the average. This provides a sense of consequence to giving the scores. Each time, there is follow up that stamps a seal of meaningfulness onto what the students have just done. Raquel consequently reports back on her ratings and justifies them: *"I gave Sara an average of seven because her answers were…"*. This provides a sense of consequence to adding up the scores. I hope you can feel how the students in this scenario would now be taking the role of listener more seriously.

To top it off, while the speaking activity is in progress, the teacher can be circulating and evaluating the evaluators. That is, stopping to listen to one of Sara's answers then looking at what points Raquel has awarded, giving a nod of approval or a raised eyebrow where she might have been a little mean.

Games

A game creates tension almost by its very definition. It has structure and rules which force behaviour into a certain pattern in order to see who best flourishes under those limitations. As pointed out by Vygotsky in an essay on play (published 1978), the compensation for adhering to these rules is the chance of winning. All activities, and especially games, have their natural breaking point, but the most common one is when it becomes clear to one player or team that they no longer have any realistic possibility of winning.

Multiple winners

In the Tour de France there are a number of winners every year. There is the overall winner by time, who wins the yellow jersey. There is the racer who is fastest climbing the mountain stretches throughout the event. They win the red polka dotted jersey. There is the rider who accumulates the most sprint finish points who wins the green jersey. In addition, there is a team prize and the *prix de la combativité*, which is awarded each day for the rider deemed to have ridden with the most competitive spirit, attacking and breaking away from the main body of cyclists.

For younger teens we can do a similar thing during games. The winners by points are the ones that finish with the highest score in the classic sense, but then the teacher can award the titles of best sports (those who played in the most civil manner) the best effort (those who tried the hardest) and the best teamworkers (who showed unity and consideration for their own group members). Cutting out a T-shirt template with a different colour scheme for each award will help make it more tangible. The existence of these alternative titles will give all teams something to play for, taking the focus off simply trying to accrue the most points by any means necessary.

Small explosions during gameplay

The teacher plays two main roles in a game. First, they set the game up, explaining the rules and assigning teams, but then their role shifts to one of umpire, judge or referee. In some cases, students may seem to take the teacher-as-game-starter very seriously but once play is underway, take less notice of the teacher-as-referee. Here it is worth remembering that when Sonia explodes on her teammate because he did not listen to her and gave the wrong answer for their team (which costs them a point and possibly the game) it is not a challenge to the *teacher*. It is because Sonia has become involved in the game itself. It has become so important for her in the short-term that the teacher on the other side of the room motioning for her to relax seems a very small and distant figure indeed.

Specifying the format for answers

When your students are desperate to give you the answer to a question in a game, but are doing so with L1 translations of the prompt word where you want synonyms in English, or when they are giving you one word answers where you wanted complete sentences, or when they are shouting out answers where you wanted them to put their hands up, it is because you have still to establish the exact and specific currency of the game.

If students are managing to exchange their answers (L1 translations, one word or shouted out offerings) for a point, a valid move or any other similar officially sanctioned progress in the game, then they will continue to do so. Early on, it is therefore useful to lay some ground rules by stipulating the exact answer format to be accepted (making sure that students have access to any supporting language necessary such as sentence length scripts) and

4. Task design and instructions

then adhering to that uncompromisingly over the first couple of rounds so that it becomes an accepted standard.

Super-charged instructions

Giving instructions is a time when we often feel strained, either because our students are not listening or because they are not managing to understand. One solution, if we know what our instructions will be in advance, in the case of a set task, is to super-charge the moment with significance by turning the instructions themselves into a listening exercise. The teacher reads out a complete version of the instructions several times and afterwards the students get a gapped version, such as the example below, which they then complete from memory. To check they have the answers correct, the teacher reads the complete paragraph once more. By first making the instructions the object of study, we better ensure their uptake. At this point, the students have already heard the full instructions three or four times. In addition, this approach has a residual effect as, once they begin the task, they have a full written set of instructions to refer back to should they need to.

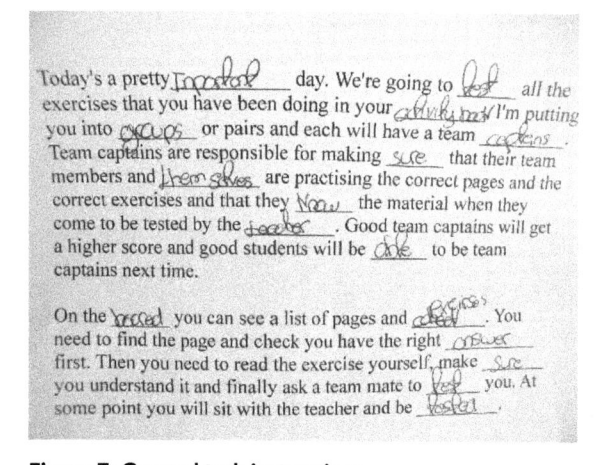

> Today's a pretty _____ day. We're going to _____ all the exercises that you have been doing in your _____. I'm putting you into _____ or pairs and each will have a team _____. Team captains are responsible for making _____ that their team members and _____ are practising the correct pages and the correct exercises and that they _____ the material when they come to be tested by the _____. Good team captains will get a higher score and good students will be _____ to be team captains next time.
>
> On the _____ you can see a list of pages and _____. You need to find the page and check you have the right _____ first. Then you need to read the exercise yourself, make _____ you understand it and finally ask a team mate to _____ you. At some point you will sit with the teacher and be _____.

Figure 7: Gapped task instructions

Echoed instructions

Another useful twist is to give your instructions as usual then ask a student to stand up and say them again, repeating the instructions as faithfully to your version as possible. This can even be turned into a challenge with the teacher awarding a hypothetical mark out of ten for accuracy and asking if anyone else would like to try to score higher.

Recorded instructions

What makes giving instructions such a testing time is that part of you, the teacher, is trying to concentrate on your delivery (logically sequencing the information to be conveyed, grading language and making each step as clear as possible), while another part of you is trying to concentrate on making sure the class are listening. It is so much easier to ensure that students are paying attention to the audio of a listening exercise because you the teacher are not simultaneously generating that audio content yourself.

A novel workaround to this problem is to turn our instructions into an audio or video recording that the students listen to or watch, leaving the teacher able to sit back and observe who is listening and who is not. Suddenly it is as if there were two teachers in the room. If the class needs to hear the instructions again we simply hit replay. If just one or two students need to hear the instructions again they can come to the front and listen again – with or without headphones. For new teachers, those training them or anyone else wishing to hone their instruction-giving, this is a useful approach. Like the super-charged instructions technique above, it requires you first to think carefully about how to stage your explanations. It also allows you to hear yourself *as your students do* and to check that you have not left out anything important.

Teacher trainer Sue Cowley (2013) suggests recording demonstrations of activities so that students can actually watch the task in question being completed. While this would perhaps be more appropriate for craft-based lessons with younger primary students, an audio of the teacher talking through either the set up or even the answers to a grammar exercise could provide additional support for struggling students while still leaving the teacher free to attend to other students or the activity as a whole.

Give them a rest

Sometimes we ask students to do a task and when they finish it we give them another. Then they finish that and they get another task, and another and another. Yes, we want our classes to be efficient and productive. However, driven by the conviction that a good class is one where everyone is engaged in activity all of the time, we might overlook the value of two, three or five minutes of occasional rest. Respite is good to reorder self. I am not sure we need to 'deal' with fast finishers at all. Instead of desperately trying to find them another thing to do, I suggest the following scenario:

"Finished, teacher!"

"Okay good. Chill out and relax. Have a rest now until the next bit. You've done your work, so you have five minutes to enjoy having done it."

Now you probably don't want to leave five minute pockets like this in assessed lessons on courses for a teaching qualification, but in general I think we are always going to have a better lesson when we remember we are teaching young people that get tired.

Questions for reflection

- Do you have classes of tweens you should be treating more like primary students?
- Do you have any classes of young adults you should be treating more like teens?

Things to try

1. Plan one of your lessons as normal then look over it and try to identify track switches, as discussed in the chapter, where students will need to change back to English if they have lapsed into L1.
2. Dissect one of your lesson plans carefully. Try to identify what the consequence of completing each stage successfully will be in subsequent stages of the lesson. How does each activity help to make the one before it meaningful?
3. Try scripting the instructions to a task as described in **Super-charged instructions** on p62.

Things to share

Partner up with a colleague who teaches the same level as you. Record yourselves on video giving instructions to a task that neither of you have yet done. Swap recordings. Give the recording of your colleague a guest spot in your lesson, using them to introduce that task. Share your thoughts later with your colleague/s on:
- Your experience of scripting and staging instructions.
- Your experience of the recording process.
- What you learnt from your colleague's recording.

References

Cowley S (2013) *The Seven T's of Practical Differentiation*. Bristol: Sue Cowley Books Ltd.

Vygotsky L (1978) *Mind in Society*. Harvard: Harvard University Press.

5. Group dynamics and order

Discussion

Too much individual, not enough group

I was getting on a plane – it was a Seville to Barcelona flight – and we did everything wrong. Who were 'we'? I am referring to the 200 or so passengers. I am afraid we were all over the place. We lined up badly for a start. I say 'we' because I perceived us as a group – albeit a temporary group united by fairly arbitrary factors of circumstance. There was meant to be one queue for seats 16 to 32 on the left and another for seats 1 to 15 on the right. Even though they had announced this four times over the tannoy, most of us, myself included, were dithering about between the two lines then getting up to the front and finding out we were in the wrong one and having to go to the back of the other.

Things did not improve on the plane. When we found our seats, we stood in the middle of the aisle getting this that and the other down from our hand luggage and making the line of people behind us wait, instead of moving in and sorting the finer points out later so that everyone could sit down at least. It took twice as long for everyone to be settled than it needed to and I hate to imagine what the flight attendants must have thought of us. We were so wrapped up in ourselves that we had forgotten we were travelling as a collective. Here is a simple schema:

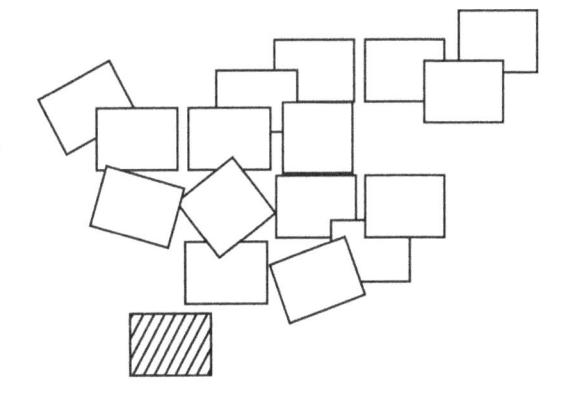

Figure 8: Too much individual, not enough group

In our teens' classes this sort of dynamic results in students all clamouring for the teacher's attention, shouting out answers, jumping turns, worrying about how to do a task before listening to the instructions and their overuse of the words 'I' and 'me'.

Too much group not enough individual

The opposite thing happens with groups of tourists that you see following a guide through frequently visited cities on day trips. If you look closely, you will see that often these people (who may be highly successful and independent individuals when they are not on holiday) are shuffling along in a way that suggests that they do not really know where they are going and may not know exactly where they are. To all intents and purposes, the people in these groups (and again, I have been one of them many times) have stopped functioning as autonomous, thinking individuals. It is another case of good people, poor dynamic. Here is the schema:

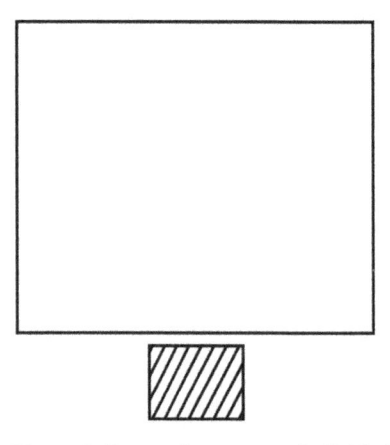

Figure 9: Too much group, no individual

In our teens' classes this would manifest itself in the form of nobody knowing what page they should be on, low energy levels, lack of initiative and a tendency to wait for the teacher to explain everything. A related phenomenon is the idea of *social loafing* (Latané *et al*, 1979) in which individuals hitch a free ride upon the collective energy of the group and do not try as hard as they would if alone.

Getting it just right

For a good English class, we cannot work very well with either of the above dynamics. We cannot use the first because there has to be some level of coordination, an awareness of forming a collective and making conscious decisions that benefit the whole. We cannot use the second because we need each individual in the group to be thinking for themselves – looking for answers, being ready and wanting to progress.

We want something like the schema below, which involves both collectivising the individuals and individualising the collective.

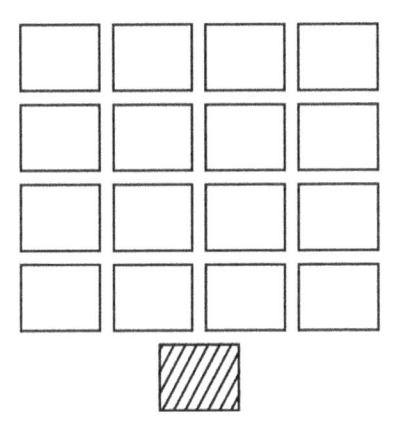

Figure 10: Individualise the collective, collectivise the individuals

Each and every class that you ever teach, no matter what age or level, will lie at a point between these two. It will never be a static point but it will always have a bearing upon what type of class you and your students experience.

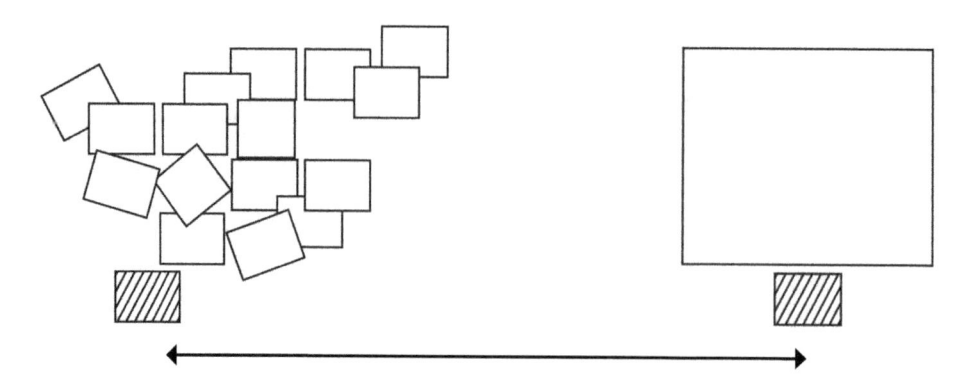

Figure 11: Finding the right balance for your class

Much of what I have to say both here and in later chapters on the subject of classroom management, order, control, discipline and general well-functioning of classes has to do with trying to edge closer to a middle point. The beauty of teenage classes is that, where primary levels are too young to understand the concepts and where adult classes might take offence, teenagers will often listen to and take on board explicit guidance in this area and we shall cover this in greater depth later.

Class vs teacher

There is another type of dynamic, related to the schema of too much group not enough individual. It is when a class goes somewhat feral and turns upon the teacher. In these cases, an 'us against the teacher' situation can develop. Teens are more peer-centred than younger age groups and nearly all the teachers of teens I have spoken to have felt hostility of this type at some point or another. Early writers on the behaviour of large groups such as Gustave Le Bon (1896) talked about the pack behaviour of crowds and later writers such as Festinger *et al* (1952) have talked about the members of large groups experiencing both a reduction of their individuality and a diffused sense of responsibility, which allows them to behave in a less inhibited way. These concepts and others have been used by writers on crowd psychology to explain the extreme behaviour of normal individuals – for example, during riots. Our classes are not crowds and they are not rioting but some of the collective processes may run parallel.

When you are met with silence

Remember that moment when you ask a class a question which is meant as a lead in to a whole group conversation and nobody answers? Can you recall that moment when you ask for a volunteer or for the answer to question 1 of exercise 2C on page 37 and get nothing back? What is happening here is that students are taking refuge in each other rather than taking upon themselves the task of negotiating a legitimate and productive relationship with their teacher. In some ways, they are hiding because it feels easier and safer. Action and the social responsibility it entails can weigh heavily upon even an adult sometimes. We need to tease our students out of this dynamic by convincing them, over time, that they have nothing to lose by the honest expression of the best English they currently have.

Practical applications

Asking specific students

As teachers, we may tend to field questions to an open class. It is part of the habit we have of talking to the collective before us as if they were just one person, as discussed in Chapter 3 on classroom micromechanics. If we can avoid fielding questions that end in *"…anyone?"* then we are on the right track. True, nominating a student does put them on the spot but it also sends a more clearly structured message about who is expected to respond and what is expected of them. It also frees the nominated individual from any danger of looking too eager to please the teacher in the eyes of their peers.

Avoiding a stand off

If a teacher tells a class off using a generic *"you"*, then to some extent, every student in the class is going to feel told off. It may be that only a handful of individuals are truly deserving of reprimand but by telling the entire group off we effectively put everyone on the same level. Students who feel they have done nothing wrong may feel the injustice of this quite keenly. As a result, individual students with behavioural patterns that are normally very different to each other might start to feel pushed together and seek alliances where they did not before – against the common enemy, the teacher. Yes, we are looking to foster a collective awareness but we need to do it positively.

Reducing the amount of time we stand in front of a class criticising them as a group is another very good step. It is, however, sometimes a hard habit to break and one that is very easy to relapse into, especially when we have lost our patience or temper.

Reaching individuals on a personal level

To better individualise the collective, we need to cut through the pack 'thing' and highlight that each student's relationship with **their teacher's judgement** is what should concern them first and foremost – at least for the duration of the class. There are several techniques we can use to do this. The first is to ensure that there are regular moments of one-to-one interaction. Even in a large class, there will be times when the students are working from their activity books and we have an opportunity to invite individual students to sit with us and talk, read us a text or something they have written, or to have some work corrected personally, thus emphasising the student's performance + teacher's evaluation connection. We shall consider these further in Chapter 19 on personalisation.

Personal feedback

You will remember that one of my tenets for teaching teens is to make things explicit. Things that we think should be obvious to teenagers are sometimes not and we can save an enormous amount of time and energy by sharing our thoughts. A conversation I have had numerous times goes like this:

> Teacher: *"Please remember, class, I teach you as a group but I evaluate you as an…"*
>
> Students: *"…individual, teacher?"*
>
> Teacher: *"Exactly. Now let me ask you a question. If there was something that you personally were doing in class that meant you were going to get a lower mark at the end of term, would you want to know what it was?"*
>
> Students: *"YES, teacher."*
>
> Teacher: *"Or would you prefer I didn't tell you?"*
>
> Students: *"No, we'd want to know."*

Teacher: *"And if there was something you were doing well would you want me to tell you so that you could keep doing it to get an even better mark?"*

Students: *"Of course, teacher."*

Teacher: *"Okay, so if you want to, you can come to me at the end of any class and I will give you a rough percentage for how happy I've been with you that class and if there's anything really good or even a little bit not so good, I'll tell you specifically what it was."*

Some students will come and it is often those whose performance fluctuates that look for such validation so this will provide an ideal entry point to further discussion and goal setting.

Letting students know that you noticed them

Another useful strategy is to hold little meetings. Again, highlighting the importance of individual class members' relationship with the teacher, not 'the pack'. We can keep a couple of students back after each class to comment on any point, not necessarily even a bad one.

Teacher: *"Helen, Alex and Mary, can I have a quick word with you?"*

Helen: *"What did I do, teacher?"*

Teacher: *"I just wanted to let you know that I did notice you knew all the answers to the listening, even though you didn't get a chance to give me any of the answers."*
[Helen is now standing two centimetres taller.]

Alex: *"And me, teacher?"*

Teacher: *"You had a good lesson."*

Alex: *"That's it?"*

Teacher: *"Yep."*
[Alex shrugs but you can see he likes that].

Mary: *"And me?"*

Teacher: "You brought a notebook this time. Well done."

Mary: "And a pencil, teacher."

Teacher: "I noticed that as well."

A positive dynamic

In this chapter, we have looked at a number of less than ideal group dynamics, but I would like to end by remembering that being in a group can also exert a very positive influence. For every class that is not working so well I am sure you can bring to mind another where students tend to encourage, help and learn from each other – one where there is an atmosphere – or what Holliday (1999) terms *small culture*, perhaps even *micro*-culture – of productivity and enthusiasm which feeds into itself. One of my personal catchphrases is: *That's why we do education in groups!* You will hear that in my classes when I see an example of peer support or of students making decisions that go beyond themselves and benefit the collective. It can be your catchphrase too, if you want it.

Questions for reflection

- Where is your most challenging class at in terms of individuals vs group?
- Do you need to individualise any group?
- Do you need to collectivise the individuals in any group?
- Do you have a group that is running on a wild 'pack mentality'?
- How do you 'reach' the individuals within your groups?

Things to try

1. In **Downloadable resource 2**, you will find a template with the two schemas and the sliding scale as in Figure 11. For each of your classes, try plotting a cross along the line to see where you think they are in terms of individual vs collective dynamic.
2. Monitor your own use of questions. Are you fielding questions to the void, as it were, or are you nominating individual students?
3. Explore the possibility of increasing in-class one-to-one time with students, remembering that it is not necessary to get through all the students in one lesson or even one week of lessons.

Things to share

Observe your classes in progress and note down any instances of collective apathy or when classes seem to band together against you.

- What were the triggers?
- Was it something you said or asked them to do?
- Was it a specific activity type or a certain time of the lesson or day?
- How did you react and how satisfactory was the outcome?

Try doing the same type of observational recording for examples of positive dynamic: peer support and students making decisions that benefit the group.

Share your observations as a sequence of mini-case studies in a short workshop or discussion group and invite your colleagues to comment.

References

Festinger L, Pepitone A & Newcomb TM (1952) Some consequences of deindividuation in a group. *Journal of Abnormal and Social Psychology* **47**: 382–389.

Holliday A (1999) Small cultures. *Applied Linguistics* **20** (2): 237–264.

Latané B, Williams K & Harkins S (1979) Many hands make light the work: the causes and consequences of social loafing. *Journal of Personality and Social Psychology* **37** (6): 822–832.

Le Bon G (1896) *The Crowd: A study of the popular mind*. New York: The Macmillan Co.

6. Affect: speaking positively to our students

Discussion

Need for attention

We have mentioned that teenagers want to receive their teacher's attention. In fact, they want attention in general. I think we all do, but I am going to go a step further and say that perhaps attention is the defining phenomenon for teens – or it is that by which they define themselves.

Erich Berne, creator of the Transactional Analysis (TA) model of social interaction, likened paying someone attention to giving them a psychological stroke (1964). The strokes we receive can be positive or negative but as Berne and later writers on TA point out, often any attention is better than no attention at all (Stewart & Joines, 1987). This is especially so with teens.

For teenagers, recognition of any type reaffirms themselves to themselves. They form themselves from it. Some of them will throw out sound rather like a bat emitting sonar, bouncing words off the world and observing the results. When you are a teenager, everything you say is at once a gamble and an experiment.

If you think I am going too far with this, please listen to a group of your teens as they stand outside your teaching centre, in the schoolyard at break, in the canteen, or as they chatter together inside or outside of your classroom between lessons. Time and again you will see one of them taking an utterance or a behaviour and throwing it out there. You will see moves that form part of a more purposeful strategy such as securing one's own position by boosting another group member's status – agreeing with them or laughing at their jokes. You will see much more basic moves such as an intrusive noise, repeated over and over again – aimed at simply getting its issuer noticed. It might be annoying. It might not be well thought out. It might not be what that teenager will wish they had said in retrospect, but it is what they have in the moment so they throw it out there and see.

A snapshot of the need for recognition

While the rest of the class completes some workbook exercises, I am testing students one-by-one on a list of vocabulary we have looked at. Right now I am testing Julia (we are both sitting by the teacher's table at the front) but while I do so, Aaron, sitting to my left, is clicking his ballpoint pen continuously, shifting in his seat and sighing loudly. Without actually misbehaving, he is making as much noise as he can. Why? Is he trying to catch Julia's attention or to impress her? No. He wants desperately to be tested.

"Do you want to go next?" I ask him. Aaron shrugs, but he takes little time to move over to the seat Julia has just vacated.

Does the teacher like me?

Irene Caspari wrote a very insightful book called *Troublesome Children in Class* (1976). Perhaps the title was deliberately provocative or perhaps our terminology has simply moved on. In any case, she reminds us that in a class of teenagers the teacher is the only adult and that the question at the forefront of our students' minds will always be: *"Does the teacher like me?"*

Who is the students' favourite teacher?

While working in the private academy sector, and over a number of years, I asked my students who their favourite teachers at school were (first reported, with some of the material below, in Roland, 2013). Unfortunately, I did not systematically collect the data but I did form a strong personal impression of the general profile of respected teachers. It was the teacher that cared, in that they embodied the rules and ideals of the institution and was not afraid to tell students off, but also the one that did not hold a grudge afterwards. On the other hand, it seemed to be the feeling of having been irredeemably negatively judged that students found least bearable.

Asking a student: *"Why do you hate that other teacher so much?"* will invariably give you an answer along the following lines: *"I hate that teacher because that teacher hates me."*

It is an extremely simple equation. As teachers it is obvious to us that we do not hate our students – but for them it is not such an obvious given. I cannot reiterate this enough:

There is a huge amount of value to you as a teacher of teenagers in making sure that your students know you do not hate them.

How do they get to know this? You tell them so. You make your reassurances explicit.

If Pablo is whistling, you can tell him: *"Pablo, I like you but I don't like that sound."*

If Ana and Conchita are nattering: *"You guys are great, but you'd make me really happy if you started that exercise."*

When we need Lorenzo, a 15-year-old boy who is quite happy sitting with his mates to re-partner with one of the other students we can tell him: *"Lorenzo, you're a fantastic person. Could you switch places and work with Almudena?"*

How can he not switch places now? We have just told him he is fantastic. If he objects to switching places, then instead of asking him again, we just tell him that he is fantastic again. Lorenzo is shaking his head, even as he is switching places, and he is thinking:

"What can I do? I don't want to switch places. I want to tell this teacher where to get off but the teacher's telling me I'm fantastic and I know they might only half mean it but they can't hate me at least, and nobody's told me that I'm fantastic all day and IT'S THE ONLY THING I WANT TO HEAR!!!!"

When a student gets an answer wrong, I try to include an acknowledgement of their effort to contribute in my response, such as "No, but I appreciate the energy" or "No, but thanks anyway" or "No, but good try".

While it *is* important to establish clearly when an answer is incorrect, especially when going over exercises, this, like the other examples above, is an example of what Carl Rogers (1961) referred to as 'unconditional positive regard'. It demonstrates a caring attitude and blanket acceptance of the student which does not depend on them getting questions right, knowing answers or achieving a certain score. It does not even depend on them behaving in a certain way. It underlies all of that.

The dial goes back to zero

I would like to describe an imaginary meter. It has a needle and markings. At one end the markings are deep green and say, *"I'm very happy with you"*. This is the zero-point of the scale. The next point along the scale is lighter green turning to yellow: *"I'm happy enough with you"*. If the needle moves further over it reaches *"I'm not happy with you. Trouble is brewing"* in orange and at the extreme end of the meter we read *"I am extremely unhappy with you and we have a problem!"*. This is the ten-point of the scale.

When Carlos convinces all his 14-year-old friends to ride into your class on imaginary horses, the dial may flicker temporarily to orange. By the middle of the lesson when he is coughing deliberately loudly, so that the sound reports across the classroom like a gunshot, then telling you it is just his bad throat, you might have hit red and feel that some sort of disciplinary measure is needed to minimise the damage Carlos is doing.

Regardless of what a student does, how much it bothers you or what classroom management manoeuvre you finally take, we need to reassure students that our responses and our measures are not rejection of them. This is part of what Ellis and Maclaren describe as rating the behaviour and not the person (2005). Again, we can do this explicitly by answering the *"Does the teacher like me?"* question right at the start of any response: *"I like you, but I'm not happy with your performance right now so we're going to do this, this and this until it gets better."*

Once Carlos's actions *do* get better though, the dial has to go back to zero. That is to say, when a student starts behaving better – it could be in the same lesson, it could be half a term later – then they are treated objectively, neutrally and the same as everyone else. This will help them realise that what you are doing when you move them about, send them out, add a comment to their report or such like is you in your professional capacity and a systematic response to their own slump in performance – from which there is always a return.

Jack's a bit daft

I would like to offer a slightly different perspective now and would ask you not to take my words too seriously, at least until you get the basic drift of the point. Jack is a 14-year-old boy. By all reasonable adult standards Jack is bit daft. He says daft things. He does daft things. His idea of what is cool is a video clip of track-suited youths moshing in an abandoned warehouse waving automatic handguns, sticks, rocks and bottles of beer. His idea of charming the girls in the class is to wind them up with smart but harmless comments rather than engage them with sentences that have any meaningful content. He often knows the answer to the teacher's questions but is not very good at waiting his turn and he also has an annoying habit of trying to spin his pen around the outside of his thumb and back to its original position – which regularly results in the pen clattering to the floor during his teacher's explanations.

Here is Jack.

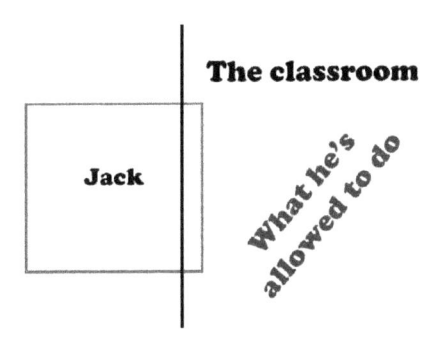

Figure 12: A student operating within a very limited sphere of action

The line represents how much of himself he is allowed to express. If we make him work on an exercise in silence and then we go over the answers as a class with students putting their hands up and answering a question but not much more, there is relatively little room for Jack to express his daftness.

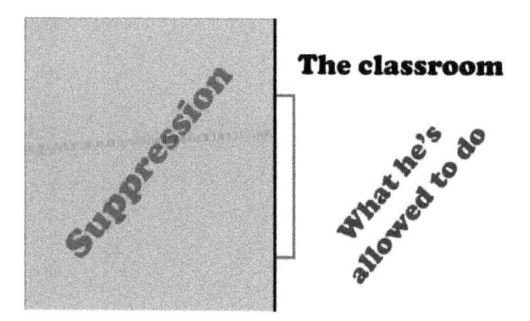

Figure 13: The illusion of a well-behaved class

This might look like a very well-managed, well-controlled class because we have largely suppressed all action, BUT, if we want a truly communicative class, if we want to invite our students' 14-year-old personalities out to play, then naturally we are going to see more daft behaviour. They are people in the process of forming themselves. Their judgements are often flawed, their perspectives very subjective and that is *fine*.

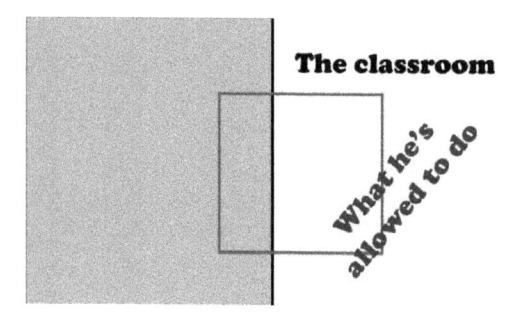

Figure 14: Getting it right

I believe that it is much better to give Jack the space and the freedom to be himself and be involved in the class albeit with some daftness than to have him in total lockdown. Yes, Jack is daft but he is 14 and in general 14-year-old boys are a little bit daft. I accept Jack when he tries to be good and I accept him when he is daft as well. He reminds me of myself when I was his age and a little of myself as I still am now.

Ana's too loud

Ana is a 13-year-old girl. Ana is loud in class. What her teacher has only half considered is that Ana is naturally loud – or at least, she is habitually loud when interacting in her peer groups.

Sometimes when she gets an answer wrong and another student makes a comment or corrects her, Ana will go into loud mode to reassert herself, perhaps with a retort. Part of her has to do this, in spite of the teacher (not in defiance of the teacher). If we can give her a prompt to come back into class mode without making a massive issue of such episodes or pushing them to a point of confrontation, then we will have a much easier time accommodating Ana into the group.

Yes, we want our students to care about what their teacher thinks and to prize that over what their classmates think. However, we will never and should never want to separate a teen from their group either. Ideally, recognition from the teacher will be seen as a respectable thing by both the individual and the whole group.

"What about the one's you don't like?"

I sometimes get asked how I deal with the students that I really do not like. My answer is the following: **right from the start I try to treat them all as if I do like them and so the issue never really arises**. Is this self-deception? Am I tricking myself or lying to myself? Am I being false? Not really. Often by behaving in a certain way you can bring a desired situation into being. We are using a simulated jump-start into a genuinely productive dynamic. By not allowing yourself to foment negativity you can stay in benevolent mode, as it were.

Again, with particularly challenging individuals we can include assertions of positive regard in our utterances: *"Yes, Carlos, my friend. You have a question?"*

Put crudely, the words we use can help get our brains moving in a certain direction. It is hard to wholeheartedly dislike someone with your head when you are simultaneously calling them friend and telling them you like them – and you will sometimes see that positivity register as a surprised flicker across Carlos's face.

The quiet ones

Paying attention to the quiet students can have a very positive effect on your class dynamic. I am talking about the ones that never say anything in open class – never offer an answer unless prompted. There is a subset of quiet students that, when prompted, you will notice, come back with the correct answer nearly every time. These are the students that are silently awake and silently shining. They were with you all along. They just need you to see that. They might not want showy praise but with some indication that you value them they will get behind you (albeit quietly). It is a different kind of cooperation and a different kind of energy but it evens out a class.

Goodwill

Students, especially teenagers, are able to detect on a very primal level a teacher who harbours goodwill towards them and one who does not. After all the mini-confrontations, rules established, broken and enforced, and when all the warnings and exam comments and passes, failures, disappointments and pleasant surprises are worked out, the question is: *"Does this teacher maintain a generally benevolent mindset towards their students or not?"*

Practical applications

Ways to enjoy your students and classes

So what gets in the way of a benevolent mindset? Seeing students as an obstacle to getting through your syllabus or getting through your day is one. Recognising where students are at, accepting their actual level, and enjoying the progress that they do make is a more positive path. If a student gives a good answer or asks a relevant question, taking just a fraction of a second to savour that with them by remarking, "Good question" or "Good answer", is a way to enrich the script that unfurls between you and your class. Referring back to contributions is another: *"Jack, what did you say the translation for ____ was?"* Or: *"Ana, what was that phrase you were using to talk about…?"*

Extending goodwill to the teachers' room

How we talk *about* our students in the staffroom is one indication of how healthy our mindset is. This may involve training (or retraining) ourselves only to speak about them in a way that, even if critical, would be considered acceptable were they or their parents present. Such a strategy will make everything discussed in this chapter easier and can reduce levels of toxicity in teachers' shared spaces.

Negative to positive

Ultimately our aim is to wean a student off getting attention for the wrong reasons and onto getting it for the right ones – off negative strokes and onto positive ones. We can reduce the frequency with which we say their name when they are off task, limiting ourselves to short prompts which are neutral in tone. However, we do not want to overcompensate by giving positive strokes when not fairly earnt – that is appeasement.

The best type of attention we can give students is attention to the *language they produce*. This means listening to them when they do make the effort to speak English and looking at their writing when they have managed to produce something with gusto. Acknowledging language production is the first step. Finding something to praise in it is the second. Encouraging them to push further is the third. Recognising their attempt to do so is the fourth. The message is clear: **if you really want this teacher's quality attention, do something in English.**

Asking genuine questions

One student arrives two minutes before the others.

> Teacher: *"Did you have a good weekend?"*
>
> Student: *"Yes."*
>
> Teacher: *"Did you do anything interesting?"*
>
> Student: *"I studied."*
>
> Teacher: *"Yeah? What subjects?"*
>
> Student: *"History and maths … for an exam."*
>
> Teacher: *"Were the exams today?"*
>
> Student: *"Yes."*
>
> Teacher: *"So how did they go?"*

At this point the student realises that you are actually asking her about herself. To begin with, she was economising, saving you both the trouble of expending energy on something she imagined was simple formality.

> Student: *"The history good. The maths, I don't know."*
>
> Teacher: *"So what was the history on. I mean, what period of history was it?"*

The conversation then gets interesting and together you manage to arrive at *the Enlightenment* from the student's L1. By this time, she is volunteering information about her history syllabus. The conversation has turned into a real exchange in English with personalise language input. It often takes students three, four, five or six questions to realise you are genuinely asking about them and their day and that you are making space for them to give you an answer.

Mountain pass politics

As a keen hill walker, I have noticed something. Please imagine you are in the city walking along a narrow pavement. Someone you do not know comes the other way. You make room for each other but you probably do not say hello. Now imagine you are walking along a narrow trail on a mountainside and someone is coming the other way. Do you say hello? I think so. Why? Because at high altitude, in the wilderness or during extremes of weather, a primal sense of community kicks in. Mutual recognition opens the way for mutual aid. Up high, you want as many friends as you can get. You might fall and break an ankle and it might be the person you have just said hello to, three hours later on their return journey, that helps to get you down.

My first recommendation with respect to this analogy is that whenever you see your students in the street, you make the effort to at least say hello and, if possible, to go over and talk to them briefly – even if it is a bit awkward. Neither play the teacher nor try to look cool. Just a simple exchange that will leave the friends they are with, who may not go to the same school, asking afterwards: *"Who was that? They seemed okay"*. Your students probably have fewer meaningful exchanges with adults than you imagine and your value as a positive reference point in the adult world may be substantial.

Please now imagine another scenario. A teacher enters and tries to start their class. Two girls in the front row look at him and start to giggle, though it is unclear whether they are giggling at him or something else. The teacher would prefer they were not giggling so he acts as if he cannot see or hear them. Now invisible barriers spring up. The girls realise that there is an unacknowledged reality running parallel to what the teacher would like to be happening. In it their smirks, snorts, chortles or whispering about the lesson or the teacher or anything else will go ignored and unanswered. This is when we need to imagine we are on that mountainside and that our continued survival depends upon a franker level of communication and successful negotiation. Rather than letting things go unspoken, speaking to students normally can be far more effective and when needed, quite disarming.

"Girls, are you giggling at me?"

"No, teacher."

"Okay. Thanks. That's nice to hear. It's still a bit distracting though."

"Okay, sorry."

Cross talk and clouds

An upper intermediate class were wearing me down. I drew a horse shoe of crosses on the board.

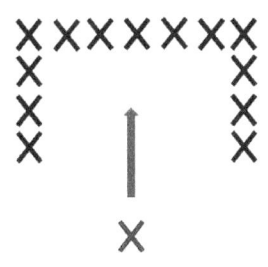

```
X X X X X X X
X           X
X           X
X     ↑     X

      X
```

Figure 15: Teacher talking to class

"This is you [I told my students] *and this is me here. The arrow is when I talk to you."*

6. Affect: speaking positively to our students

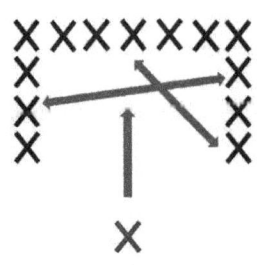

Figure 16: Cross talk between students

"This is cross talk. That is the name teachers have for when you are talking to each other about … anything – especially when I'm trying to explain something to you."

Figure 17: How the teacher feels about the students

"This shows that I care about you."

Figure 18: What happens to that care when there is lots of cross talk

"When there's a lot of cross talk, dark clouds roll in and they start to block out that care. It is still there but it doesn't reach you."

This is a very simple schema but I have found it exceedingly useful to convey the extreme frustration that unsolicited student inter-chatter can have. The actual board work looked like this:

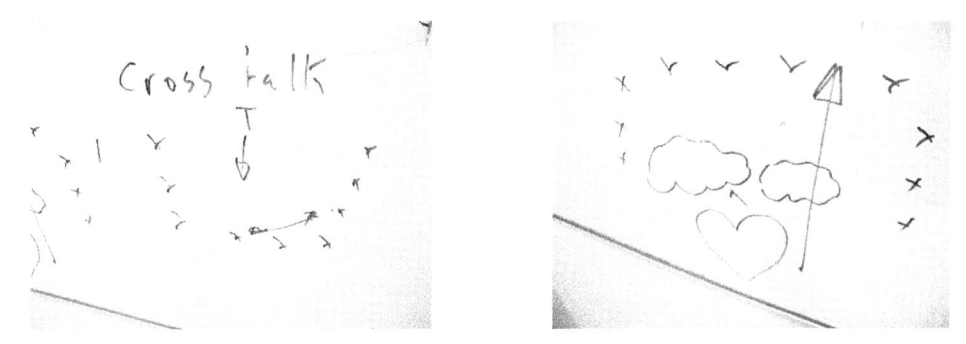

Figures 19 & 20: The cross talk analogy as it was illustrated to the class

My partner and fellow teacher, Raquel Gorosito Villalobos, liked the analogy so much that she sometimes uses a cardboard heart and cloud, stuck to the top of the board, to indicate to students how close the dark clouds are.

Questions for reflection

- How do your students know you do not hate them?
- How much of your students' personalities do you want to work with?
- How much attention do you pay to your quieter students?
- Does your dial always go back to zero?
- Do you see any value in sharing with your students how you feel, as in the dark clouds schema?

Things to try

1. Next time you ask a student if they have had a good day or if they did something interesting at the weekend and receive a curt reply, try following up with additional questions so that they see you are genuinely interested.
2. Consider integrating positive affirmations into your exchanges with students such as: *"I like you but…"*
3. Monitor yourself. What do you sound like when you talk about your students to colleagues? How would your students feel if they could hear you?

> **Things to share**
>
> Observe a student whose behaviour you find challenging or who you are struggling to like. Seek out something genuinely positive about them from their own perspective, a classmate's or yours. Share this in a positive comment about them:
>
> - to a colleague who knows that student, seeing where the conversation goes
> - to the student themselves, if appropriate
> - on their report card.
>
> **Note:** This does not mean ignoring behaviours that need to be changed.

References

Berne E (1964) *Games People Play*. London: Penguin.

Caspari I (1976) *Troublesome Children in Class*. Boston: Routledge and Kegan Paul.

Ellis A & MacLaren C (2005) *Rational Emotive Behaviour Therapy*. California: Impact Publishers.

Rogers C (1961) *On Becoming a Person: A therapist's view of psychotherapy*. Boston: Houghton Mifflin Company.

Roland C (2013) Let's talk about discipline. *English Teaching professional* **89**: 4–6.

Stewart I & Joines V (1987) *TA Today: A new introduction to transactional analysis*. North Carolina: Lifespace Publishing.

7. Logistical questions: homework, L1 and seating

Discussion

A rationale for homework

None of us wants to impose upon our students' time or add to an already considerable workload from other subjects. It would be worse, though, to allow students to go through the machinations of attending English classes – for however many hours, weeks and years – and not be able to communicate reasonably at the end of it. For me, there are two levels of homework. Simple homework tasks can help increase exposure time to core language covered in the lesson, acting as a reminder and fixing language. I share the rationale like so:

> *"This homework will help you remember what we have done in class. It's short, it's simple, but it's important."*

A higher function of homework is to provide the opportunity for more carefully and creatively crafted responses than are always possible in the classroom. This is ideal for those students who want to stretch themselves and explore the language as a medium for personalised expression.
I generally offer these type of homework tasks as optional but I extend the offer to all students, regardless of their level.

When L1 use is unwanted

I hope that most English language teachers have no problem with students using their first language to help them understand and form utterances in English. It is much more than a *bona fide* resource. It is their world. What most teenagers' teachers actually object to, I believe, is:

a. Cross talk – short or extended exchanges between students that are tangential, irrelevant or even detrimental to the language task underway (and which are normally conducted in L1).
b. L1 use when time has been made in the class for English to be practised – equating to students being off task – which may be felt by the teacher to be a particular loss in contexts where students have little chance to practise outside of class time.

Neither of these are objections to the L1 *per se* but more a concern for class dynamics.

Seating

Seating can quickly become an issue in teenage classrooms. When students are allowed to sit where they want, place boundaries can become part of their classroom identities. That is, they get used to sitting in a certain seat or next to certain classmates, and feel that those choices reflect who they are and become quite protective if they feel someone has taken 'their seat'.

One solution is for the teacher to assign seats on a monthly or termly basis in a roster type fashion. Another is to assign seats randomly at the beginning of the class by handing students a number card as they come in and having them find and sit in the correspondingly numbered chair.

Whether a system is used or not, it is important that seating remains the prerogative of the teacher. I personally do allow to teenagers to sit where they want, most of the time, but I try to make it very clear at the start of the year that seating is a teaching issue:

*"Everything you do in this classroom has the end purpose of helping you learn more words and sentences in English. That includes where you sit – in relation to the board, in relation to me and in relation to your classmates. I **will** ask you to move – quite often in fact. It will sometimes be for reasons that are not obvious to you in that moment – reasons connected to language practice, language learning and group dynamics. However, it will always be to help you and not to punish you. If you co-operate without making a fuss, then the rest of the time I can keep letting you sit where you want."*

Practical applications

Choosing tasks for homework

In general, homework is something our students just want to get done. They are not analytical experts or linguistic researchers. They will not normally be able to figure out rules for themselves. If they do not know the answers to an exercise, they will often get them wrong. Standard, regular homework, for me, is less about covering new ground and more about increasing familiarisation with existing knowledge by following up classwork.

Audio homework

Homework that involves students recording themselves speaking or reading something out then submitting that electronically is very well suited to the rationale outlined above. I regularly set a range of different tasks including:

- Reading out a piece of writing that they have had corrected, integrating my corrections into their spoken version.
- Rehearsing a presentation that they are going to give in class.
- Reading out grammar exercises already corrected in class as consolidation.
- Working through a vocabulary list, reading out L1 translations.
- Responding to conversation questions on a topic already covered in class as an opportunity to integrate the language that was provided then.
- Describing a picture already looked at in class, again as an opportunity to recycle vocabulary specific to it.
- Reading a text already looked at in class as a pronunciation exercise.
- Reading a text already looked at in class providing a spoken translation into L1.

Our default blueprint for homework is that it is paper based. Audio-based homework shifts us towards an emphasis on spoken fluency and pronunciation. I shall explain further how I respond to these in Chapter 10.

I recommend setting up a dedicated email address to receive students' work so it does not mix with your personal correspondence. For transparency and professionalism, I advise making parents aware of this additional channel either by a consent letter or on parents' evening. In fact, where my students do not have their own email address, they often use a parent's. In addition, if submissions are acknowledged and replied to during working hours and exchanges always asynchronous, with chat in real time avoided, the purpose and function of the system will remain uncompromised.

Working to these guidelines, in four years of using email-based homework extensively with teens, I have had no incidents of inappropriate material, disclosure of overly-personal information or students just wanting to chat.

Returning work

With a group that is challenging, I recommend starting off the lesson by returning some written work or some tests that you have marked. Even if you did not get time to mark everyone's offerings, just handing back three, four or five pieces to a number of students will work in your favour for several closely linked reasons.

It reminds students that the big question is their individual performance and progress – as evaluated by the teacher. It may give students a reason to talk to you on a one-to-one basis, to query your comments for example. Also, it focuses students' attention on something other than entertaining themselves at the beginning of the class, and students that do not get work back will be curious about the other students' work.

In addition to this, giving something back represents a symbolic exchange. It is almost like getting presents: the curiosity, the possible reward and even the chance of occasional disappointment. There is a whole realm here, explored by Marcel Mauss in his essay *The Gift* (first published 1954). One of his central points, which I shall crudely summarise, is that nothing is for free. Any kind of exchange places some sort of obligation of reciprocity on the receiver. On a very reasonable level, students might hypothesise: *"Teacher, why should we do any more work for you when you have not held up your part of the bargain and recognised our efforts from last time?"*. They might not actually articulate this in quite those words. On a slightly more calculated level, classes will sometimes use what they can, especially if you are still at a class vs teacher stage. Asking a teacher if they have marked the last writing assignment and the teacher having to say no apologetically forces that teacher onto the psychological low ground right at the start of the class. It is only a slight strategic disadvantage, but it is significant and one worth avoiding nonetheless.

L1: decisions

In terms of L1 use, I have found that the following line of reasoning often works well to lay an initial foundation of understanding:

"You won't hear me say 'No [L1 or L1s]!' in this class. I love languages, all of them. BUT this is an English class. I can't make you speak in English but I can see when you have made the decision to try to speak it yourself. So, the deal is this: if I see you making the decision to speak English as much as you can – to me and to each other – then I will write that down and it will convert directly to better grades and better comments for you."

L1: cutting in

When you do find yourself witness a very open cross talk exchange between two students in L1, and you consider that the theme is neither too private nor inappropriate to make public then one option is to intervene. Often at this point students are expecting a simple rebuttal such as *"stop talking"* or *"get on with your work"*. One interesting strategy is to first look as if you are headed in that direction but then put a more positive twist on it:

Student: [Cross talk utterance in L1]

Teacher: *[Looks up at S1]* *"You can say it in English. Come on, I've got faith in you."*

Student: *[Reformulates last utterance in English]*

Teacher: *"Well done."*

I recently let an L1 conversation involving five students continue for two minutes before stopping it and reenacting it with them, speaker-by-speaker, in English. When they were not quite sure who had said what at a given point, I reminded them – as I had been noting the turns and contributions from the start.

L1: opportunities

Very recently one of my students was not speaking any English in class. I had even been in contact with her mother about it. Prior to one lesson I said:

> *"Look, I don't know if you have consciously decided not to speak English or if you just get blocked or embarrassed but I'm going to tell you what we are going to do today and where the opportunities to speak English will be if you decide to do so. First, you are going to test each other on the vocabulary. You'll be able to speak a little bit there. Then you'll be preparing and practising the presentations. Again, there's a chance for speaking there. After that we've got some exercises, so not so much there, but to finish the lesson there will be some conversation questions about sport – so that will be another chance to speak. If I see you speaking, it's points for you but otherwise I'm going to back off. Okay?"*

Instead of undefined pressure, she now had a clear roadmap with stages and options. Three months later and she is regularly interacting with her peers in English.

Seating: not moving

When two students are not working productively together, one approach is not to move them:

> *"I know you two are friends but you are not working well. We could separate you but I don't want you working well apart, I want you working well **together**. I want you to use the good relationship you have to help each other."*

Students are used to being split up. This alternative tack is less predictable and addresses the underlying dynamic in a more constructive and perhaps more humanistic way.

Seating: actually moving

If we do need a student to move, we can make sneaky use of the teacher's chair: *"Rami, come and sit in my chair for a while"*.

Few students will pass up this opportunity but as Rami leaves his own seat, we smoothly reposition the teacher's chair to the location that we want Rami for the next activity.

Seating: letting them know why

I have found that much of the resistance teenage students put up when asked to switch seats has to do with the perceived intentions of their teacher. *I'm being moved because I'm talking* is the most common interpretation. This often results in said student digging their heels in and trying to stay where they are. Presenting students with an alternative rationale for moving can often help them out of that particular rut.

"Ana, can you do this next activity with Fatima and Angela, please?"

"Why, teacher?"

"Well, it's conversation questions about favourite films and at the moment you're sat next to your sister and your best friend. You already know what their answers to the questions will be. With Fatima and Angela, it will make the conversation more real."

Or...

"Albert, can you work with Tommy for the next activity? It's gerunds and infinitives and you were particularly good at those last lesson. You can go back to sitting with Mary and Andrea later."

Or...

"Laura, can you sit with Jose for the next task?"

"With, Jose?"

"Yes. I've never seen the two of you work together, and I'm curious."

The combinations

I was pairing up 14, 15 and 16-year-old students in an intermediate group for a collaborative writing activity and had asked Mary to sit with Toni.

"No, teacher," said Mary. *"I can't put up with him."*

I looked at Toni.

"It's true," Toni said, *"we can't put up with each other"*.

"That's tragic!" I exclaimed.

"No," he replied, *"I don't hate her. We just can't work together."*

"Is that true, Mary?"

"Yes, teacher."

I use this anecdote to remind teachers and to remind myself that sometimes students really do find it hard to be with each other. They are trapped in a room with their classmates just as much as they are trapped in a room with their teacher. To this end I have developed what I call 'the combinations'. I say to a class:

"When I say: 'Combination A', I want you to get into groupings like this."

Combination A
Malcom+Inés
Joe+Marina
Dan+Pablo
Sydney+Antonio
Maria+Alonso
Elena+Sam+Carmen

"When I say 'Combination B', it's like this:"

Combination A	**Combination B**
Malcom+Inés	Malcom+Dan+Carmen
Joe+Marina	Joe+Elena
Dan+Pablo	Inés+Pablo
Sydney+Antonio	Sydney+Maria
Maria+Alonso	Antonio+Alonso
Elena+Sam+Carmen	Sam+Marina

"… and when I say 'Combination C' it's is like this:"

Combination A	**Combination B**	**Combination C**
Malcom+Inés	Malcom+Dan+Carmen	Dan+Inés+Joe
Joe+Marina	Joe+Elena	Malcom+Elena
Dan+Pablo	Inés+Pablo	Pablo+Sam+Maria
Sydney+Antonio	Sydney+Maria	Sydney+Alonso+Carmen
Maria+Alonso	Antonio+Alonso	Antonio+Marina
Elena+Sam+Carmen	Sam+Marina	

This allows us to sit at home and figure out at our leisure who we think will work best together for a speaking activity, who will best help each other focus on grammar activities, and which pairings might be best when we want them to be moving around in a responsible way. The chart can go next to the board in case anyone forgets.

Questions for reflection

- What is the purpose of homework for you?
- Does the homework you usually set reflect this purpose?
- When do you find L1 use amongst your students an issue?
- How much resistance do you get when you ask students to move places?

Things to try

1. Draft out a plan for different groupings as described in the 'combinations' section.
2. Set up an email channel for audio homework and experiment with that.
3. Make a list with your class about how L1 use can help in class and how it might hinder.
4. Try explaining to your students why you are setting each particular homework assignment, what the underlying principles are, what they should learn from it and how they will be able to tell if they have done so.

Things to share

Tell your class that their next round of homework will be marked by another teacher. That teacher can also be invited in during a guest spot to give the students feedback in person. Meanwhile you do the same for that colleague's class. This will:

- make the assignment feel special and improve overall quality
- allow you to share thoughts on the quality of work and student needs with your colleague
- allow you to share thoughts on students' in-class performance and conduct.

References

Mauss M (1954) *The Gift*. London: Routledge. Taylor & Francis e-Library.

8. Tidy learning, messy learning and simple clutter

Discussion

In this chapter, I will argue that both tidy learning and messy learning have their places. I will explain how I am using both terms and give a number of examples. On a very practical level, we shall also look at two areas where physical untidiness might hamper our lessons: in notebooks, as far as our students are concerned, and on the teacher's table and shelves as far as we are concerned.

Tidy learning

I use 'tidy learning' to describe when a class activity can be reduced down to one very specific operation – as for example when you are going over an exercise. When learning is tidy, logistics are straightforward, everyone is equipped with the right materials, seating is satisfactory and it is clear what is going on even to an outsider popping into the class briefly. I may use it in a positive sense to talk about real organisation and efficiency. I may use it in a more negative sense to talk about a simplified classroom dynamic which gives the impression of organisation and efficiency.

Messy learning

This is some slightly exaggerated rhetoric I use when talking to my students:

> "You go into a class and the students aren't talking. They aren't moving about. Everyone's in their places. They are still and you could hear a pin drop. It's like a temple. Is it a good class?"

> "Yes, teacher. A very good class." (Someone will say that.)

"Well, to me it isn't a class at all."

"Why not, teacher?"

"Nobody's talking. Nobody's even moving. How are you going to learn a language that way?"

As suggested in the previous chapter, if the majority of action on the part of students is suppressed and they are operating at a fraction of their potential level of agency then we cannot really cite good behaviour or even good learning, just inactivity. This may be the darker side of tidy learning.

What I shall call 'messy learning', on the other hand, involves everyone *not* doing the same thing at the same time, but being engaged in various inter-related activities. It involves, as far as logistics allow, freeing students from having to be in the same seat all the time and on the same exercise as their peers, allowing them to work at different paces and on areas appropriate to their own needs as language learners – but still from a pre-determined set of possibilities. If everyone gets on with what they need to be doing then the whole will work. Systems theory writer Russell Ackoff uses mess to describe a set of problems (1974) – and in this sense I have taken liberties with the concept. The only problem messy learning poses, as used here, is for the casual observer trying to figure out what is going on and why all these young people are moving about in different directions.

Under a tidy learning paradigm, there is a level of synchronisation and standardisation. We deliver a lesson pitched to where we think students ought to be and we proceed as one. Sometimes this results in increased efficiency, sometimes it does not. Under a messy learning paradigm, we are working with a fragmented classroom, with individuals who want and need different things and who may not benefit from being treated as the same person. The reader will sense that I am echoing the idea of collective vs individual here and it will come as no surprise when I say that we need both tidiness and messiness.

In my own practice, once I have reached a satisfactory level of tidiness during a lesson or task, then I will deliberately create additional mess by allowing more activity that is individually centred or tailored which will result in an increase in random variables such as movement, interactions, dialogue and noise. As a result of messing things up like this, the class again becomes harder to monitor and harder to manage – or at least requires monitoring and managing in a different way. Having introduced this new level of mess, I then try to accommodate, systematise and regulate it – in a nutshell, to tidy it up again. This cyclical process of ordering an increasingly complex realm of activity, in our case language practice, is what constitutes for me the highest level of ELT artistry.

Practical applications

A case study with both tidy learning and messy learning

Right at the start of the school year I try to reconcile students to the idea that they are going to need to listen to each other – and that includes in open class. However, fighting all your energetic impulses in order to listen, not even to the teacher but to a peer, can require serious effort, or serious structure.

In this example, the students in a young teens class have each prepared a one-minute presentation on an invention of their choice. They have researched the inventor and various other details such as the date of the invention and its inspiration. We would now like each student to read their work to the class and to be able to enjoy having the class listen to them.

Remembering the importance of appearances and of consequence, let us formalise the situation by giving everyone a blank grid. Each student puts the names of all the class members along the top row then writes the name of the first speaker in the first row down the side. At this point the grid looks like this:

	Estela	María	Carmen	Ductor	John	Enrique	Pablo	Mig	Javi
Estela									
María									
Carmen									

Estela comes to the front, sits in the teacher's chair and reads her piece to the class. Every student is responsible for completing their own grid and this starts with them putting an 'SP' in Estela's box because she is the speaker.

Students then repeat back to Estela details of what they have heard and understood from the presentation. They do this by putting their hands up and waiting for Estela to nominate them. If they are nominated they tell Estela one thing that they heard. If she deems the detail to be accurate, she publicly awards that student one point and everyone puts a 'Q' in that student's column (for having answered a question).

	Estela	María	Carmen	Ductor	John	Enrique	Pablo	Mig	Javi
Estela	Sp	L	L	Q	Q	Q	Q	Q	Q
María									
Carmen									

If the detail is shaky but along the right lines Estela decides if it earns a 'Q' or not. When feedback on her contribution starts to dwindle Estela invites the next speaker. The students who have not earned a 'Q' during Estela's turn all receive a listening point in the form of an 'L' in their boxes, provided they have been attentive. 'Ls' are worth the same as 'Qs' but the teacher encourages students to aim for a mixture of both. After several turns, the grid may look something like this:

	Estela	María	Carmen	Ductor	John	Enrique	Pablo	Mig	Javi
Estela	Sp	L	L	Q	Q	Q	Q	Q	Q
María	L	Sp	Q	Q	Q	Q	Q	Q	Q
Carmen	Q	Q	Sp	Q	Q	Q	Q	Q	Q

This activity incorporates both tidy and messy learning in so far as it is heavily structured and measurable but the individual contributions – the presentations – are original and student generated. There is no fixed order to the responses, there is a stream of students transitioning between roles and for the duration of their turn each speaker has control of the activity. I have run this with groups of 12, 13 and 14-year-olds for the last five years and it has always worked, with listeners often asking speakers to reread their pieces once or even twice. With more personalised presentations (for example if each student has written a paragraph about their favourite hobby), rather than simply reporting back details, the rest of the class can be charged with asking pertinent follow-up questions.

A second case study with both tidy and messy learning

With a pre-B1 teens class (aged 12-15) that I currently teach, we had a lesson with the following set up.

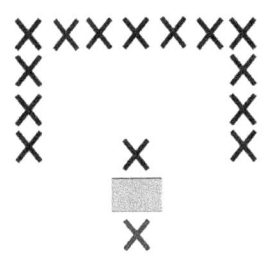

Figure 21: Students sat in horseshoe formation with additional one-to-one set up at the front

The students had prepared a presentation based on a text about a self-made millionaire. I had provided them with the simple schema below.

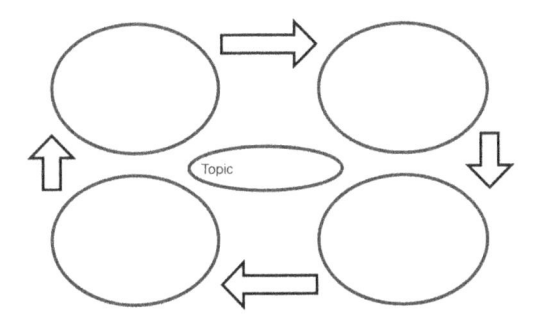

Figure 22: A simple schema provides students with a sense of security

The four bubbles corresponded to the four paragraphs of the text and inside each bubble they put up to 10 key words to help them later convey the content of the paragraph. They did not have to provide a word-for-word reconstruction but rather to convey the main message.

After practising in pairs, each student came and sat opposite me and spoke. I used the flash tools timer on my interactive whiteboard (IWB) desktop to give them two minutes to work through their presentation, though there was no obligation to get to the end. I had also established a marking criteria which was: a possible 10 points for preparing key words in bubbles, another possible 10 for how obvious it was that they had practised and up to 10 more marks for the delivery itself.

Up to here I was working on a tidy learning paradigm with a structured template, timing and criteria. Meanwhile, the rest of the class were doing one of three things:

a. Finishing off their schema.
b. Practising their presentation with a partner.
c. Working on an end of unit revision page.

This is where I allowed an element of messy learning. Not everybody was doing the same thing and so student behaviour and productivity was harder to interpret. This is where an element of trust came in. Students had to decide when to transition from one task to another and how much practice was enough.

Before starting, I explained to the class:

> *"Sometimes, when one student is speaking to me, what happens is that the other students look and think: 'Hmmm, the teacher's not paying any attention to us. Maybe the teacher isn't interested in us right now. So we'll do something to get noticed.' Or they think: 'The teacher isn't paying any attention to what we're doing right now. That means the teacher doesn't care what we're doing right now. So we'll just do anything.' That's not the case though. I DO care, but in order to give this person my full attention, in order to give this person the quality listening they deserve, I need to focus on just them for a short time – and remember, this will be you at some point as well."*

Here I am fronting classroom management and priming students by making the implicit explicit. This is nothing my teenagers could not have worked out by deduction, but just because they *could* have worked it out does not mean that they *would* have, or that they would operate along the conclusions of those workings.

The first few speakers spoke and the rest of the class, prone to chattering, behaved impeccably. At this point I decided to make things messier. I paired up students who had not spoken and sent them off to various parts of our teaching centre, such as reception and an open area next to the teachers' room, in order to practise. Students who had already spoken were also allowed to act as listeners on the condition they actively helped the speaker.

Between listening to presentations myself, I would send a student off to recall individuals or to check everyone was on task. This meant that at any one time there was a varying number of students in the classroom itself and a varying number of students on a given activity. I was deliberately leaving holes in my task design for the students to fill with their own efforts and initiative.

In less than 40 minutes of a 90-minute lesson, all 13 students had spoken. At the end of the phase I congratulated the group.

> *"Today I was able to concentrate fully on the person in front of me. I hope you feel that it was worth it. This was possible because of you and the way that you conducted yourselves. Well done."*

I believe it is possible for a teacher to build up a tolerance to productive and principled mess. By this I mean the ability to cope with students in a class being engaged in an increasing number of different activities at any one time. My purpose in describing this activity to you is to show how a foundation of tidy learning and tight task design, coupled with flexibility and the accommodation of a certain amount of randomness, can be a very fruitful combination.

What this may look like from the outside

Lessons like these may give the impression of disorder. To appreciate them we need to look more closely at what individual students are doing in terms of purposeful initiative. Such lessons take skill to orchestrate and are also harder to interpret for an observer.

What you can do with a particular group depends on that group. If students struggle to work with each other nicely in class, the time is not right to send them to another location independently. If they struggle to go over an exercise as a whole group, they may struggle even more in smaller ones. In this sense we need to increase the complexity of our classes step by step.

Notebooks

So far we have been discussing order on a somewhat abstract level – that of task design and group dynamics. Shifting now to the sphere of classroom materials, we come to the issue of clutter – when things are not in their right places and are most probably acting as an obstacle to learning.

Helping students organise the physical dimension of their study has benefits for the time we share in class with them. If *every* student has a notebook, we can ask them to record important language covered without the lesson losing impetus as the teacher looks for pieces of blank paper. In any case, those loose sheets of paper often get dog eared and lost, sometimes not making it out of the classroom at all. In this respect, notebooks are as much about keeping things together as they are about hard work and copying. In addition, if each student has a notebook, the teacher can take these in as a class set for marking.

If students have been given guidance on the internal organisation of their notebooks and divided them into sections – one for vocabulary, one for rough work or exercises and one for writings – they will be able to find required material more easily.

Where students are submitting written work on loose paper we might provide each one with a plastic wallet to keep them in.

Improving notebooks

One useful follow up task when language has been recorded in notebooks is for students to look over each other's work, awarding it points out of ten for neatness and for being correct. They can also test each other using those same pages. If students know that what they are recording will be looked at or used, then the veracity of their own record is likely to be much higher.

Copying as a safe place for students

We may also do well to remember that those who struggle with English in general sometimes try to take sanctuary in copying. Struggling students may take longer to copy due to the fact they are slower at decoding what is on the board, have issues with handwriting such as letter formation or dysgraphia, or are less effective at organising what they put on the page. Some learn that if they take even longer copying they can use this as a reason not to answer questions from the teacher in the following stage of the lesson: *"Sorry, teacher, I'm still copying"*. As we tend to treat copying tasks as sacred, this can start to become their 'safe place'.

Copying as a safe place for teachers

Similarly, when students ask: *"Shall we copy, teacher?"* a novice teacher or even an experienced one finding the class an uphill struggle may simply say yes to take a breather for a few minutes and use up some class time. Obviously, this is hardly the ideal and originates from a 'just get to the end of the lesson' mindset.

Before asking students to copy, we might ask ourselves: *"What are they recording this for? Are they going to look at it again? If so, how am I going to structure, support and measure that follow-up study?"*

Sometimes it might be preferable to provide a printed handout or to display reference material and have students begin the assimilation process by working with that in pairs as soon as possible, reserving the notebook for recording their own original responses and explanations or vocabulary items that come up during class.

Decluttering your classroom

If you are an organised teacher of teens, you may wish to skip to the boxes at the end of this chapter. If, like me, you struggle with order now and then, read on.

In his television series *Kitchen Nightmares*, Michelin-starred chef Gordon Ramsay visits failing restaurants where he spends a few days tasting, inspecting, observing and talking to staff before providing a full analysis and recommendations to the owners.

I sat in my empty classroom not so long ago and imagined that Gordon Ramsay had just walked in and that I was accompanying him as he had a look around and questioned me on my set up, just like he does with the restaurant proprietors. Here is a very short excerpt of how I thought the conversation might go – though I have toned down the expletive language customarily heard in the television programme:

GR: "Let's start with this shall we?" [Gordon points to a collapsed stack of papers and books on top of a cupboard.]

CR: "Okay."

GR: "What have you got in here, Chris?"

CR: "Not quite sure."

GR: "Wow. Okay. What's underneath it?"

CR: "I don't know, Gordon."

GR: "Let's just have a little look, eh? Let's bring this down… [Gordon nudges the stack gently and a mini-avalanche of random ELT materials slide off each other and topple to the floor. He then starts to sift through the debris]. *So, what have we got? What's this?"*

CR: "It's an upper-intermediate teen's writing file."

GR: "What's it for?"

CR: "For the upper-intermediate teens to put their writings in."

GR: "How long have you had it?"

CR: "Two months, Gordon."

GR: "What are these? …letters to students from Admin. …and look! Someone's even carefully worked out how many you'd need for each class. When were these meant to be given out?"

CR: "Last month."

GR: "So that's how much respect you've got for your co-workers in the office is it? Great. And what are these?"

CR: *"Homework charts for the students to keep a record of what they have to do."*

GR: *"Have they all got one?"*

CR: *"No, but…"*

GR: *"But what?"*

CR: *"But some of them have been asking for them."*

GR: *"Well there they are, Chris. There they are. And what's all this doing over here?* [Pointing to two more similar stacks of papers on the teacher's desk]. *What is this piece of furniture in the middle of the room anyway?"*

CR: *"It's my desk, Gordon."*

GR: *"For working at? For sitting at? Or for trying to squeeze round without knocking anything over?* [As if on cue, Christopher's arm catches the edge of the desk and a number of board pens clatter to the floor. Gordon tuts.] *This isn't a classroom. And this?"* [picking up a textbook which has fallen down between the side of the cupboard he was standing next to before and the wall].

CR: *"It's an intensive B2 exam preparation resource book. It's a good book, Gordon."*

GR: *"Are you teaching intensive B2 exam preparation this year, Chris?"*

CR: *"No, Gordon."*

GR: *"Then whose book is it?! Don't answer. Don't even answer cos I know whose it is. It belongs to one of your colleagues who's been looking for that book for two weeks. And what does it say on this stapler, Chris?"*

CR: *"It says 'STAFFROOM DO NOT REMOVE'."*

As you can see, order is not one of my strengths but I believe I am not the only teacher that suffers from ELT piles – stacks of uncategorised papers which may conceal anything from your register to an essay that a student has been insisting they gave you for weeks. For some teachers, the above scenario will make very little sense. Others will know exactly what I am talking about here. For the latter group, being proactive and stepping outside of yourself, as it were, to take an aggressively critical look at your own document filing systems, organisation, storage and workspace can be a useful exercise.

Questions for reflection

- How often do you have students working on different activities at the same time?
- Do all your students have notebooks?
- If so, how much guidance do you provide on their organisation?
- What purpose do your students' notebooks and their contents serve in your classes?
- What would Gordon Ramsay say if he visited your classroom?

Things to try

1. Try spotting when struggling students take refuge in copying from the board.
2. Try using student notebooks as the basis for follow up activities.
3. Take a lesson you are about to teach and think about where an additional layer of complexity or 'mess' might be productive. Think about how you will structure that and how you will explain it. If it seems feasible, have a go.

Things to share

With one or more colleagues, read the two examples of classes that contain both tidy and messy learning. There is also a case study in Chapter 14, p175 (with tidy learning, messy learning, autonomy, technology and movement). Then discuss:

- whether you have done any similar lessons
- whether you would use any elements from these lessons
- if your institution sanctions lessons like these
- if you see any value in the concepts of tidy vs messy.

References

Ackoff R (1974) *Redesigning the Future: A systems approach to societal problems*. New York: John Wiley & Sons Inc.

9. Autonomy and student-fronted classes

Discussion

The argument we have been building is that the more teenagers get to do in class, the more they will engage with the language. The more systems that a learner has 'online' the more alive they will be to that language. Numerous methodology books and articles invite the reader to reflect upon the different roles a teacher performs in a classroom. An alternative task would be to list all the possible roles that a *student* might perform – such as interviewer, listener, analyst, or partner – and then try to incorporate these in lessons so that language will need to serve our students across a wide range of functions.

Autonomy in the ELT classroom with teens is more than just about students doing things on their own. Nothing comes for free, least of all freedom, and any increase in liberty involves an increase in duty (for an interesting discussion see Fromm, 1947). Autonomy for teenagers involves students actively making decisions on how to execute language tasks and where they are informed, prepared and supported by the teacher so that they can go about doing so in a responsible and efficient way.

These elements form a whole. In order to make decisions, students need to be active. In order to be active, they need to use some initiative during the exercise, but they also need to have been given the space in which to act. In order to give them that space, the teacher needs to feel confident that their students will acquit themselves reasonably and not let the group down. This is especially true where another group, teacher or transition from the classroom to another space is involved. Students knowing how to perform a task well and in an acceptable manner is something that the teacher can guide by suggesting guidelines, parameters, structure and by clarifying the dynamics and conduct they expect.

Allowing students out of the classroom

Allowing teenage students outside of the classroom is not by itself granting them autonomy (which requires decisions and control over task content and execution) but it does presuppose that the elements outlined above are all in place. What an individual teacher is free to do will depend on their institution's rules, established levels of supervision and custodial care, the institution's layout and whether there are common spaces which are monitored. My golden rule, as a teacher trying to maximise opportunities to use space and spaces, is to check with your director of studies, centre manager or department head.

Being the teacher

We have seen a number of examples of students 'being the teacher'. These may involve students testing each other, leading a dictation, evaluating one another or going over exercises. We have also seen how the teacher can provide supporting scripts so that this increased responsibility can be exercised in English. In my own classes, this is the basic building block for further autonomy. *"If we can get this right,"* I say to my groups, *"we can do more stuff. If we can't get this right, we're stuck here."*

Early on in the academic year, I make sure everyone has had two or three goes at being the teacher, highlighting when someone does well: *"So, what made her/him a good teacher?"*

Depending upon the case, possible answers might be:

> *"He kept checking and asking: 'Has everyone got that?' before going on."*

> *"She wrote the spellings on the board to check we had the difficult ones right."*

> *"She went quite slowly."*

> *"He didn't go too slowly."*

> *"We could hear him."*

> *"She asked everyone."*

> *"He decided who to ask quite quickly."*

> *"She waited till we were all quiet each time."*

When appropriate, I also include the following rhetorical snippet: *"What's the other reason she/he was so good? No? It was that you all helped her/him."*

Having got to a point where students can perform the tail end of a language task, we can then choose to make them responsible for introducing and monitoring tasks.

Practical applications

Teens teaching teens

Although first in this section, this activity is perhaps the most technically challenging to oversee – but one of the most rewarding projects I have undertaken with intermediate level teenagers (first outlined in Roland, 2016).

To set up the activity, students are put into groups and each group is assigned a page from the coursebook and a date on which they will teach their lesson. For example:

> *"Ana, George and Tami, you'll be teaching page 44 on the 23rd of this month. Raymond, Pascual and Viktor, your page is 45 and you will be teaching that on the 25th."*

When each group is clear about their page, the class is given time to plan and prepare their lesson. About an hour of class time is required for this, sometimes a little more. During this time students need to look at their page, decide what they are going to do and what they are going to leave out, decide who in the group will introduce each activity, who will be monitoring and who will be going over the answers.

During the planning and preparation stage, the classroom becomes a busy place with each group looking at different pages. Students have at their disposal the teacher's book and any digital materials that they might need (as well as the teacher for consultation).

Each member of a group gets a lesson plan template and is responsible for completing it. The earliest lesson plans I used for this activity were student-produced collages of photocopied teacher's book answers cut out, glued to coloured paper and annotated with their own scripts. More recently I have used a variant of the template below:

Page number _____ Exercise number _____ What type of activity is it?	What will your instructions be? What explanations will you give? Write out exactly what you will say.	What language will the students be learning? How will students get a good evaluation from you?	Write the answers to exercises here. For readings or listening, what words might they ask you for?

During the preparation stage, those groups including a listening exercise will need to decide on who controls the audio and to locate answers in the transcript. Those doing a reading will need to study the text, deciding what words their classmates might ask about and how they will explain those in English. All groups need to think about instructions and find the answers to their exercises, penciling those in.

If a class needs it, I may make the planning and preparation stage an evaluated activity in itself, monitoring groups to see if there is even participation, if the lesson plans are complete and most importantly if each member of a group knows what the group is doing at any given moment, which I ascertain by asking them.

On the day of their lesson, the group that is teaching sit at the front. They have a grid into which they enter the names of their classmates and are also responsible for evaluating the performance of their students along parameters that they themselves have decided. They normally take great relish in this. Past categories have included participation, teamwork, attitude, pronunciation and getting the answers correct.

> Student: *"Will these scores go on their reports, teacher?"*
>
> Teacher: *"Not in that exact format but I will look at them and take them into consideration when I do write the reports, yes."*

I position myself with the rest of the class and make notes on how the student teachers are performing as well as how much each of the other students is helping them. I will intervene to answer content related queries – principally from the student teachers (so as not to undermine them) and also to step in and remind individuals that they could be more cooperative when necessary.

When allowed to moderate coursebook material for themselves, students can be surprisingly innovative and resourceful. Students teaching their own lessons is an incredibly powerful vehicle for functional language. They get to demonstrate not only their communicative skills but their powers of organisation and fairness as well. On all but a few occasions, my own groups have risen to the task admirably. I have had otherwise very reticent learners come alive and would recommend the activity to anyone wanting to take their teaching further. Furthermore, this activity is all perfectly contained within the room and does not require splitting the class or students needing to go to any other additional spaces.

Teens teaching primary

If you teach in a language centre and have both young learner and teenage classes, or you are in a larger school where there is both primary and secondary and have a colleague who is willing to collaborate, then another option is to invite your teens to teach the younger ones. This could involve your students staying after their class has finished and teaching a segment of your own or another teacher's primary class or going to another teacher's class during their regular class time. Either way, this works best as a voluntary project – though I do reward volunteers with an additional positive comment on their report cards.

Most recently I provided a group of five intermediate teenage girls, aged 14-16, with two sets of flashcards – food items and beach objects. They rehearsed with these during several 20-minute slots that we freed up for them in class time and then they taught these to a group of upper primary students using a number of word and mime games they had devised.

The primary class were mostly girls as well, and the 'big sister' role model effect was obvious. The teens got a little nervous before the class but they enjoyed the experience and the primary students certainly enjoyed it. One of the little girls asked if the older ones would come back. One of them asked if they, the primary students, could teach the infants in the class next door and one of two little boys in the class even offered to pay the teens to come back. He only offered one euro cent but that was more than he ever offered to pay me, so I took it as a positive sign.

I asked the teenagers to do a brief diary-type write up of their experience, so that there was personalised and reflective language work in it for them as well. Here are a couple of their comments, with any language assistance from me in bold.

> "*I **imagined** that this would be a good experience and **I wasn't** wrong.*"
>
> "*…the truth is that you're very nervous and it is very different **to what** you **expected**.*"
>
> "*…all of us **took away** that no matter what age you can always have fun teaching and learning things.*"

To tighten the activity even closer to our B1 syllabus, I used the simple beach vocabulary (towel, goggles, sun cream, shampoo, etc) they had worked on with the children as the basis for a collaborative speaking activity. I wrote the following on the board and stuck the flashcard images around it:

> *"You are going to spend the day at the beach and then in the evening attend a party there with a barbecue. You only have a small bag. Decide with a partner which three of the objects you would leave behind."*

Class-to-class presentations

Another activity that I have run recently, again for students who volunteer for it, is an inter-class presentation. This activity is promoted on an institutional level by the language academy where I am based.

Typically, this activity involves a group of students from an upper-intermediate class (who have already done the B1 level and exam) giving a short presentation to classes of pre-B1 students, explaining what to expect from the year to come and their recommended study tips. The older students talk about what they did last year. The younger students hear about what they are going to do next year.

I provide the presenters with an empty classroom and some class time to practice. So far they have not let me down. Some of the most imaginative and original work has come from my students when I have given them some space and let them get on with it. Last year we went a step further and the presenters first gave their talk to their own classmates who provided feedback, before departing as ambassadors for their group and level.

When we put two classes together we want to ensure both sides benefit as equally as possible. In order for the younger group to interact with the presenters, we prime them by allowing the preparation of questions in advance. I would also recommend allowing thinking time after the older students have spoken in which to generate more questions or modify the ones they had, in light of what they have heard.

I would also recommend that, where possible, the students presenting come from a class at least two levels higher than their audience. We have found that their additional maturity and increased language proficiency creates a stronger impression and serves as a more inspirational role model. During the last round of talks I was informed by a colleague that a pre-B1 student asked one of my presenters, *"How did your English get so good?"* Apparently, she looked surprised for a second, as if the answer were self-evident, before replying curtly, *"With practice"*.

Making it meaningful

Teens teaching teens, primary or inter-class presentations all provide an urgency and a sense of realism to the use of language. One of the most impressive examples of the positive effect that I have seen was during a teaching conference in the Canary Islands. The attendees were offered a guided tour of a small natural history museum in the city of La Laguna. The museum itself was part of an annexing school and on this day, our guides were a handful of teenage students from that school. They had prepared and practised their information and each took turns to curate a section of the museum. There were about 50 teachers there and we were divided into two groups in rotation. Each student therefore spoke to one group, had a break of ten minutes then spoke to the other.

In terms of ratio, we had a single teenager holding the floor to an attentive group of 25 adults (and English teachers at that) which ironically is the exact reverse of the ratio we normally have in a classroom. For those students, and for their audiences, the moment and the word were infused with purpose and relevance just as the rounds of applause they received afterwards were infused with encouragement and recognition. That experience had a considerable impact on me and makes me think that, in terms of the ideal future of language teaching, what we need are structures and systems that get aspiring young language speakers out there speaking in situations that in some way matter.

Questions for reflection
- What does student autonomy mean for you?
- What is the most responsibility that you give to your students?
- Do you agree with this chapter's initial argument for increased student agency?
- How can we make language practice more real for our teenage students?
- Would you enjoy setting up a series of student-led classes?

Things to try

1. If you have not already, try letting students be the teacher and inviting feedback from their peers on how well each has done.
2. The next step is to allow students, or groups of them, to give short explanations or to lead games in short slots.
3. Set up full-blown student-led classes like the ones described above.

Things to share

Talk to your director and/or a colleague about:

- some of your teenagers leading a short lesson with younger ones
- a group of your teenagers giving an inter-class presentation.

With this, as with the student-led lessons, keep a record of how you structured the activity, high points, recommendations and evidence of learning. Present this to colleagues in a short workshop.

References

Fromm E (1947) *Escape from Freedom*. New York: Farrar & Rinehart.

Roland C (2016) Teens teaching teens. *English Teaching professional* **107** 8–10.

Special thanks to TEA, the Canary Island teachers' Association, in particular Juan Morales its president, and to the students and staff at IES Canarias Cabrera Pinto.

10. Teenagers and technology

Discussion

Technology is what technology does

I would like to argue here that we should evaluate technology in our language classrooms by first identifying the underlying function it performs, then considering if the newer systems or equipment are more or less efficient in fulfilling that function than the old ones.

Whiteboards and markers are slightly more user friendly than chalk and blackboard – no dust and no occasional scraping sound that makes some students wince – but they are both essentially the same. With the arrival of interactive whiteboards (IWBs) we got IWB pens. These, however, are less suitable for writing quickly as their sensors are unable to pick up erratic movements. In addition, some IWB systems do not allow two pens to be used at the same time so multiple writers at the board are not an option. In these respects, the interactive whiteboard may not represent a technological advancement.

CDs replaced cassettes. The advantage of CDs was that the teacher could find tracks much more quickly but if the underlying function of audio equipment is to play and *replay* stretches of speech to students, tapes had the advantage of being easier to rewind and replay. Digital sound files redressed this. Not only is it now possible to replay stretches of speech with pinpoint accuracy, we can also adjust speed and share files (license allowing) for students to replay at home. In this respect digital sound files *do* represent a technological advancement.

New technology in the classroom sometimes manages only to mimic older systems, enhancing visuals and sound effects – what Murray and Barnes (1998) referred to as the 'wow factor' – but with little increase in efficiency. For me, this includes online drag 'n' drop exercises that replicate those found in paper-based activity books or mobile apps that simply replicate, while unnecessarily digitising, whole class quizzes.

Having said this, the judicious inclusion of some technology can serve to make a classic activity more relevant and interesting for our students.

When deciding on what a certain technology contributes, our questions might then be:

1. Is it quicker?
2. Does it make language more memorable?
3. Does it mean that fewer students are waiting and more can participate at a given moment?
4. Does it increase engagement with and production of words and sentences in English?

In the second part of this chapter we shall look at some uses of both new and old technologies that I believe do enhance the teenage ELT classroom.

Whose technology is it?

First, I would like to address what I consider to be two dead ends in terms of thinking.

1. The first is the notion that our teenage students are somehow responsible for technology, as implied by terms such as 'digital natives' and 'screenagers'. Sir Clive Sinclair and his company produced one of the first slimline electronic calculators in 1972 and groundbreaking PCs in the 80s. At the time of writing he is 77 years old. Steve Wozniak, co-founder of Apple, is currently 67. Chad Hurley, Steve Chen and Jawed Karim, the creators of YouTube are 41, 39 and 38 respectively. These ages represent various generations – none of which are our current teenage students. It is our generations that grew up with calculators, PCs and for younger readers, the internet. If our teenage students appear to lack self-restraint when it comes to screen time, perhaps it is our fault for supplying it and our failure to provide a responsible example.

2. The other misconception, I think, is that our teenage students are somehow magically tech savvy. In the 1990s, before teaching, I worked for a telecommunication company. One of my jobs at night was to input line data on two different telephone exchange systems. Most of it involved resetting the PIN numbers on customers' fixed line messaging systems or removing call barring that had been put on in error. I was not a telephone switch engineer. I had very little technical knowledge. I was able to do this because there was a soft interface – a simplified operating system between myself and the actual technology – which meant that all I had to do was input binary code parameters from a reference manual. It meant that the monkey could work the machine.

The same is true for our teenage learners. Those soft interfaces give the illusion of understanding. As mobile technology becomes more user friendly, the gap between being able to slide one's finger across a touchscreen with confidence and any real grasp of the processes behind that widens. There is also a difference between having acquired the operating skills necessary to be a smartphone end user and the sort of computer literacy that is useful in a learning setting: being able to compose, manage, edit, save and send documents. These skills need to be learnt, as do higher level capabilities regarding layout, organisation, knowledge of genres, selection and critical evaluation of sources. I have learnt this the hard way by presuming my students had some of these skills and discovering that this was not uniformly the case.

When designing lessons that introduce a new digital technology, my advice is to provide operating instructions as an integrated part of the English language input for that lesson.

Practical applications

Audio files and email

I would like to reiterate here that the combination of recording software, sound file and email has huge potential for our students. This is the fourth year I have set audio homework tasks and the first year they have outweighed paper-based tasks.

In terms of processing the work, as most of the task types I use (detailed in Chapter 7) are geared to providing students with practice, an exhaustive listening is not always required. My general strategy is to play recordings as I prepare my class and to pick out one or two salient pronunciation points for each, acknowledging receipt and mentioning these in my reply. Recent responses have been:

> *Well done for sending that Hugo.*
>
> *Is it possible that sometimes you say "olives" when you mean "grapes"?*
>
> *Also, remember that homework never has an 's' on it (uncountable).*
>
> *See you tomorrow – and keep up the good work!*
>
> *Chris*

> *Good! Well done for sending that.*
>
> *When you say "furniture" put a ch sound in there.*
>
> *See you in a bit!*
>
> *Chris*

> *Cheers for that!*
>
> *Remember, when you say: "She hates my guts" to make the "s" on hates.*
>
> *See you in a bit!*
>
> *Chris*

> *Some good stuff there Ana!*
>
> *You could say: "We had a small Christmas party at school" and it's "physics and chemistry" (like kemistry).*
>
> *Come and ask me about that if you remember.*
>
> *Finally, you could say:*
>
> *"The family is more together" or "The family is more focused on the celebrations" depending upon what exactly you are trying to convey with the sentence.*
>
> *BW*
>
> *Chris*

I have found that listening and responding to audio-based homework takes no longer than its paper-based equivalent with the added advantage that students are getting additional speaking practice outside of class time.

Keyboard mediated classes

A colleague at ELI in Seville, Clive Jenkins, gave me the idea of writing my instructions to the class on screen rather than speaking. I trialled this with a pre-B1 group. I entered class and typed onto the projector screen that I had lost my voice, could not talk and that they would have to read what I said all lesson. For the next 90 minutes I did not speak one word. Everything went up on the screen.

The whole lesson, with every interaction in words between myself and the students is available as **Downloadable resource 3**, if you wish to get a feel for how the activity panned out.

For the first few minutes they implored me to try to say something, just so they could hear my poorly voice. I did not speak though. Was I lying? In a way. It was an artificially engineered situation to benefit learning and the scenario needed to be convincing. In the lesson we did grammar exercises, for which they were the teachers and did the corrections, we did speaking in pairs and we watched some clips at the end.

Looking at the excerpt here you will see there was a narrating element to my articulations which I found served in the moment to make all the students aware of what I was referring to and that kept us in touch with each other.

> Carlinhos Brown is a singer – he came here in 2005.
>
> Cris asked because his photo is on the opposite page.
>
> Can you make sure that you have the same answers as Lucía… or Miriam.
>
> Okay Helen, close your book and work with Mary. I appreciate your honesty.
>
> Now it's time to test our knowledge. Can you please do C and D? Cheers. (It means thank you Marco.)
>
> 1805 (That's the time we are at now). One sec.
>
> Okay!

> María T., can you be the teacher for exercise C, please?
>
> I really like the technique that you guys have developed of repeating questions so that everyone gets a go.
>
> Mirlam, can you do exercise D, please?
>
> Alex, can you correct your brother's while he is in the toilet? Thanks.

I resisted the temptation at the end of the class to tell the students that I had not really lost my voice because that might ruin it for the next teacher – or indeed if I wanted to do it again.

So why might you want to do this? We always need to talk to our class. Here we have simply changed the medium – and in doing so given students the most real reason to read English possible: to find out what to do and see if what is typed up there refers to them. The text in their coursebook will never refer to them personally.

Keyboard mediated instructions also have a calming effect. Changing the dynamic like this slows down the pace as students shift to a different type of processing. It takes the lesson beyond their initial expectations and beyond their conceptual horizons.

Interestingly, when you ask Alex to stop chatting and get on with his work with your voice, the words are gone in a second and he starts chatting again. When you type it up, it is there as reminder for some time. If you type Alex's name up someone in the class will let him know about it even if he has not seen it himself. If you correct an error or provide the meaning of a word, likewise your response remains for students to use as reference, or for when the next student asks you the meaning of the same word.

Teachers do lose their voices sometimes. If you have any throat problems over the next school year, I recommend not straining yourself even a little but trailing this alternate form of delivery. I have also since used this for shorter slots in classes too, with no pretense.

Countries map quizzes

The majority of our coursebooks have countries in them, but in the English class we tend to focus on the country word, forgetting that countries are places *in certain places*. By focusing on placing the country as a game, with the country word used as means to an end, we take out the pain and learn something of factual value. Both Lizard Point Geography and Seterra Geography offer such quizzes. The programs give you a country and you place it on the map. Players receive points and can try to better their own times. You can choose the continent and whether to test countries, capitals or cities. While the quizzes look great as a large projection, one laptop set up at the front so that only the current player can see the screen, will provide less of a distraction to the rest of the class.

YouGlish dictation

YouGlish, a programme designed by Dan Barhen, will find examples of a word item you have typed, embedded in a succession of real snippets of speech from YouTube's video archives. If you type in *mountain*, you will get that word said by different speakers and in different contexts. Without allowing students to see the computer screen we can explain that they will hear four snippets of speech all containing the same word. They have to identify the word in common and write that down, as a dictation. I first saw this technique demonstrated by trainer Annie McDonald (2017) and have since been using it to work through our regular vocabulary lists. It allows students to hone their ears to different accents and takes them beyond what Cauldwell (2013) refers to as the 'citation form' – the standard dictionary pronunciation of a word when it is said in isolation.

Going backwards

Recently my students have been disappearing off in pairs to interview and record each other using an old Dictaphone machine, loaded with micro cassettes. These machines and the cassettes are available online for very little and put a novel twist on pair work for students.

Online IPA chart

Weston Ruter's online international phonetic alphabet (IPA) chart can be used to prepare stretches of language in phonemic script. These are the symbols that most coursebooks use to familiarise students with the basic sounds of English. They often appear in a chart at the back of the book and in its pronunciation sections. Being able to include these symbols quickly and easily in our own teacher-produced worksheets is really very useful. We shall look at some of the ways that these can be used with classes in Chapter 15.

Screenshot tools

Later I will talk about images and clips. The beauty of the screenshot tool, available on any operating system is that with it we can take part of a clip and use that as thumbnail on a presentation or handout as a visual link to the vocabulary that came up. The clips we show can thus become an integral part of our course syllabus.

Local shots

One of the surest things you have in common with your students is sharing, in some way, the village, town, city or province where you teach them. There is nothing particularly new about digital photographs but if you walk out the door of your teaching centre, go 100 meters, take a photo and display it in class you will have students jumping up to tell you that it is just down the road, that their grandmother lives in one of the blocks of flats in the photo or that their uncle owns the shop you can see on the corner.

Simple prompts such as these can form the basis of more in depth descriptions, both spoken and written:

> "I know this part of town well because…"
> "This place is quite near to…"
> "In this picture we can see…"

Figure 23: A street in Seville

I learnt from my students that one of them lives on this street, a minute's walk from our centre, another three live near it, one uses it daily on her way to rowing club, there is an estate agency on it (which I have never noticed) and apparently one of the best chicken grills – which I smell every day on my way back from coffee.

Continuing your stroll and taking a photo every so often will provide you with a very useful image bank. A lot of course syllabi and exams involve students describing their neighbourhoods. Practising with visual prompts such as these will enrich those descriptions.

Questions for reflection

- Does the technology you use in class increase participation or mean more waiting?
- Have you ever lost your voice in class? If so, how did you cope?
- Would you consider using older forms of technology such as Dictaphones?
- How much do you use images of the village, town or city where you teach?

Things to try

1. Try playing on one of the geography map quizzes yourself. Did you enjoy it?
2. If so, try setting that up as a parallel activity for students in class.
3. Look at YouGlish. Would a dictation using that work in your classes?

Things to share

Using Weston Ruter's site, try one of the following:

- Typing up a short message to the class in phonemic script, including that on your next worksheet or presentation.
- Typing the instructions on a worksheet or presentation in script.
- Typing out students' names in script, to generate interest in the symbols (this may involve using symbols that represent sounds not considered phonemes in English).
- Typing out commonly mispronounced words to raise awareness.

Share any successes that you have with colleagues.

References

Cauldwell R (2013) *Phonology for Listening: Teaching the stream of speech*. Birmingham: Speech in Action.

Lizard Point Geography. Available at: http://lizardpoint.com/geography/ (accessed July 2018).

McDonald A (2017) *Making Listening Memorable: Listening in chunks*. Presentation given at GRETA Teachers' Association. CEP de Granada.

Murray L & Barnes A (1998) Beyond the "wow" factor – evaluating multimedia language learning software from a pedagogical viewpoint. *System* **26** 249–259.

Seterra Geographay Free Map Quiz Games. Available at: https://online.seterra.com/en (accessed July 2018).

The International Phonemic Alphabet, Weston Ruter. Available at: http://westonruter.github.io/ipa-chart/keyboard/ (accessed July 2018).

YouGlish. Available at: https://youglish.com/ (accessed July 2018).

11. Differentiation

Discussion

The term

Carol Anne Tomlinson, writing in mainstream US education, popularised the term 'differentiation' which refers to how we help struggling learners, challenge the advanced learners and cater for all those in between (2001). In ELT we have traditionally used the term 'mixed-ability' but the difference with Tomlinson's approach is that instead of trying to accommodate everyone and squeeze them all together, she promotes exploring diversity in terms of level and ability.

Reframing the term for ELT

Together with Daniel Barber, I first explored how to translate differentiation principles to an ELT context in an article for *Modern English Teacher* (Roland & Barber, 2016). We shall start by revisiting some of those ideas until moving on to an even simpler conception of the issues.

Managing the class as an event vs managing learning

There is a degree of event management to teaching of all ages, including teens. We have to organise and supervise a group of young people for a specified time period, making sure they are safe, working harmoniously and with a semblance of order. None of that is about learning English in itself, but how well the class works on a logistical level will ultimately determine where the ceiling is for learning. Managing learning involves taking each child and adding to what they have in terms of words and sentences in English – their ability to recognise them and use them.

Goals

In terms of goals, we are trying to help our students get towards the same language use. The diagrams that follow illustrate this point. Imagine our aim is to help our students use some regular past simple verbs to talk about what they did yesterday.

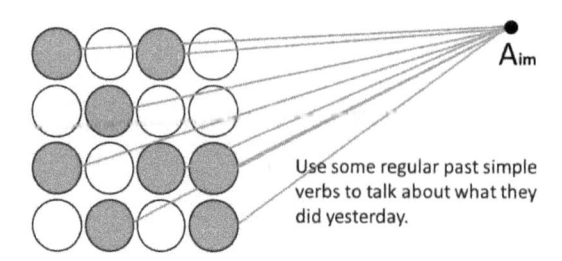

Figure 24: Most students achieving our lesson aims

As we see in the first diagram, most of the students will get there, more or less.

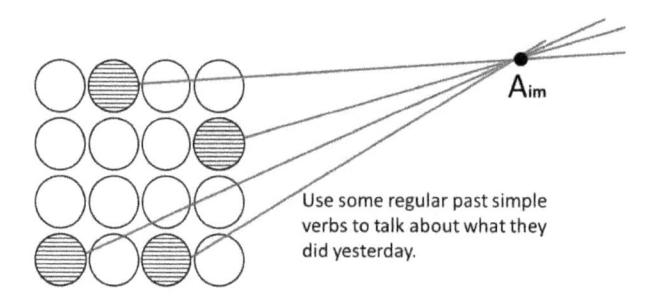

Figure 25: Some students going further

The advanced students might get further and be able to mix in continuous and irregular verbs as well.

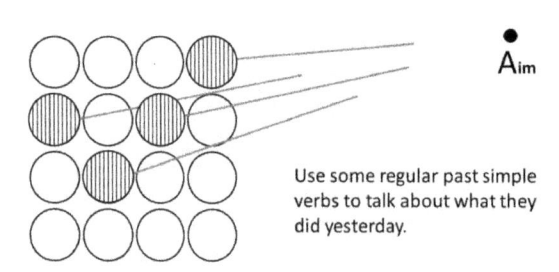

Figure 26: Other students on their way

Some students will not get all the way there. They might not be able to remember what the verbs mean. They might have other obstacles. Maybe they keep confusing 'yesterday' with 'tomorrow' and 'morning' with 'afternoon'. So we stop these students – while the rest carry on – and we say: *"Okay, have a rest from speaking and look at four sentences I've just put on the board."*

"Yesterday I listened to ___ different teachers in class."

"In the afternoon, I studied for ___ minutes / hours at home."

"In total, I chatted to ___ different people."

"Last night I watched YouTube clips or Netflix for ___ minutes / hours."

What we have done is to make a class within a class. We make sure these students understand the four sentences, then they read them to each other and now they are making small steps in the right direction.

Fragmenting the class

We may at times acquire the habit of teaching a class in lockstep as if it were one person. Splitting the class up and having students working on different variations of tasks results in what I termed 'messy learning' in Chapter 8. It is without doubt a skill. It may also be what teaching needs to evolve to but it requires a shift in mindset on the part of teachers and students who have to be more responsible and cooperative for this sort of instruction to work.

Types of differentiation

Daniel and I distinguished two types of differentiation. 'Differentiated support' is what we termed on-the-spot interventions on the part of the teacher to help students struggling on a task or to tweak the difficulty to make an activity more appropriate for an advanced student. 'Structured differentiation' involves pre-planned variations on a task such as one version of a worksheet that has questions for conversation and a second version which also has language prompts for struggling students to structure their replies. Professional development courses, especially at diploma level, may require evidence of this latter form of differentiation in either preparation of materials or task set up.

Two red herrings

One measure that teachers often employ to differentiate is the pairing of weaker and stronger students. This in itself, however, does not always result in benefits to either party. If the stronger student is simply supplying the other with the correct answers to questions, neither may be moving forward. If, on the other hand, the stronger student has the opportunity to actually explain language choice to their classmate, and the weaker student the space in which to take that on board, and even practise, then we have a healthier situation.

Extending the scope or complexity of a task so that advanced learners can benefit is not the same as just dealing with fast finishers. When trainee teachers use this latter phrase, it tells me that they are still thinking about the class as an event – keeping everyone busy – rather than thinking about levels of learning.

Practical applications

A shift to the simple

To reframe the issue in the simplest language possible, differentiation for us is how we help students who cannot do a task and how we make sure that the 'good ones' learn something when it seems too easy. In order to help make the leap from concepts to classroom, I have drawn up two tables (see pages 137 to 142) – one to help target where students might have problems more precisely and the other to help identify how we can stretch a task in terms of complexity and depth.

Helping stuck students

There are two reasons a student might not be doing the task we have set them – they do not want to or they cannot. Not wanting to includes becoming distracted, forgetting what they are meant to be doing, not having enough energy or focus to manage another exercise or actually having made a conscious decision to reject the task and the teacher's requests.

Not being able to do the task means 'being stuck'. Being stuck is a situation most of our students find themselves in every day. It is worth looking at more closely because when we talk about how to support struggling students in an ELT context, it will nearly always be when they are stuck – but what exactly is happening and how can we help?

Being stuck means being unable to proceed to the next part of the task. When students get stuck, they are like cars stalling on a motorway. In one way, each case will be unique to its owner but in another, each case will be determined by the task type, hence the stuck student troubleshooter guide below. If you can identify where a student is stuck and get them moving again, your role is like that of a tow truck. If you can figure out where they are going to get stuck and cater for that in advance, you become more like a ministry of transport.

Differentiation troubleshooting chart

Reason for getting stuck	Support to help 'unstick' students
Grammar or vocabulary exercises	
Does not understand the task.	■ Check instructions with student. ■ Explain in L1 if necessary. ■ Do the first few questions with student as example.
Does not understand the forms required (grammar exercise).	■ Explain the forms required for those specific questions on a one-to-one basis. ■ Make the various forms required for the exercise available to the student, either as a chart or as options. ■ Complete the first few questions with the correct form, explaining why that form is used and what the sentence means. ■ Allow student first to see the answers then to complete the exercise as a memory task.

Does not have the lexis required (vocabulary exercise).	■ Show the student the vocabulary bank or unit page that corresponds to the exercise so that they can access the language. ■ Ask the student to look over the corresponding vocabulary before continuing with the exercise. ■ Allow student to work through exercise with access to a dictionary. ■ Allow student first to see the answers then to complete exercise as memory task.
May know lexis or forms but does not understand keywords in the questions, gapped sentences or input material.	■ Ask student what it is that they do not understand in the input question and provide explanation or L1 translation.
Reading comprehension or text	
Does not understand the text as a whole – its basic idea, theme or gist.	■ Provide a short, simplified synopsis: *"This is a text about…"*. Repeat in L1 if appropriate. ■ Provide a simple paraphrased version of the title and first paragraph. ■ Provide a line-by-line spoken translation of the title and first paragraph.
Does not know a specific word/s.	■ Provide explanation or translation at the point of need. ■ Allow access to paper-based or electronic dictionary. ■ Allow students to scan text prior to task and ask about unfamiliar items.
Cannot understand key sentences.	■ Ask student to identify those sentences (underlining or highlighting). Paraphrase into graded language or L1.

Does not understand any of the text.	■ Indicates serious decoding issues. ■ Allow student access to paper-based or online dictionary and ask them to work through just the first paragraph, translating it – then together look at the translation. ■ Provide a line-by-line L1 translation spoken. ■ Move student off task to vocabulary work, which will serve as the basis to understanding of the text – or the vocabulary that the text is meant to serve as a vehicle for. ■ Then later: provide a simplified text. ■ Provide a version of the text double-spaced with an interleaved L1 translation.
Does not understand the wording of questions on the text.	■ Ask what it is the student does not understand. Provide graded paraphrasing or L1 translation.
In-class writing	
Does not understand rubric to writing task.	■ Identify if this is because there are individual words in the rubric that are unknown and if so, explain them. ■ Where the level of unknown language is higher, paraphrase the rubric into graded language or provide L1 translation. ■ Where the underlying basis for the genre is unknown, explain it. For example: *"An 'article' is something you might read in a magazine or on a web page"*. ■ Show student a model answer to the question to give them an idea of format and register.
Does not know the word or phrase for something.	■ Provide word or phrase as teacher input or allow access to paper-based or electronic dictionary.

Does not know how to express an idea in English.	■ Allow student to explain what it is they want to say. ■ Reformulate student utterance providing input language, adjusting word order or forms. ■ Help by providing entire phrase or longer utterance.
Cannot think of anything to write.	■ Explore with the student what the input rubric and question prompts might mean for *them*. ■ Provide some basic ideas. ■ Allow student to look briefly at what a classmate is writing.
Is struggling to write anything.	■ Provide entire model answer and allow student to look at it. ■ Follow up with either a reconstruction activity or allow student to work through translating the ideas into L1.
Speaking activity	
Does not understand the question, scenario or prompt.	■ Reformulate or explain question. ■ Provide L1 translation where possible or appropriate.
Does not have the word to express an idea.	■ Provide word when and where needed.
Does not have a combination of words, phrases and forms to express an idea.	■ Listen to student's utterance and reformulate. ■ Provide student with required input language.
Did not understand partner's last utterance.	■ Ask partner to repeat, reformulate or explain. ■ Paraphrase partner's question. ■ Provide simplified question on the same topic.

Cannot think of anything to say in response to a question or scenario.	■ Provide additional prompts. ■ Try to help student personalise answer by exploring what the question might mean for that student. ■ Give own personalised responses as example: *If I was answering that, I'd say…*

Listening comprehension activity

Does not understand the general context, theme or dynamic of the audio.	■ Explain this. For example: *"In this recording there is a mother and a daughter speaking etc"*. If possible, once the recording is playing, pause and reorientate the listener. For example: *"That is the pop star and this… is the interviewer. Can you hear the different voices? So the pop star is the woman and the interviewer is the young boy"*.
Does not understand the question because of unknown words or phrasing	■ Explain unknown terms. ■ Reformulate question or translate into L1.
Is unable to locate the answers that correspond to the questions in a comprehension as has become 'lost'.	■ Pause the audio, class permitting, and orientate student: *"Now you are about to hear the answer to no. 4. Have you looked at that? Are you ready?"*
Is unable to decide on the answer to a question because of one or more key words being unfamiliar.	■ Identify with student what words might tell them the answer. ■ Provide clues or even answers in citation form then replay key stretches of audio to see if student can hear them for themselves.

Is unable to decode the stream of speech because of accent, speaker speed or unfamiliarity with spoken words out of citation form.	■ Employ a combination of the above strategies. ■ Slow down the recording if a digital audio. Provide answers in clear citation form yourself then allow students to try to hear these on the audio. ■ Move from comprehension task to the open analysis of several stretches of speaker speech.

Making things harder

At times we may need to increase the level of the challenge to engage more advanced learners. This graphic equaliser-style sliding scale shows the easier aspects of a task on the left and the more challenging ones on the right. Where a student has coped with a task easily, you can ask them to do something further with it, moving to the right.

Slide right to increase task challenge

knowing language	1	recognises language	recalls language	easily recalls language	memorised language	automaticity with language items	full assimilation of language items
pronouncing sentences	2		pronounces individual words correctly in citation form	able to pronounce longer phrases correctly		able to pronounce full sentences with stress that helps enhance message	
generating language	3		can read model sentences containing target language	can generate variations on given sentences		can independently generate original sentences containing target language	
level of personalisation	4		can work with text or audio about a neutral topic	can produce language about someone else from information collected		can produce language/adapt text so it accurately describes self	
operating systems	5		can get answers right to grammar/vocabulary questions	able to pass a test on these	able to explain structures or meanings to a colleague		able to design a test for a colleague
working with text	6		understands a text	able to translate or help a classmate with the text	able to retell the text	able to write questions on the text	can interpret, critique and add to the text
understanding audios	7		understands the gist of an audio	understands most of the words	can transcribe the audio accurately		recognises accents and pronunciation differences between speakers
spoken interactions	8		can answer simple questions	can make questions for a partner	can provide extended answers		can have back and forth conversation reacting to partner's contributions
sounds and symbols	9		produces individual sounds/matches them to IPA symbols and words	recalls sounds and symbols and able to make connections independently		able to transcribe to and from IPA	

Figure 27: **If the underlying functions performed by a student are more complex, we increase task challenge, the amount of language practice and hopefully learning outcomes**

So for example, if a student has answered questions on a text easily (looking at arrow 6) we could move to the right several steps and ask them to go off and record a spoken synopsis of the piece, to write an additional five questions on the text for a classmate or to write a short paragraph saying what they liked or did not like about the text. See **Downloadable resource 4** for further examples of increasing challenge to illustrate the scale.

I would like to offer a few words of caution. There is a world of difference between a student finishing an exercise quickly and finishing an exercise easily. Before adding challenge, we need to look at how a student has performed on the exercise. In the case of students who really are coping very easily with the task, we do not have to wait until they have finished before extending their learning – we can move them straight along the scale, and thus avoid them feeling that they always have to do double.

Finally, our conceptions of struggling learner and advanced learner need to be fluid. A student who coped easily with yesterday's vocabulary activity and was thus given a more challenging variation on that task, might be struggling with today's listening comprehension and will require more support. Rather than pigeonhole students as struggling or advanced learners, period, we need to base our evaluations upon the task they are currently performing and to reevaluate their performance as often as we can.

Questions for reflection

- How much do you tend to teach the class in front of you as if they were one person?
- Have you seen any of CA Tomlinson's YouTube clips on differentiation?
- In general, how do you get on with the concept?

Things to try

1. Try pinpointing more closely than usual where your students get stuck on a task.
2. Use the sliding scale above to adapt tasks for your more advanced learners.
3. Experiment with setting up two or three different class tasks at the same time.

Things to share

Take an element of your institution's set syllabus such as a mandatory coursebook page, worksheet, exam task or curriculum feature. Make three versions of a related worksheet:

- A standard version.
- One that has additional support built into it.
- One that has an element of extra challenge in it.

Trial your worksheet and share your experiences with colleagues.

References

Roland C & Barber D (2016) Untangling Differentiation. *Modern English Teacher* **25** (2) 64–66.

Tomlinson CA (2001) *How to Differentiate Instruction in Mixed-Ability Classrooms* (2nd edition). Virginia: Association for Supervision and Curriculum Development.

12. Repetition, assimilation, memorisation

Discussion

We often underestimate the number of times most students need to hear most words to remember them. Coursebooks make a systematic effort to recycle vocabulary. A core item will normally first appear within the context of a reading or listening text, or in its own dedicated exercise. It will normally appear again in an end of unit revision exercise, in the workbook and in a vocabulary summary or index at the back. This will often result in students seeing the item five, six or seven times in total. I have found, however, that students regularly need to see a new word anything up to 20 times – and sometimes more – in order to remember it (Roland, 2013).

If the teacher keeps revisiting and reworking new language, it will get assimilated. The essential ingredients are patience and persistence.
We might also try to give students a variety of 'looks' at the same language. Some words they will take to immediately – either because they like the shape or the sound of them, because those words strike them as something that may be useful in the future (for a more in-depth look at how we appraise new language, see Schumann, 1999) or because they are able to connect them to existing language (for an explanation of all the crisscrossing networks of associations involved in knowing a word, see McCarthy, 1990).

Most of us probably already give students a word set as it is in the coursebook – within the context of a reading or in an exercise where they match words and thumbnail photographs. After that, we might try creating personalised associations: *"Who has a* [+new noun] *at home? When was the last time you* [+new verb]?*"*. We might also provide the words in a list and work with L1 translation or provide sentences containing new items which will work as definitions or examples of use. However, in this and the next chapter we will look at numerous things we can then ask our learners to do with the language. Each time students do something different with new words, phrases and sentences, each time they look at them in a different way, we increase the chances of them making connections that will stick. For a fuller range of memorisation activities see Bilborough (2011).

Practical applications

Flagging up recurrences

Words recur. Items that you have looked at in course material will reappear, for example, during a whole class discussion or during a YouTube clip. Our most useful function when this happens is to make the recurrence explicit by pausing the exchange or the clip and drawing everyone's attention to it: *"Did you hear that? Can you remember it from the word list?"*.

Sooner or later, your students will start picking those words out and tossing them back to you as well, having made their own connections. Recently I was guiding an intermediate group through their first B1 practice listening exam. *"Candidate,"* said one of them as we looked at the initial instructions, *"That's on our vocabulary list"*. Then, later as we were going through and discussing the answers (to a question that asked: *Which version of the story does the woman prefer – the novel, play or film?*) one student told us all she had understood a key line, *"I **still** prefer the book"*, because *"That's what you say teacher when we get an answer wrong – I **still** like you"*. Here students are becoming their own language detectives.

Saying it again

In a busy class, it is easy to respond to a student request for language by writing it on the board, waiting for their nod and turning your attention to the next hand in the air. However, language does not happen by magic and if a learner has never said a word *inside* the classroom, it is unlikely they will manage to say it outside while on holiday, in an interview or on a video call. I recommend sharing this line of thinking with your students too.

Taking a few more seconds to get a student to actually say a new word is an invaluable investment, even though there may be other distractions clawing at the periphery of your attention. Getting students to say a new item more than once will add further value. After two minutes, you might ask them again. Then after ten, after half an hour or just before the end. Once they cotton on to the fact that you are making 'a thing' out of their word and 'a thing' out of remembering then it becomes a type of game. Teenage students will generally not mind this at all because it means that you keep coming back to *them* as a person, to *their* word and to *their* learning – they are getting your attention.

Working with lists

At the back of many coursebooks, vocabulary appears in lists. These may be organised by theme, unit or in alphabetical order for the whole book. If we want to be able to play with these lists – for example, in rapid-fire quiz style games – and if we want to do so without recourse to L1 translation, then it is useful to put the items into simple sentences that explain the terms (first discussed in Roland, 2012). So, if our word list reads like this:

Jobs
Actor
Architect
Bank manager
Builder
Dancer
Electrician
Engineer
Firefighter
Greengrocer

We might produce something like this:

An **actor** plays the roles of different characters.
An **architect** designs buildings.
A **bank manager** may agree to lend you some money.
A **builder** works with bricks and cement.
A **dancer** needs to have a sense of rhythm.
An **electrician** makes your lights work.
and so on…

Now students can use these explanations to show the teacher that they understand the words. This is particularly useful in international classes

12. Repetition, assimilation, memorisation

where students have a range of L1's or where the teacher is trying to establish the space as an 'English only' zone. The inclusion of full sentences also allows us to extend learning above and beyond core items.

Now when we ask Fernando: *"Builder?"*

He can tell us: *"A builder works with bricks and cement."*

Queens and clowns

The following is a game that requires no additional materials, is easy to set up and I have used it with consistent success for nearly 20 years. It is ideal for classes sitting in horseshoe formation of about 12-15 students.

Figure 28: The sequence of turns when students are sat in horseshoe formation

With students seated in fixed rows it can still work by establishing the order of turns clearly at the start (see Figure 28) and with larger classes again, it can still work if students collaborate sufficiently for gameplay to progress swiftly.

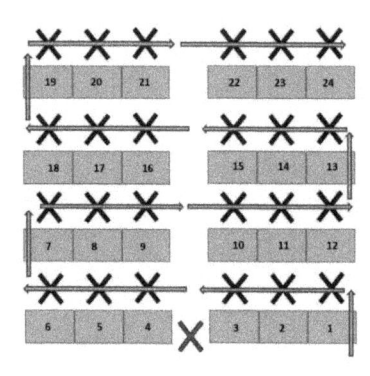

Figure 29: The order of turns for a larger class with a more traditional seating plan

12. Repetition, assimilation, memorisation

First we assign roles starting with the queen or the king. The context is an imaginary medieval city. I use the roles in the table below, with a few additional explanations. I will add or omit roles depending upon the number of players and I have recently made them closer to popular series such as *Game of Thrones* or *Vikings* depending upon class tastes. Additional roles might be general, soldier, squire, blacksmith, physician or innkeeper.

Seat No.	Role	Back story
1	Queen or king	You are top dog. You are the owner of all you see. Nice life!
2	Princess or prince	You do what you want, when you want. There's only one person you have to listen to.
3	Minor royal	You live in the palace, you enjoy its security and its luxuries.
4	Prime minister	You have the queen's/king's ear and you invent all the laws.
5	Queen's/King's champion	You are considered the bravest and most skilled warrior in the land.
6	Queen's/King's bodyguard	You are considered the queen's/king's most loyal warrior.
7	Noble	You are part of the aristocracy and have extensive lands beyond the city.
8	Friend of the family	You are not nobility but are well connected and are seen at all the best parties, with none of the responsibilities.
9	Rich merchant	You own the entire market. Nothing comes in or out of the city without you knowing about it.
10	Stall holder	You work in the market. You have your own stall. It's a steady job.
11	Assistant stall holder	You help the person who has a stall in the market – on Saturdays when you're not at school.

12	Stable girl/boy	You work with the horses. You spend a lot of time with a shovel in your hand.
13	Hermit	You live just outside the city walls in a little stone building. People think you're a little bit crazy but sometimes they come to you for advice as well.
14	Wildling	You live in the forest on the hill. You run about with a big sword and when the people in the town see you and your friends coming they light fires and ring bells.
15	Court jester	You live in the palace. You eat well and have a warm bed at night. The only thing you have to do is to make the queen/king laugh three times a day. For this you have a hat and a stick with bells on them.

Next we explain that the character roles are connected not to people but to the chairs so that whoever is in position 1 is the queen or king, anyone in position 2 becomes the princess or prince, etc. The aim is to keep your top spot if you are the monarch and to try to get to the top spot if you are not. It is all about being upwardly socially mobile.

Gameplay works as follows. We ask the queen a question, for example, "What is an actor?". If she can give us a definition sentence such as: *"An actor plays the roles of different characters"*, then she is safe and maintains her position (the game can also be played with straight L1 translation). If she cannot, that question goes to the next player. If they get it right, they swap places with the queen. If they do not, the same question goes to the next player and so on until somebody gets it right upon which they swap places with the queen. It is always the person who eventually gets the question right who ascends to the position of the person who first got that question wrong. All the players in between stay where they are. If a question goes right round the class with nobody able to answer, the teacher gives the word.

Students like this game because there is always a chance they will get the next question right. Language learning happens because students hear not only their question but also the questions that other students get right (or that the teacher has to give) so it is important that everyone is controlled enough to listen to everything. If they are not, we can pause the game and explain this.

In terms of pitfalls, occasionally a student might prove reticent to move. I have played this hundreds of times with dozens and dozens of groups and the simple fact is that the game stops working if a student is allowed not to move – so it is worth insisting, with a smile. The game also stops working if students shout out answers. I explain first: *"If you know the answer, it could be your ticket to success. The question could come round to you so keep it to yourself."*

Blank exercises

"With exercises from the book," I tell my students, *"the real work starts once we have completed the exercise – that is, after we have filled in the gaps. It's fine having a coursebook full of completed exercises that you can't remember, but that won't help you to speak English when you're on holiday, in an interview or on a video call"*.

So we do the exercise, correct it, check each other's corrections and test each other. To this end, I have made increasing use of blank exercises (photocopies made before the gaps are filled in) for students to test each other's memory in pairs or for me to test individual students on a one-to-one basis to make sure they have paid attention to, processed and retained the language of an exercise.

Student generated audio lists

If you give students a list of words and ask them to study at home for a test, the chances are that some will do so and some will not. It is impossible to know exactly who has or has not looked at them, and even test results will give only an indirect indication. An alternative is to ask students to record themselves reading the list and then send you the audio. Granted, reading a list out loud is not the same as learning it by heart but at least you have a tangible way to measure task completion. This is a way of guaranteeing everyone has looked at the list outside of class time. To increase exposure, we can ask students to read the list again but this time backwards, starting from the last item.

Recycling language from the board

One of the advantages of a coursebook is that, simply by virtue of existing over time, it acts as a record of the core language presented therein. At other times though, new language will come up in our conversations with a class and as part of their spoken or written production. You can decide how much importance to place on this additional language. Personally, I see it as the outcome of our hard work to set up meaningful interactions. If students are requesting language it is because they need it to express themselves. A board full of language at the end of class indicates there has been an attempt by students to go beyond what they know. In classes without a coursebook, it is items from this language that can be selected and turned into both a record of the class and a retrospective lesson-by-lesson vocabulary syllabus. In all classes, language on the board can be revisited at the end of each lesson (first discussed in Roland, 2013).

Imagine you are in a lesson about food and that the following has accumulated on our whiteboard:

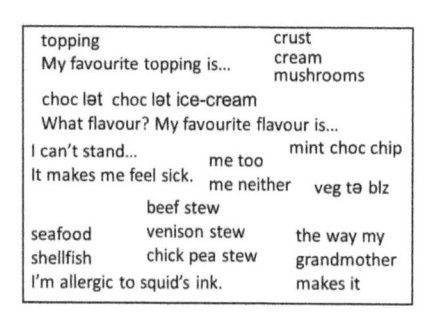

```
topping                      crust
My favourite topping is...   cream
                             mushrooms
choc lət  choc lət ice-cream
What flavour? My favourite flavour is...
I can't stand...                mint choc chip
                  me too
It makes me feel sick.
                  me neither   veg tə blz
              beef stew
seafood       venison stew     the way my
shellfish     chick pea stew   grandmother
I'm allergic to squid's ink.   makes it
```

Figure 30: Language that has been boarded while a class has been talking about food

While students are on another task, the teacher can quickly rub out certain words, replacing them with lines and numbers like so:

```
t¹_____                         crust
My favourite ²_____  is...      cr ³___
                                  mushrooms
choc lət  choc lət ice-cream
What  ⁴___ ? My favourite ⁵___ is...
I can't stand...                  mint ⁶___ chip
                    me t ⁷___
It makes me feel ⁹___ .  me n ⁸___   veg tə blz
               b ¹⁰___ stew
sea___¹³      v ¹¹___ stew      the ¹⁷___ my
Shell___¹⁴    c ¹² p__ stew     grandmother
I'm allergic ¹⁵ squid's ¹⁶___ . makes it
```

Figure 31: By testing each other's memories in pairs, students get to engage with that language one more time

Now for the last five minutes they can work in pairs to try to remember the different items, providing another point of contact with the vocabulary.

Recording language from the board yourself

If the teacher records language from the board themselves, this sends the message that what is up there matters. It also puts the teacher in a great place to recycle items in subsequent lessons. One small turn I like to put on this is to face away from the board myself and ask students, one-by-one, to read out the words behind me. As they do so, I copy them down. This gives me one more chance to guide pronunciation and it gives the students yet another point of contact with the words.

This technique can be doubled up with the previous instant board gap-fill to serve as a refresher for the items students did not manage to recall. When a student inevitably suggests: *"Teacher, why don't you just turn around so you can see the board?"* We can respond with a smile and a flourishing gesture as we remind them: *"The whole of this, you coming here, calling me 'teacher', it's all for one thing and one thing only – to get you saying words and sentences in English. You're clever. You know that really. So... this is just more of that"*.

Organically evolving language

The teacher is then free to take recorded language away and play with it between lessons. Vocabulary that was written on the board as single word items can be put into sentences. Imagine the following words were written down at the end of a lesson:

go-karting
initials
I'm looking forward to it
affectionate
vulture
wristband
great grandfather and great grandmother
stationer's

From these we can type up something like this:

Have you ever been **go-karting**? If so, where? If not, would you like to?
What are your best friend's **initials**? And yours?
What future event are you **looking forward to**?
Which do you think are more **affectionate**: cats or dogs?
What is the closest you have ever been to a **vulture**?
Are you wearing any **wristbands** today? Do you have any others at home?
Do you know the first names of any of your **great grandfathers** or **great grandmothers**?
From which **stationer's** do you buy most of your school equipment from?

The items are now included in fully grammaticalised questions, so the next time the students see them, the language has grown, evolved towards something that can be used for either pair or whole class communicative speaking – while still revising the original vocabulary.

Image + gapped sentence + target item

The first set of vocabulary that I covered with two intermediate teen groups that I teach at the time of writing was a wide selection of seafood, meat, fruit and vegetable items. As usual, first we matched words to pictures. In subsequent lessons we reworked the vocabulary in both teacher and student-led dictations. We covered the words and tested each other using the photographs and I also sent out the lists as a recording. Nothing worked. On short one-to-one tests with both groups it became clear that many of these words such as *courgette, cabbage, beetroot* and *raspberries* were not sticking.

As a solution, I took a Google image of each item and placed it on its own PowerPoint slide, with a gapped sentence underneath such as: "_____ *can be light or dark green and are also called zucchini*". I then duplicated the slide and restored the word to the gap on the second one. In this case it read: "**Courgettes** *can be light or dark green and are also called zucchini*". This way I could flick through the presentation giving students a chance to try to remember before the correct word was displayed. I showed the document once a lesson and by the third showing the whole class had it. *"It's easy like that, teacher,"* they said.

Although somewhat reminiscent of the operant conditioning scene in the film *A Clockwork Orange*, this combination of image and gapped contextualising sentence followed by a second slide with the target word restored has proven the singular most effective memorisation technique with my own students. I now have numerous PowerPoint documents in this format.

Questions for reflection

- How much importance do you place on language that 'comes up' during class?
- How much recycling of language do you consciously include in lessons?

Things to try

1. If you are working from single item lists, try turning those into sentences.
2. Follow up vocabulary exercises with testing to measure retention.
3. Try the Queens and Clowns game if you have never played it.
4. Turn the contents of the board into a quick refresher gap-fill at the end of class.

> **Things to share**
>
> Take a set of approximately 20 vocabulary items that both you and a colleague need to teach.
>
> - One of you write conversation questions including all those items, as described in the chapter.
> - One of you make a PowerPoint with images and gapped sentence on the first slide and restored item on the second as described above.
> - Trial your own resource followed by the one created by your colleague.
>
> Compare your experiences on the processes and the outcomes.

References

Bilborough N (2011) *Memory Activities for Language Learning*. Cambridge: Cambridge University Press.

McCarthy M (1990) *Vocabulary*. Oxford: Oxford University Press.

Roland C (2012) Teen-angles. In: Díez MP, Place R, Fernández O (Eds). *Plurilingualism: Promoting co-operation between communities, people and nations*. TESOL Spain, University of Deusto.

Roland C (2013) Some considerations for teaching low-level teens. *Teaching with Technology and the Human Touch*. TESOL Spain. Ed Rebecca Place, Olga Fdez. Vicente.

Schumann JH (1999) A neurological perspective on affect and methodology in second language learning in *Affect in Language Learning*. Ed: Jane Arnold. New York: Cambridge University Press.

13. Remembering irregular verbs

Discussion

How do we feel about the chart?

At the back of most coursebooks we will find a list of the irregular verbs: *be*, *was*, *been*, *become*, *became*, *become* and so on. Are irregular verb forms useful? Yes. Do students need to know them? Yes. Is the three-column format the best one? Perhaps. Perhaps not.

I remember having lunch in Damascus, years ago, with a mixture of locals, people from the Spanish embassy and English teachers from the British Council. We had settled on English as the lingua franca and one of the Spanish diplomats wanted to ask one of the Syrians if the part of town we were eating in had expanded in recent times.

"Has this part of the city…"

Then I saw his eyes drift upwards and move across in increments as he silently mouthed the words grow, grew before settling on:

"…grown?"

Then in his mid-20s, he was using the three-column format which he had learnt at secondary school as a prop to production.

So when people ask me how I feel about the irregular verbs chart, my reply is that it can work, just as any list can, but we need to remember that a list is merely an organising principle and not a pedagogic technique. There are things we can do and places we can take those verbs to restore a little more meaning to them and help fix them in our students' minds.

The importance of irregular verbs

The first step is to instill the importance of the irregular verb forms in our students' minds. *"You need these"*, I tell my students. *"Without the participles, you can't make clean sentences in the present perfect, past perfect, conditional or passive. Without the past you can't tell anyone what happened today at school, stuff about when you were younger or anything about the lives of your parents or their parents. You become like a musician in concert that can't play certain notes and whose amplifiers are giving screeches of feedback now and again."*

Another analogy is the following: *"Knowing your verb forms is like having a good basic posture or stance in dance or sports such as MMA, fencing, or tennis. It enables you to make a series of effective moves or shots from a strong central position."*

Practical applications

Identifying patterns

One of the most frequent objections to the irregular verbs chart is that it consists of decontextualised items so there is no clue to meaning or guide to use. This is a very reasonable point and one we will address shortly, but we might also look at things in a different way. Decluttered from any surrounding language, the three-column format enables us to focus *purely* on form.

Taking the time with a class to stop and appreciate this form may be a new experience for them. We can explain to them that just as there are patterns in nature (such as the veins on leaves, snowflakes or other crystals) so too are there patterns in the verbs. With class sets of colours or highlighter pens, they could begin by marking in yellow all the verbs that follow the i-a-u pattern such as *begin-began-begun* and *drink-drank-drunk*. In a different colour they can highlight those verbs that have the same form for each column such as *hit-hit-hit*. Then there are the verbs that end in ght for the past and participles (*buy-bought-bought* and *catch-caught-caught*) with the teacher drawing attention to the silent *gh* and the fact that two combinations make the sound *ou* and *au*.

The next group of verbs to be categorised could be those that follow the ew-own pattern such as *fly* or *grow*. Another group are the verbs where the participle form ends in *en* such as *give* or *ride*. A further general category might be those remaining verbs that follow a 1-2-2 pattern, where there is one form for the present and where the past and the participle are the same – for example *understand-understood-understood*. Of the remaining verbs, some will also follow a 1-2-1 pattern where only the past form is different such as *come* or *run*.

Creating images to learn the irregular verbs

I have also gone to considerable lengths to provide additional context to the irregular verbs. I even made a set of Rorschach-style ink blot flash cards with a sentence for each column and an abstract image which evolved slightly across the forms.

It's good to **be** here.   Yesterday I **was** there.   I have **been** both here and there this week.

Figure 32: Inkblot images for *be/was/been*

Small children **fall** over a lot.   She **fell** over last night.   Someone has **fallen** off the roof.

Figure 33: Inkblot images for *fall/fell/fallen*

You're not allowed to **feed** the animals. We **fed** the animals at the zoo. We've **fed** the animals each day this week.

Figure 34: Inkblot images for *feed/fed/fed*

I want to **sell** it. I **sold** it yesterday. I have **sold** them all.

Figure 35: Inkblot images for *sell/sold/sold*

The idea here was that, being suggestive only, the images require students to put some of their own imagination to the activity of viewing – to complete the interpretation and help fix the item in memory. I am still trialling these, so unlike the other activities in this book, I cannot provide guidance on the best way to use them or a final verdict on overall effectiveness. However, if you would like the full set to try out go to **Downloadable resource 5**.

"Sentencyfying" the verbs

The above activity is artistic and creative but it begs the question: *Whose creativity?* If we deconstruct the inkblot activity, we see that the first step was to put the verbs into sentences. This is in itself a creative activity and a useful starting point for anything else. Students could just be given sentences with boxes as below to allow them to create their own illustrations or to paste their own images in.

I need to **leave** 10 minutes early to go to the doctor's.	When the teacher **left** the room, the students went crazy.	I think I've **left** my mobile in the toilets. Can I go and look for it?
Can somebody **lend** me a pen?	She **lent** me her headphones but I broke them.	Have you ever **lent** anyone your trainers?

This approach, more appropriate for younger teens encountering all the verb forms for the first time, is worthwhile if you are going to undertake it systematically, providing a stapled pack or plastic wallet where students can keep all their illustrated verbs together.

Creativity vs language

The downside of any craft-based project though, is that while a student is drawing a picture, they are not engaging with language. As Hugh Dellar (2012) has pointed out, it is often best to get students working with language at a basic level and having repeated exposure to it. In my own trajectory, I have progressively favored encouraging direct creativity with sentences themselves – that is engagement with and production of language. Going back to our verbs in sentences, such as these below, we can ask: *"Can you make a similar sentence, leaving the verb intact but changing the rest so that the sentence is different, more interesting or more relevant to you?"* Using the first sentence in each case as a point of departure, students might generate second sentences such as these:

*I need to **leave** 10 minutes early to go to the doctor's.*
*I need to **leave** 30 minutes early to go to the dentist's.*

*When the teacher **left** the room, the students went crazy.*
*When the teacher **left** the room, the students continued to work.*

*I think I've **left** my mobile in the toilets. Can I go and look for it?*
*I think I've **left** my bag in the canteen. Can I go with Alex to look for it?*

This provides a point of entry for students to interact with the original sentence and a chance to create their own as context for the form. Similarly, we could ask them to provide a follow up sentence which in some way extends the original.

*I need to **leave** 10 minutes early to go to the doctor's.*
My mum will pick me up from outside the school.

*When the teacher **left** the room, the students went crazy.*
Roger and Sergi started kicking each other.

I think I've left my mobile in the toilets. Can I go and look for it?
Okay, but don't be long.

Audio lists

There are numerous internet tutorials which take students through the verb columns. As 'Fluency MC', Jason R Levine (2010) has even gone as far as to put two massive whiteboards full of irregulars into rap. Recording yourself reading the irregular verbs is very easy and has the advantage that what your students hear will correspond exactly to the list in their own book – as lists tend to vary slightly from publication to publication.

Again, in terms of completion, asking students to listen to the audio then send you a sound file of *them* reading the list, is a tangible and measurable task. If any 'clangers' jump out at you while giving the audios a cursory listening, students can be asked to listen to your model audio again then re-record (signposting them to the verbs they need to pay particular attention to in terms of pronunciation). Students could also read their verbs on a one-to-one basis to the teacher in class. Having a machine set up at the front or in an adjacent class for students to listen to using headphones is also an option.

Image + gapped sentence + target verb

Just as I have found the most effective form of vocabulary revision to be gapped sentences with a corresponding image (with the target item restored to the sentence on the next slide), I have also found the same to be true for the irregular verbs. I show these to pre-intermediate and intermediate teens classes over the first month of class.

In order to avoid complications regarding copyright and distribution, I have included a template from which you can make your own photo-illustrated gapped irregular verbs document – see **Downloadable resource 6**. The sentences are already in place on the slides and where the images need to go, I have suggested a search phrase that will take you to a number of suitable images, leaving the reader responsible for requesting permission for whichever images they settle upon where necessary.

| I need to _____ 10 minutes early to go to the doctor's. | I need to **leave** 10 minutes early to go to the doctor's. |

Figure 36: Example slides from the photo-illustrated verbs template

A *regular* verbs list

The methodology in this book is meant to compliment conventional practice rather than challenge it. You will notice I have not railed against any ELT industry standards and, apart from the inkblot flashcards, have kept my coverage of experimental practice rather low. There is, however, one thing that we do that strikes me as rather odd. When our students ask us about the past or participle form of a new verb, we often tell them: *"If it isn't in the irregular verbs list, it's regular"*. However, if our students still do not know the irregulars very well then this back-to-front process of elimination, defining the easier verbs by the more difficult, is going to be of limited use. What I would like to see is the inclusion of a *regular* verbs list in our coursebooks and on several occasions I have created my own regular verbs list for the particular coursebook I have been using by scanning through it page by page and making the list up that way. This is also something that could be done in class with your students over the course of the year as you work through the book.

admit	admit**t**ed	admit**t**ed
agree	agreed	agreed
answer	answered	answered
argue	argued	argued
ask	asked	asked
ban	ba**nn**ed	ba**nn**ed
believe	believed	believed
blame	blamed	blamed
book	booked	booked
call	called	called
cause	caused	caused
change	changed	changed
cheat	cheated	cheated
cook	cooked	cooked
copy	copied	copied

Once we have a list of regular verbs, we find they are not so regular either. We can listen to them with our students, crossing out all the 'e's in -ed endings that are not pronounced. Then we can look at some of the letters that double up and where the 'y's turn to 'i's. This sort of initiative on the part of the teacher does not have to run counter to course materials but is an example of how we can take practical but principled steps to make things just a little easier for our students.

Questions for reflection

- How prominently does the irregular verbs chart feature in your teaching?
- Would you ever focus on form by having students colour code the irregular verbs?
- Does the idea of allowing students to flesh out the irregulars with their own example sentences appeal to you?

Things to try

1. Record a model audio of yourself or your students reading the irregular verbs and work with that.
2. Create a digital irregular verbs resource with images and gapped sentences.
3. Try working the other way. With any text, ask students to find and underline examples of verbs in the past and in the participles. These can then be further categorised as regular or irregular and meaning explored.

Things to share

Over the course of one or two weeks, choose a group and record every error that students make with verb forms in written assignments, marking up the frequency on an irregular verbs chart (and noting errors with regulars). After this period of data collection:

- Can you discern any patterns?
- Is there any follow up you feel appropriate or needed?
- Is there anything you feel worth sharing with other teachers in your centre?

References

Dellar H (2012) *The Curse of Creativity*. Available at: https://hughdellar.wordpress.com/2012/09/17/the-curse-of-creativity/ (accessed July 2018).

Levine JR (2010) *Learn and Speak English Irregular Verbs Grammar Rap*. Available at: https://www.youtube.com/watch?v=gZzKe1BC2XU (accessed July 2018).

Roland C (2013) Some considerations for teaching low-level teens. *Teaching with Technology and the Human Touch*. TESOL Spain. Ed Rebecca Place, Olga Fdez. Vicente.

14. Movement and space

Discussion

Structuring the moment

Agnes Richter was an inmate at Hubertusberg Psychiatric Asylum, Germany, in the 1890s, and as a seamstress she decided to embroider her straightjacket (which can be viewed online) with her own personal codification of thoughts, reflections and biographical details (Hornstein, 2018).

Luang Pho Daeng was the abbot of a Bhuddist temple on Ko Samui island in Thailand (Barrow, 2012). He spent his life meditating and when he died in 1973, he was still meditating. Forty-five years later, his mummified remains, still cross-legged, are on display in a glass case on Ko Samui.

Agnes and Luang both managed to structure their moments to find a release from the worlds they were in. Our teenage students' world is that of the classroom. With or without us they will find a way to survive it but if we can make the present slightly less suffocating by introducing an element of movement, space, freedom or fun then that shared world becomes more inhabitable for both parties.

In this chapter we shall look at ways to achieve this without compromising either our learning goals or principles of good teaching practice.

Practical applications

Making the most of space

This plan is very similar to the centre where I work.

14. Movement and space

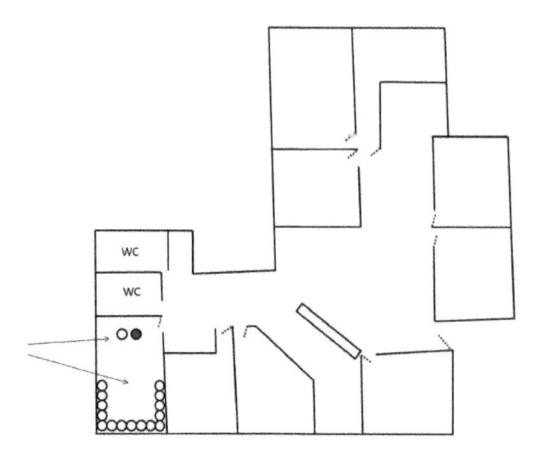

Figure 37: A centre plan

As you can see above, the students normally sit around the outside of the room but sometimes I have them sit at the front and talk me through some work. I might also ask them to read me something they have prepared, such as a mini-monologue, just outside of the door. This involves a sense of transition but I am still able to keep an eye on the whole group.

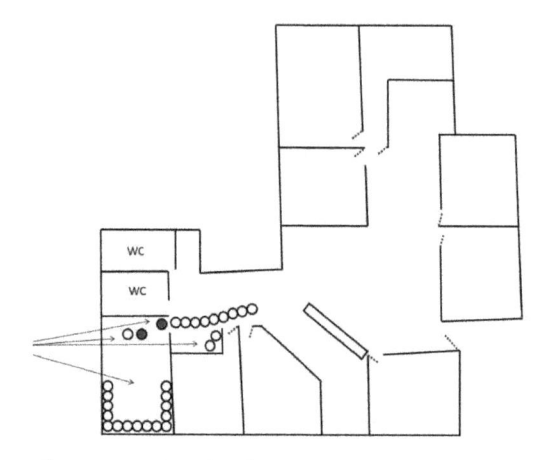

Figure 38: Using the classroom and nearby spaces

Right at the start of the lesson, I might create a pressure spot at the door, requiring that students produce some spoken language by completing a sentence before I let them in. Such sentences might be: *"If you let me in I will ... "* or *"So far today I have learnt about ..."* (see **Downloadable resource 7** for a document containing over 100 such questions).

During the lesson, I might send a couple of students out to try to complete an exercise that I have previously stuck on the wall outside. This has the advantage of allowing two students who need a break (or who the others need a break from) to have time out without any blame, conflict or overt disciplinary measure. A variation on this task is to supply one of the students with the answers and ask them to test the other.

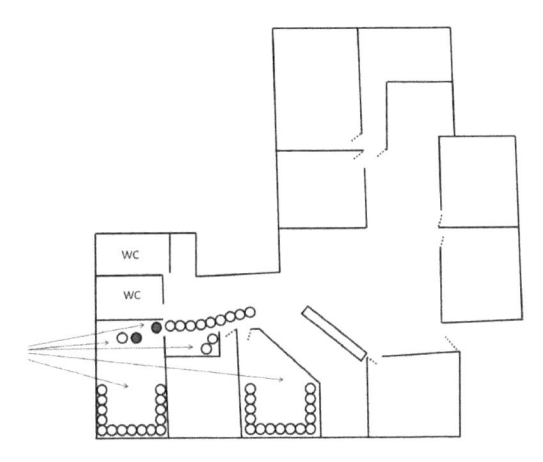

Figure 39: Using a spare classroom

If another classroom is free, we may all go together and sit in that for a change of scenery. If students have to prepare or practise something they can do it in the spare classroom and return to ours when they are ready. This normally works in the teacher's favor as, contrary to expectations, most students do not want to be the last ones left in the other room, away from the majority of the group. A writing activity that has been a favorite of mine for years involves students making a poster-sized company information sheet edited down from the corporation profiles found on Wikipedia (including information such as company history, product lines and philosophy). A spare classroom is an ideal space for them to practise talking a reduced audience of one or two classmates through their creations.

14. Movement and space

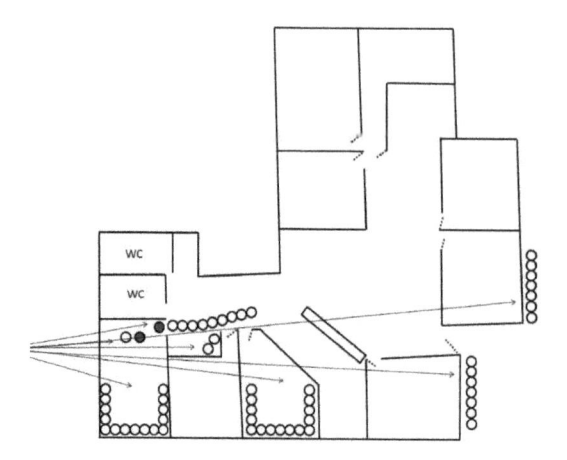

Figure 40: Using the outside of the centre

While working in a large school with both primary and secondary modules, I walked out into the schoolyard and stood with my back to a large iron gate. From there, I wrote down everything I could see. The list included basketball courts, covered walkways, chapel roof, palm trees, chimneys and a construction crane. I then produced a mini-photo dictionary of these items with their words and a space for students to insert an L1 translation, which they did in our next lesson. I then took them out and had them stand with their backs to the same gate, draw what they could see and write a paragraph length description of it – using their picture dictionaries. This helped them describe the space they had been playing in since they had come to the school as five year olds.

I do a similar activity with my current language academy students. They stand with their backs to the building and draw the street scene opposite the centre, which consists of residential flats, balconies, a pelican crossing, traffic lights, a park and railings. They also complete a write up using the picture dictionary I have made for the setting. So here we are using even the outside of the building as a resource.

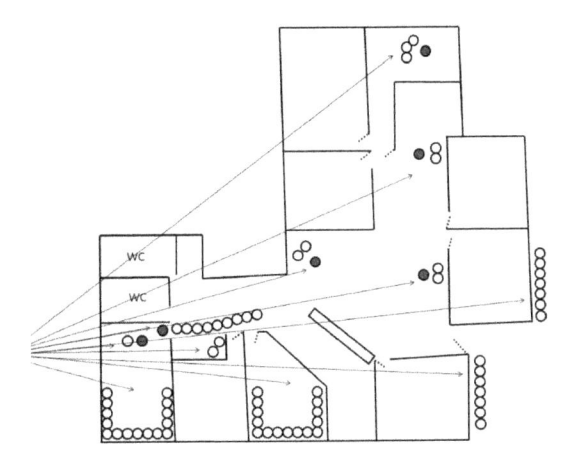

Figure 41: Using all the space available to us

Finally, we can set students up in small groups around the centre with one in each group appointed as speaking examiner, complete with scripts and questions, photos and stopwatch and have them examine each other. This creates a sense of responsibility and it is surprising which students can rise to the occasion here.

We can use the physical space of our school to create various sensations and useful tensions within our students, in order to activate their energies and maximise productivity.

Multiple writing surfaces

At the very moment I write the line you are reading, I have been sitting in my chair for an hour and a half composing the paragraphs above. Just being able to get up and move to another location (in my case the living room, with a pen and notepad) provides enough stimulation to keep going without having to leave off.

A little over five years ago I was given permission by my institution to install four whiteboards in my classroom, enough for all the students to write simultaneously. These have since become an integral part of my teaching and I wholeheartedly recommend multiple writing surfaces to anyone considering the setup of new classrooms or anyone who has a say over their existing ones, for these reasons:

1. Students get to stand up.
2. Writing on the board still holds something special for them.
3. Allowing them to do so challenges the traditional default blueprint of the classroom and increases ownership of the space they are in.
4. Students are able to see what each other has written and learn from that.
5. It is much easier for the teacher to correct – when a student asks for a word or phrase, the teacher can see the context into which that language needs to fit.
6. Students can incorporate corrections at the time of writing when they are relevant.

For any teachers, trainers, directors or school owners interested, my use of multiple boards in the classroom is further documented in Roland (2014).

Movement away from norms

We often talk about fun, but where does the fun in a fun activity come from? I have suggested that it comes from what we perceive as movement away from the norm (Roland 2013; 2016). We enjoy being in different places, doing new things, looking at unusual objects. I have categorised this movement into a number of shifts. So far in this chapter we have looked at 'spatial shifts'. Allowing students to be the teacher, as in Chapter 9, is an example of 'power shift'. Being allowed to graffiti a whitewashed cabinet, write about education on house bricks or use correction fluid to write maxims found on the internet onto beach pebbles are all examples of 'text shift' (see Roland, 2015). While such a transfer of words and sentences to atypical surfaces lies outside of what is central and necessary to practice written English, if the writing has been guided, drafted and checked then it can prove stimulating to students and they can get pleasure from the end products.

'Object shift' describes the sense of curiosity we get from seeing something inside the classroom that is not normally there. Importing objects as 'realia' for vocabulary (e.g. bringing in fruit to teach fruit words) is probably not worthwhile in terms of the mileage we can get out of it, but if the imported object serves another function then it might. Beads, monopoly money or casino chips can represent points in a game. We can invite students to throw splat balls or other sticking projectiles at word items written or projected onto the board. With both chips and splat balls, the basis of the activity can remain student-generated or student-processed sentences.

If ever I have a large cardboard box, I challenge the students to see who can sit down in it without breaking it. We call it 'the box challenge'. When I am dieting, I bring in a set of scales and once a week each student gets the chance to try to guess my weight before I step on. Again, the drive for the first challenge is towards the construction: *"Alejandro fits in the box. Felipe nearly fits in the box"*. For the second, students need to produce full sentences for their predictions: *"I think you weigh…"* and they get practice with decimal points such as: *"a hundred and two point seven"*. Such incidents provide a little light-hearted relief but we still have not let go of the language.

Student-initiated play

If we are reading through a text together in class, I will sometimes ask a student to read a sentence then nominate the next reader, with the condition that they cannot nominate one of their neighbours. During one such reading I noticed that some students had arrived at an unspoken accord that they were going to keep nominating their friend Pablo. So Pablo, while finding the attention fun (I was careful to make sure he was not feeling picked on), ended up reading a little more than he normally would.

Some years ago, during some project work, my students were in pairs at PC terminals. One in each pair was responsible for reading a text to the other, sentence by sentence, who would then type it up. While monitoring, I noticed that in two or three cases the reader was trying to confuse the typist or go too fast for them and the typist was trying to go faster than the speaker.

Both episodes are examples of students finding a way to turn a task into a game. They were playing. In both cases I could have intervened: *"You can't ask Pablo anymore"* or: *"Read more slowly please"*. That was my first instinct but in both cases I resisted. Their play ran parallel to my own agenda but did not seriously damage it. Students find opportunities for this sort of play all the time. It is one of their survival strategies. Sometimes it will run counter to what they are supposed to be doing and threaten to derail the official task. Other times it will not. In the case of the latter, my question is: why jump in at all? We therefore need to be able to discern what type of play we are dealing with. This is something we already do but can get better at by actively observing this aspect of student behaviour over time.

A case study incorporating numerous shifts and play

A small group of pre-intermediate teens in an academy were surprised when they entered the room and saw that I had turned the two central tables that we normally sat round into a ping pong table using extra wide packing tape strung between pencils for the net – but nobody objected. They took turns to play in doubles and I let them go like that for 20 minutes. It was an unexpected slot of pure recreation.

Then they got this:

Complete the sentences so they are true for you.
a. I played with _____.

b. I played against _____.

c. I spent about _____ minutes playing.

d. I spent about _____ minutes watching.

e. My best shot is my serve/forehand/backhand/slam.

f. I have the most trouble with my serve/forehand/backhand/slam.

g. The strongest player in the group seemed to be _____.

h. I enjoyed playing against _____ the most.

i. We played for points/didn't play for points.

This exercise asked them to personalise their experience and reflect on the games they had played. Many of your students will play table tennis, real tennis, squash, badminton or mess about with a bat on the beach, and in any speaking test that I know of, if a candidate manages to come up with: *I play tennis. It's fun. My best stroke is my backhand*, they are going to make an impression on the examiner. There was no turning to me and saying:

Teacher, I don't know what my best shot is. They had just been playing. They knew. Then they read their sentences out one-by-one and everyone listened to everyone else because each other's names kept cropping up.

This is an example of *supplementing* the English that we teach with real and common experience – or supplementing that real and common experience with English. A survey like the one above could be adapted for various sporting activities, team games or board games.

A case study with both tidy and messy learning, autonomy, technology and movement

This example comes from a lesson I gave in the large school mentioned previously. In pairs, I asked students to choose three locations around the school and to record a one to two minute video for each using their mobiles. Each recording would explain the function of the location, its importance, why they liked it and/or what memories it held for them. Before recording, they needed to prepare a script and bring that to me for checking but they were allowed to go to the location in order to write in a more inspired way.

They were also allowed to interview other students or staff members provided they were not keeping anyone from their studies or work. All interviews needed to be in English which might involve *them* providing language support where necessary.

The school was self-contained with common areas such as hallways, reception, cafeteria and school yard either staffed or monitored, thus I was able to let the children move about freely. Normally I would circulate myself, providing additional supervision and assistance but this time I remained in the classroom providing a constant point of reference and base of operations.

The agreement was that every 15 minutes each pair had to report back, without fail and with evidence of progress. Not doing so meant being recalled and confined to the classroom. For my part, I had a grid with each pair along the top and time intervals down the sides. As they reported back, I entered ticks in each pair's square, complete with notes about progress. This combination of structure and freedom was a perfect cocktail. During the next hour I had a regular stream of slightly out of breath but highly energised students coming to show me paragraphs, scripted dialogues and recorded presentations that were some of their most productive work of the term.

Lying to your students

To close our discussion of movement, I would like to describe a few short forays into the realms of the incorrect and the inaccurate. When asked for the spelling of a word, I will occasionally write on the board something that is deliberately wrong such as fourgotten or threwout and wait for my students' instinct for English to kick in – which it nearly always does.

> *"How did you know?"*
> *"I just knew, teacher."*
> *"You see, the Force is strong with you."*

Sometimes when handing out lists of useful language for a certain writing genre, I might tell them: *"All of these words and phrases will get you extra points in your writing except three which I completely made up and which will actually lose you points because they are not real English"*. Suddenly the room is full of young people hunting through words trying to find the bogus ones rather than putting those lists straight into their folders.

Once in a while, I will tell my students I have been to an exotic holiday location or done some outlandish and risky sport over the weekend. What follows is normally an exchange of questions and answers that not only reveal the sad truth of my deception but that also work the past simple tense:

> *"But teacher, I saw you in the supermarket on Saturday."*
> *"You saw me on … Friday, didn't you?"*
> *"It… it was Saturday."*
> *"That was before I left."*
> *"It was in the evening. When did you leave?"*
> *"… erm [starting to smile]."*
> *"It's impossible. You did not go to those islands."*

I call this 'truth shift' and have a double rationale for introducing small doses of it in class. First, there is some human survival programming that goes to sleep in the relative safety of an English class – the primal art of distinguishing between harmless and harmful. By serving our students the odd curve ball, we wake up their judgement just a little more. Second, there is a chain of logic that goes: if the teacher is smiling or playing that means they might be having fun. If they are having fun, that means they might enjoy being here with us. If they enjoy being here with us, they might actually like us too.

Questions for reflection

- How often do your students get to move about inside your class?
- How do you feel about the concept of shifts to describe how we experience fun?
- Would you use multiple boards if they were mounted on the walls of your class?
- How do your students know that you enjoy being in class with them?

Things to try

1. Observe instances of spontaneous play where students have turned a regular task into some sort of a game. Try to figure out the workings of that game.
2. Use spare space to allow students to practise presentations.
3. Create a pressure spot at the door so students need to produce language to enter.
4. Consider using the outside of your building as subject matter.

Things to share

With your director or head of department and/or colleagues, talk about:

- What spaces are available to exploit during English class.
- How transitions beyond the classroom might be used to facilitate learning.
- What your institution's guidelines on this are.
- What levels of supervision vs trust are acceptable.

References

Barrow R (2012) *The Mummified Monk in Samui*. Available at: http://www.thaibuddhist.com/the-mummified-monk-in-samui/ (accessed July 2018).

Hornstein GA (2018) *Agnes's Jacket: A psychologist's search for the meanings of madness*. New York: Routledge.

Roland C (2013) Cooking up fun. *English Teaching professional* **84** 22–24.

Roland C (2014) Four walls, four boards. *English Teaching professional* **93** 29–31.

Roland C (2015) Writing here, writing there. *English Teaching professional* **101** 24–26.

Roland C (2016) Being naughty in class. *Selected Papers 2014-2015*. Salamanca: TESOL Spain.

15. Getting them talking

Discussion

Why do we go to such lengths to get our students speaking in class? I can think of three reasons:

1. It allows them to familiarise themselves with and assimilate language, acting as a rehearsal for conversations beyond the classroom – in a word: *practice*.
2. Speaking tasks create the need for phrases that they might not have (as does interaction with question prompts), creating a vacuum into which we can feed new language.
3. It gives the teacher the opportunity to listen to learners and monitor accuracy, communicative competence and pronunciation.

Our three main concerns should therefore be:

1. To set speaking activities up solidly so that students are motivated to keep speaking for a reasonable length of time.
2. To provide support by feeding in new language before, during or after the task.
3. To find a way to effectively hear their production and give them feedback on it.

Sentence quota

One of the issues in the teenage classroom might be reticence to speak – either because students do not want to make a mistake in front of their peers or because speaking in English seems so much more of an effort than speaking in their L1 – or simply not speaking at all. To drive home the fact that one important function of the English class is as a space for students to practise, you might try taking a sentence quota. This involves putting a list of your students' names on the board at the start of class and asking:

"How many sentences have you spoken in English today?" (or yesterday, or at the weekend).

It may be their first English class of the day at 9am. It may be an extra-curricular class after school. Whatever the situation, we are not trying to score points off other teachers but I can assure you (if you are teaching in a country where English is not the first language) that it is never going to be many sentences for the majority of the students. I like to write on the board the approximate number of sentences for each student next to their name. A typical list might look like this:

Marina   3
Myriam   10
Ricardo   5
Patri   2
Natalia   20
Manuel   0
Berta   3

Then we can say: *"Right, let's see how many you can speak in **this** class."*

Whether you do a count up at the end, ask each student if they think they spoke more or do nothing, this reasoning helps students to see that here is an opportunity. It also gives you an insight into how English fits into their day.

Pronunciation

From every speaking activity, be it pair, group or whole class discussion, there will be items that can be practiced in terms of pronunciation. These we can collect from individuals but examine as a group because the majority will be L1 to L2 transfer errors shared by various members of the class (we have a natural tendency to pronounce a new language as we do our first). Pronunciation is one of the key criteria in official speaking exams and it brings presentations and public readings alive. Moreover, poor pronunciation will often mean that our students are overwhelmed when it comes to *listening* tasks because they are not hearing words as they expect them to sound (Walker, 2014). Again though, teenage students may sometimes feel silly working through pronunciation drills and/or be unwilling to have a go on their own *unless* we can broach the issue by turning pronunciation practice into something more lighthearted, which helps them forget about being so self-conscious. We shall look at several activities designed to do just this.

Practical applications

Getting the most out of questions

Postman and Weingartner (1969) suggested a whole syllabus made up of questions – of lines of inquiry worth pursuing. I have developed my own bank of 300 conversation questions (see **Downloadable resource 8**). The questions, alas, are not as progressive in spirit as the above authors' seminal work but do range over 20 common topics and are suitable for A2 to B2 levels. I would suggest using that document as a starting point for getting teens to speak more in class, adapting and adding new questions to better suit your own context.

Extending conversations

When setting up conversation in pairs, providing students with ten to 15 questions is probably the ideal number. With fewer, students finish before you have time to settle down and really listen to anyone. With more, they will start to skip questions or cover them superficially – not doing justice to the preparation time you have put in. Encouraging students to work individual questions more thoroughly is also a solution.

Last month I stood in front of a B1 class and put the question on the board: *Do you like football?* The conversation then went like this:

"Celia? Do you like football?"

"No." [I wrote 'No' on the board]

"Now everyone, for me as an interviewer, that's not enough. Celia's answered me fine, but I've got to work harder. So, Celia, what sports do you like?"

"Volleyball. I like volleyball."

"When do you play?

"At school, on Tuesdays and Thursdays. Twice..."

*"...**a** week."*

"Twice a week."

"But today's Tuesday. So did you play today?"

"Yes."

"Okay! Now we're getting somewhere. So what position do you play?"

"Colocadora." [Spanish for setter]

"So everyone, we've found out that Celia likes volleyball, she plays it at school, twice a week and we know what position she plays. We make a note of that so we can look for it in English and now we can move on to the next question. Okay?"

We could also emphasise the importance of fleshing out replies and responding in full sentences but here, by putting the onus on the questioner, we are increasing their prominence in the interaction and thus the extent to which they will be listening – and if there is one factor that motivates teenage students to continue to speak it is having a partner who is listening.

Questions from the book

Coursebook units often open with two or three questions designed to act as a warmer for a topic. Similarly, with readings, once the vocabulary and comprehension work has been done, we often find a couple of questions for reflection addressed to the students about what they think of the issues in the text.

The problem is that on a logistical level, two or three questions at a time, though useful for a cursory class discussion, will not fuel a solid amount of pair work. One solution is to generate additional questions yourself at the planning stage. Another is to go through the entire coursebook putting all those questions together as a word document to create a type of core conversation questions curriculum for the particular book you are using.

It takes surprisingly little time and will provide you with a list of around one to two hundred questions which you might display on the wall, telling students: *"By the end of the year you should be able to comfortably answer all of these"*. This makes quite a lot of sense. After all, they are the book's own questions and will be supported in terms of content by the book itself.

'Big Brother' style monitoring

This technique is useful for groups that are having problems staying on speaking tasks (first covered in Roland, 2009). We pair students up in two rows, close together, with one row facing the other so that everyone has a partner opposite them. We provide questions on the board or on paper. The instructions go like this:

> *"When you hear the sound [a drum, bell or whistle] start talking. You ask a question. Your partner asks a question. Remember, every answer needs to be longer than the question. I've got a list here with all your names on it. I'm going to work down the list, looking at each of you one-by-one. Every time I look at you, I'm going to record what I see. If you're speaking English, I record that. If you're listening I record that. If you're doing anything else, I record that. When you hear the sound again, it's time to stop talking and everyone moves one seat to their left so you get a new partner."*

As the students speak, we do just that, stopping the conversation when we have either one or two entries for the whole group. It may look something like this:

Jordi	Speaking English (Sp. E), listening.
Aleix	Tapping head, choosing a question/Sp. E.
Berta	Sp. E, removing fluff from Ana's sleeve.
Mireia	Listening, Sp. E.
Ana	Looking at Kevin, Sp. E.
Kevin	Sp. E, asking me about "keen on".

We then feedback:

"So, Jordi, that was great. I looked at you twice. The first time you were speaking English and the second listening. Do we like listening? Yes, we do. Aleix, you were tapping your head [Aleix remembers doing that] *and then speaking English. Berta you were speaking English then pulling something off Ana's jacket* [Berta has an OMG moment because she now remembers doing that]…"

After feedback, students change places and go for another round or more. Far from feeling stifled, I have only ever found students to respond well to the added attention paid to their performance. The only drawback is that monitoring like this takes us out of the picture in terms of monitoring for language input and errors.

Teacher positioning

It can be tempting, having managed to set up an activity and seeing your teens all busy speaking English, to sit back and watch rather than listen. It is essential though, that we 'get in there'. We start this *before* the activity by thinking about where we are going to monitor from. I have seen teachers in observed lessons hovering, prowling or trying to monitor from up at the front of the class. Granted, you cannot listen to everyone in a single speaking phase. Here I shall suggest three alternative seating plans to help you listen to at least several pairs during each activity.

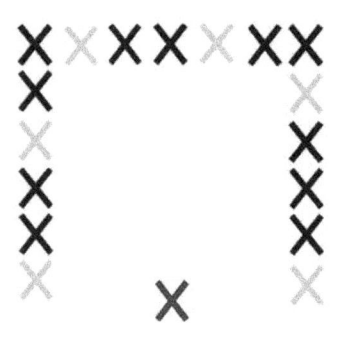

Figure 42: In a class with spare seats the teacher can leave strategic gaps to move into and listen from

Here, the teacher has explicitly asked students to leave certain chairs empty so that he or she is free to move into those places during the activity without needing to interrupt anybody.

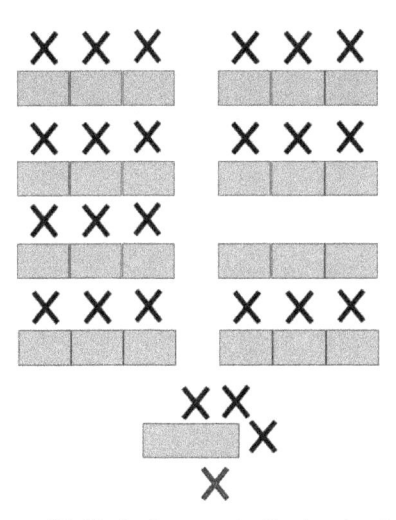

Figure 43: Students come to the teacher to be listened to

In a larger class, the students are sat in fixed rows with little space between. In this scenario, the teacher has seats set up at the front and each group spends five minutes talking there. The teacher monitors them for two or three minutes but also circulates around the class.

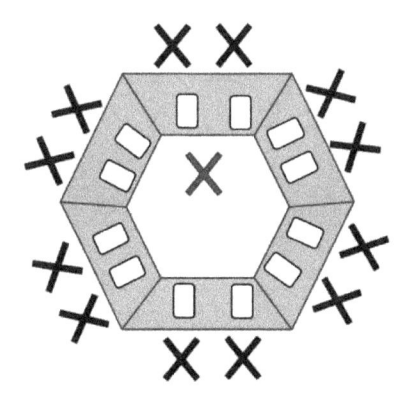

Figure 44: A more unusual 'teacher-in-the-middle' seating arrangement

Here the teacher has 'trapped' themselves in the centre of the students with a ring of tables. At any time, the teacher is able to move over to another pair – the more so if their teacher's chair has wheels on it. In addition, in front of each student the teacher has placed a sheet of paper (with that student's name on it). This acts as a sort of open file. As the activity progresses, the teacher can write feedback directly onto each student's piece of paper for them.

Whole class chats

Some of my most rewarding moments teaching teens are whole class chats where students get to give their opinions and be listened to. These can be planned or can occur naturally, as when a 14-year-old student recently started the ball rolling by asking why nobody had ever told her about a number of 'diphthongs' and commonly mispronounced words we had just covered. This led to a discussion on language teaching and education in general with all the students wanting to contribute. Another fantastic discussion on gender equality started when two girls asked me about my surname, what had happened to my mother's surname and why women's surnames in the UK disappear when they marry.

Keeping order in such debates can sometimes feel like trying to hold back the tide. I have shared the following logic with my students almost verbatim:

"I really enjoy chatting to you guys but I need to be able to justify it pedagogically. We need to have a steady flow of sentences. If the lesson was video-taped or there were 100 other teachers watching through a one-way mirror here would they say: "Ah, that's an English lesson!?" I calculate that we need about four-eight sentences produced by you or occasionally me per minute for the answer to be yes. The better the chats work, the more of them we can have. If we fall to three or less sentences produced per minute, we are in the critical zone.

Obviously, after each person has said something, if it is funny or controversial, there is a moment when we all have a spontaneous reaction because it is too much to keep inside, but then we have to listen as the speaker completes the rest of their turn.

So, imagine Andrea is speaking. It looks as if she is speaking to the teacher, but really she is just looking at me because I am moderating the chat. She is speaking to everyone. Everyone is free to respond but it has to be by putting your hand in the air. Yes, the teacher will respond first and maybe provide some language or a correction but then it is someone else's turn – possibly yours.

What happens if Barbara starts up a conversation with Albert while Andrea is still speaking? Well, the clear line of communication is blocked. Andreas's message gets broken. Other people don't hear her so well. The teacher finds it harder to moderate **and** *any good ideas that Barbara or Albert had are getting lost and not put back into the conversation."*

This is reasoned and explicit rationale and it is far more effective in tuning students into a greater awareness of and sensitivity to turn-taking than simply telling them that they need to shut up and listen. We can also offer a safety valve.

"I've given each of you a piece of paper. If, when it's not your turn, you have an idea for something that you really want to say, you can scribble it down here so you don't forget it. If everyone plays by the rules, and the lines of communication are clear, I won't end the conversation until you have been heard."

I have even had students, in the middle of a whole class chat that was getting too messy, remind each other by echoing my ideas: *"The lines! The lines!"*.

During chats, the teacher can make notes on who has said what. Then, in the next lesson, work load permitting, we might hand back to the students a short summary, asking them to check that they agree with the details. What we then have is a roomful of young people reading hungrily about themselves. We have created a common history and we can also use that text as the vehicle for target vocabulary and structures.

Pronunciation challenge

The target words for pronunciation in a coursebook unit often come in a little box. I write them as a list on the board. After explaining how each one is articulated I challenge students one-by-one to try to read the list without making a pronunciation error. I tell them: *"For this, your pronunciation has to be perfect"*. As soon as a student makes a mistake, I write their name next to that word. This game acts as a hook and students do bite. In no time at all the room is full of hands in the air wanting to have a second or a third go in order to try to get to the end. The images in Figure 45 indicate the pronunciation challenge with a small group after one, five and ten minutes of play. In the last picture, you will see a couple of the names with a small number after them –

such as Claudia[2] and Ángel[2]. These numbers indicate that the student reached that point on their second attempt and sometimes they might get a third or even a fourth try.

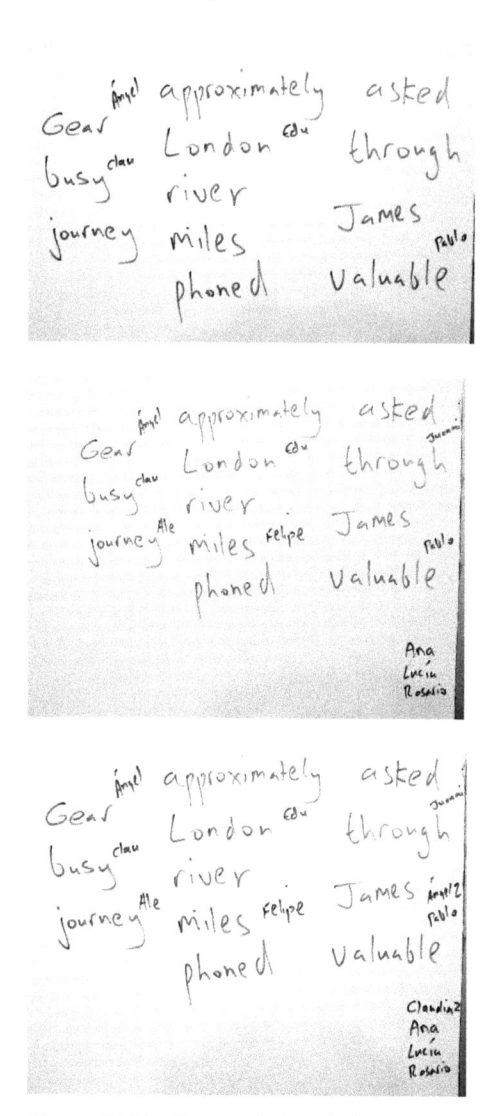

Figure 45: The 'pronunciation challenge' activity as it develops

Nuclear stress

If your students have prepared short texts for presentations or dialogues for roleplays, one very useful exercise is to help them identify where the pauses in their reading might appropriately be placed. You might also use a highlighter pen to mark up where the nuclear stress in each word group could be placed effectively. This will have the effect of helping bring what they read to life (see Walker, 2010).

Impersonation competition

One further way to encourage your learners to think about nuclear stress and rhythm is to give students the transcript of a short online presentation – just a paragraph from a talk – and tell them that in two weeks' time you are going to have an impersonation competition to see who can read the piece most like the presenter. This will give them insight into how English is spoken by a successful user, even if they are not aiming to replicate that particular accent and intonation patterns in their everyday English. The readings could be public or you could have X Factor style auditions to a smaller panel of judges, chosen or elected from the group.

Sounds and symbols

Most of the pronunciation errors your teens make will be due to the fact that they think a word is said with the wrong vowel, diphthong or consonant, and that they have not noticed this through listening to others or that nobody has listened to them closely enough and pointed this out or managed to get them to switch sounds. The other possibility is that they do not even know that one of the sounds in a word even exists. This is why working through the IPA, explaining the importance of mouth position, modelling and drilling and raising overall phonological awareness using a resource such as Hancock's PronPack (2017) is so valuable.

Pronunciation dictation

Both Paul Seligson and Carmen Dolz's original phonemic chart[3] for the English File series and Hancock's PronPack soundchart (2017) have IPA

---

3 Seligson P & Dolz C. *English Sounds Pronunciation Chart*. Oxford University Press website for English File. Available at: https://elt.oup.com/student/englishfile/elementary3/c_pronunciation/pronunciation?cc=global&selLanguage=en (accessed July 2018).

symbols integrated with or accompanied by pictorial representations of words that boast those symbols. Students can fold a piece of paper twice, making four boxes, then copy four symbols designated by you, complete with pictures, to help make the symbols memorable. The teacher then reads out a selection of words and students write them in the box that corresponds to the sound in each.

Writing messages in script

As suggested in Chapter 10, another technique to encourage familiarity with the script is to occasionally write messages to students at the top of the board such as these:

kæn aɪ hæv maɪ bʊk bæk pliːz diːmæ

θænks fɔː sendɪŋ miː ðæt lɪŋk pɔːl

haʊ dɪd jɔː bæskɪtbɔːl mætʃ gəʊ ælexændræ

Notice that we have left the name until the end to tempt more students to read the message. We can also use the IPA to provide feedback at the bottom of individual writing assignments.

wel dʌn ðæts ə gʊd piːs əv raɪtɪŋ

or

eɪt aʊt əv ten

> ## Questions for reflection
> - Do you ever alter your classroom layout specifically for speaking activities?
> - How do you keep students on task during speaking activities?
> - Are your students aware of the differences between ɜː and ɔː for example?
> - Would you consider marking nuclear stress on students' presentations?
> - Does the idea of any kind of reading competition appeal to you?

Things to try

1. Take a sentence quota, as described in the chapter, at the start of a class.
2. Encourage students to push for more details when interviewing a partner.
3. Set up a whole class discussion, then feed back with a summary paragraph.
4. Have a go with a pronunciation challenge activity.

Things to share

Over two weeks, note down for any particularly successful speaking activity:
- What the topic, the set up and the dynamic were.
- Why students were so productive, what kept them on task.
- Whether the activity could be repeated for another topic.
- Any examples of learner exchanges that stood out.

Share these with colleagues informally or by way of a short workshop.

References

Hancock M (2015) *PronPack Soundchart with Pictures*. Available at: http://hancockmcdonald.com/materials/pronpack-sound-chart-pictures (accessed July 2018).

Hancock M (2017) *Pronunciation PronPack 1-4*. Hancock McDonald ELT.

Roland C (2009) What do I do with them? *APAC magazine* **67** 21–28.

Postman N & Weingartner C (1969) *Teaching as a Subversive Activity*. New York: Dell Publishing Co.

Walker R (2010) *Teaching the Pronunciation of English as a Lingua Franca*. Oxford: Oxford University Press.

Walker R (2014) *Pronunciation Matters – Re-thinking Goals, Priorities And Models*. Presentation at British Council Madrid. Available at: https://www.youtube.com/watch?v=497emkwf_fM (accessed July 2018).

16. Listening and reading

Discussion

The starting point for listening

I say to my students: *"The first and the most important thing you can do to improve your listening, is to stop talking when I put on the audio. Really, and I say it with love, you can't hear anything while you're still talking"*. This may seem very direct to anyone who has not taught teenagers, but I suggest that the logic needs sharing: *"If the audio is on and you have stopped talking and are trying to understand some of what you hear then you have made the decision to improve your listening and you can feel proud of yourself, even if you get the answers wrong."*

Managing audios

When it comes to teaching listening, I say to teachers, your most valuable tool is the left mouse button. Where teachers have CD players it is the pause button. What I mean by this is that the ability to stop the audio, to go back and revisit stretches of speech until your students can really hear them is your biggest asset. When a student can close their eyes and mentally tick off each word from a sentence, *then* they can hear it. As trainer and author Annie McDonald puts it, we have then given them something to take to the next listening experience (2017).

Thinking small

Coursebook audios can often go on for a considerable time but we can choose to work in detail with just part of them. The obvious stretches of speech to revisit are the ones that contain answers to comprehension questions. Another option is to look in detail at the first two or three sentences of every audio we use, replaying them to students, without providing an accompanying script, unpacking all the sounds they contain. This type of listening may be the most useful of all. By doing it before playing the full recording, we have our students' ears at their freshest and we give them a fighting chance with the rest of the audio by helping them understand the opening context at least. If we unwittingly give the answer to the first comprehension question, our lesson will not suffer either.

Supporting work

As we look at stretches of recording we need to ask: what are they hearing? What are they not hearing? Do they understand how the sounds run together? For a detailed exploration into this I recommend Cauldwell's *Phonology for Listening* (2013). Where appropriate we can also ask: are they capable of copying that? Here we are back to pronunciation teaching. As suggested in the previous chapter, pronunciation and listening support each other. They are different ends of one and the same thing. Let us not forget either that it is impossible for a student to 'hear' a word they do not know, so all and any vocabulary work you do will also play a supporting role in your students' listening.

Reading

It can be hard for teenage students to go from the public context of being in a room with their friends to the private context of reading. We shall look at several techniques to encourage students to engage with text when it comes to short, in-class intensive readings.

After graduating but before teaching, I worked as a volunteer in a UK village primary school. For six months I sat with children from the top two year groups as they read their readers to me, one child after another, hour after hour, day after day. I watched them using bottom up decoding skills to grapple with new language and top down whole word recognition to speed things up and zoom across familiar phrases – as well as whole word guesswork which sometimes worked and sometimes did not. With regards L2 acquisition, I have not spoken to a teacher yet who is not convinced of the usefulness of reading to enhance spelling, lexis, grammar, collocation, register and word formation. We shall look at several ideas to make our classrooms reflect our convictions about extensive reading.

Practical applications

Micro-listenings for teens

I tell my adult students that speech hits our ears in a long uninterrupted stream. I ask them to imagine a sausage-making machine spewing meat out into its edible plastic skin. It is our capacity to match bits of that stream to words and phrases we know that acts as a cutting device, making individual sausages. Following my crude analogy for what we refer to as 'lexical segmentation' (Rost, 2011), I send them away with minute-long internet clips to transcribe. However, for teenagers, even at intermediate level, a minute is far too long. So instead I ask them: *"Who would you like to listen to?"* Last year the list included: singers Justin Bieber, Ariana Grande and Beyoncé, actors Selena Gomez, Zac Effron and Jennifer Lawrence, YouTuber Liza Koshy and footballers Harry Kane and Theo Walcott.

I found YouTube clips of each and copied the links onto a word document. I then selected a ten second stretch of each and transcribed it myself (remembering to note down the start and finish time). I have found these short excerpts perfect for focusing on features of connected speech. I play an excerpt in class, looping back many times so they hear each word and phrase ten, 20 or 30 times and challenge students to write down what they hear. Before I show them my transcription, we go around the class and they get to tell me what they heard – and everyone gets lots of praise and encouragement.

I would strongly recommend the same process to you: surveying the class, finding clips and preparing your own two, three or four sentence transcripts. It takes no more than a couple of hours to prepare a term's worth of excerpts. Up until now, I have used one a week but I plan to start using one a lesson soon.

Playing it one more time

Imagine you have just done an exam style multiple choice listening task with a class. It is very tempting to ask the first student what they got for number one then go round asking everybody before revealing the correct answer, upon which there will be some cheers of victory and a few groans:

S1 – A
S2 – A
S3 – B
S4 – A
S5 – [had C but decides to change] …A

However, not only is this another opportunity to play the script again, it is a chance to deconstruct each snippet and perhaps help some students 'hear' things for the first time. My advice here is not to reveal the answer until it comes up in the script. Until then we can work through each section eliminating possibilities and then finally helping students hear the actual answer – this is as valuable listening work as the initial test.

Making listening a little more real

I showed a group of 11 to 13-year-olds a YouTube clip entitled *How to eat a tamarind pod* (ZeppCollector98, 2012). I then gave each student a tamarind pod (with prior knowledge of allergies) and they peeled and ate it according to the clip's instructions. You do not need tamarind to improve your students' listening. My point here is that the whole relationship between listener and audio changes when he or she knows they are going to be acting on the information they are hearing. It could be instructions for preparing something, making something, setting up an experiment or recorded instructions for a classroom task.

Another way of making listening feel more 'real' is to invite guest speakers. These could be other teachers from your centre, visiting teachers or visiting friends or relatives that have a reasonable level of English. One option is to have students interview the guest (and they can have worked on questions before). Even more useful might be to ask the guest to tell the students about one or two personal experiences or anecdotes connected to a recent topic that you have been covering in class. Again, if students know they will later be doing a short write up about the presentation, we have given them that sense of rolling consequence mentioned earlier.

Reading texts

An alternative to students reading a text on their own and then answering questions is to lead them through the text with the teacher posing improvised questions that correspond roughly to each sentence while the students read on ahead to find the answers. I call this an *as-you-go* comprehension.

Text	Teacher/student dialogue
David Slater was born in Hubei province, China. His father was a Finnish engineer and his mother a South African artist. He went to school in Helsinki. He started making and flying kites when he was only seven years old. His father used to help him with the frame and his mother with the fabrics. "My kites were always easily recognised at competitions because of the different animal patterns… "	T – "What was Mr Slater's first name?" S1 – "David." T – "Yep, and his initials?" S2 – "D. S." T – "Which country was he born in?" S3 – "Hubei." T – "Country?" S3 – "China." T – "Got it. Where was his dad from?" S4 – "Finnish." T – "Which country?" S4 – "Finland." T – "And his mum?" S5 – "South African… South Africa." T – "Rock and roll. Where did he grow up?" S6 – "In Helsinki." T – "When did he start…"

At no point is anyone actually reading the text out aloud. The first time that you do this, it takes the students a while to adjust to reading on ahead for the answers. Some initiative is involved but what results is a faster flowing journey through the text.

Questions in pairs

Our default setting for going over comprehension questions to readings is most probably with the teacher leading the whole class and nominating students to answer. Another option is to make this a communicative activity from the start:

"In 10 minutes, half of you are going to be interviewed by a partner on this text. The other half will be the interviewers. Everyone needs to make sure they have read the text, know the answers to the questions in Exercise 3 and can locate those answers in the reading."

With a little attention to logistics, this can result in a class full of students discussing a text they have read in English, which will provide a great deal of practice and greater incentive to commit to the initial reading.

Pictographs

Since 2010, the Royal Society for the encouragement of Arts, Manufactures and Commerce has produced the RSA Animate series of videos which consists of talks on social issues and behaviour change, illustrated sentence by sentence with cartoon drawings that support the audio. While they are well worth looking at and considering for use with advanced-level teens if you are not already familiar with them, a short and well-chosen excerpt of one can also serve to demonstrate to students at intermediate level how to convey the meaning of multi-clause sentences in pictorial form.

Students can then be provided with poster-sized paper or card and asked to illustrate the next reading from their coursebook in a similar way. Again, this provides a very tangible rationale for them to engage with each sentence and a very obvious outcome to demonstrate that they have done so. They can then rehearse in pairs how they might talk a viewer through their illustration in what is essentially a reconstruction exercise that will require them to refer back to the text numerous times and thus reengage with it even further.

Read it to tell it

Another way into readings is the much simpler form of reconstruction that we saw in Chapter 8 (see p105). For a text of four paragraphs, I provide students with a blank template consisting of four empty circles, one for each section of text. For each paragraph they choose ten key words that will help them retell (not word for word) that part of the text later on and copy those into one of the circles. We then make time, before the next reading, for each student to practise and to present that to the teacher.

For single paragraph texts we can give students a small Post-it note and ask them to do the same. In both cases, decoding the text becomes subsidiary to – but also instrumental in – prepping their summaries, and performance on the final task is just as effective a measure of comprehension as questions from the book.

Extensive reading charts

In terms of learner coaching, Barber and Foord (2014) suggest giving students a gentle nudge by having a reader on your teacher's table, just to pique curiosity. In an attempt to make my classroom a reference point for work done outside, I have a simple reading chart for each class. Every time a student reads 25 pages of their graded reader, they get a sticker which they add to their column. The stickers I use are white rectangular labels, large enough for the student to write on the title of the book and their current page range (1-25, 26-50, etc). Therefore, the chart acts both as a very quick visual bar graph and a record of who is reading what and where they are up to.

Reading for five minutes

At the other end of the scale, Barber and Foord mention the idea of DEAR (**d**rop **e**verything **a**nd **r**ead). I do believe in the value of asking a class to read from their graded readers in silence for five minutes or so, for a number of reasons. First, it tells you where a group is in terms of management and self-control. An English lesson *should* be a place where students can all focus individually on something for at least a little while. It so often is not but this will tell you how much further you have to go. Often I find the first couple of minutes are lost and sometimes, out of five minutes, only the last one or two are quality reading, but these couple of minutes can act as a springboard for students to continue out of class, helping to get stalled readers back into the flow of their respective stories. Finally, as a fairly hefty nudge, a few minutes of class reading allows you the teacher to make sure that everyone does in fact have a graded reader (whether they are all reading the same story or students are selecting different ones).

Extended reading conversations

It is impossible for us to enter into the minds of our students when they are at home and make the decision to read for them. What we can do though, is to provide some positive reinforcement and validation when they have made that decision. The chart serves as a record of progress but an equally valuable show of interest is asking students periodically on a one-to-one basis: *"How are you getting on with your story? Anything interesting happening in it?"* Getting to have a meaningful conversation with an adult about their book, and one that is not too 'quizzy', may add worth to the act of out-of-class reading for them.

Questions for reflection

- Do you often pause audios and replay stretches to help students notice language?
- Does your school or centre have graded readers for students to take away?
- If so, is there any kind of reading scheme or program in place?
- Is five minutes of silent reading in class something you do or would consider?

Things to try

1. Compile a bank of authentic ten-second clips with speakers who your teenagers will recognise for class transcription.
2. Invite a colleague or outsider to be a guest speaker as a live listening exercise.
3. Note down any differences in your students' reactions to this compared to standard audios from course material.
4. Set up some sort of class reading chart. Participation could be a course requisite or on a voluntary basis.

> **Things to share**
>
> Try the alternative approaches to texts, as described in the chapter such as:
> - pictographs
> - as-you-go comprehensions
> - student to student comprehension questions
> - reconstruction activities which involve turning a text into a presentation.
>
> In a small segment of your next in-centre teachers' meeting, report back to colleagues teaching similar groups or levels.

References

Barber D & Foord D (2014) *From English Teacher to Learner Coach*. Available as e-book at: http://the-round.com/resource/from-english-teacher-to-learner-coach/ (accessed July 2018).

Cauldwell R (2013) *Phonology for Listening: Teaching the stream of speech*. Birmingham: Speech in Action.

McDonald A (2017) *Making Listening Memorable: Listening in chunks*. Presentation given at GRETA Teachers' Association, CEP de Granada.

RSA Animate Video series. Available at: https://www.thersa.org/discover/videos/rsa-animate?p=1 (accessed July 2018).

Rost M (2011) *Teaching and Researching Listening*. Harlow: Pearson.

ZepCollector (2012) *How to Eat a Tamarind Pod*. YouTube clip. Available at: https://www.youtube.com/watch?v=7wNkEMhEzow (accessed July 2018).

17. Grammar and writing

Discussion

Grammar exercises and the need to do more

The basic unit of a coursebook is the exercise; sometimes vocabulary, often grammar. Despite the fact that our teenagers might have spent a good portion of a lesson industriously working away on a set of exercises, there is no guarantee that the content material will be remembered. Completing an exercise and actually learning from it are two different things. The latter does not automatically follow from the former. I would go further and say that for many teenage students, the latter will hardly ever follow from the former *unless* we do something more with the exercise afterwards. A similar thing might be said for the grammar explanations we give our students, verbally or as board presentations. If our teenagers are to assimilate the workings of grammar on a conceptual level and to get to grips with the terminology we use to describe it, then there needs to be various points of engagement/analysis with it.

Grammar exercises that are too difficult

Grammar exercises are written carefully by their authors, then subjected to review by one or more editors before being tweaked or rewritten. As a result, they are normally well produced. Occasionally though, you will look at an exercise and instinctively know that your students are going to have problems with it. Perhaps they have not yet fully grasped the structures to be worked. Perhaps the exercise works too many structures at once, for them. Whatever the reason, giving your students an exercise that you already know they will have trouble with is analogous to deliberately setting up a train crash. In this chapter we shall look at ways to provide extra support from the start as well as how to provide additional engagement with grammar content.

Writing

When students hand in a written assignment, they are normally more or less happy with it. Even if they know deep down that there are errors in the text, somewhere there is a hope that there will not be too many and that everything will be alright. When that work comes back with somebody else's writing scrawled alongside and over their own, an unpleasant feeling is created. Teenage students will often take a piece of returned work and, after a cursory look at the grade they have received, tuck it straight away in their folder or rucksack without looking over the finer points in their teacher's annotations. Below we shall also look at some ways to overcome this and to use student writing as a vehicle for language input and the noticing of rules.

Practical applications

Grammar exercises: teaching for success

Where we know that students will struggle with an exercise, there are several strategies we might employ to avoid frustration.

1. **Priming students with the answers.** This is not as ludicrous as it may sound. I use the following lead in or a variation thereof.

   Teacher: *"In a moment we are going to do an exercise. It will involve filling the gaps in some sentences but first I'm going to read you those sentences with the answers in them and you repeat them back to me."*

   Student: *"What page, teacher?"*

   Teacher: *"No page, just listen. Afterwards I'll tell you the page and you can go there and do the exercise. For now, books closed and ears open. If you pay attention now, the exercise will be easy for you."*

   The teacher then reads the complete sentences to the students and, even though they do not know exactly where the answers are in what they have heard, they have at least been exposed to the completed version and will have it as residual memory to aid them.

2. **Projecting an exercise onto the board and talking it through it with your students.** This allows us to go over the exercise orally, sentence by sentence, and discuss the answers with our students, but again before they have even opened their books and before they have

written anything. In this way, the bulk of the thinking gets done together, as a rehearsal, and the individual work (when we turn off the projector and students complete the exercise in their own books) will involve memory work, reconstruction and consolidation. During their day, teenage students are given a lot of exercises, but sitting and discussing an exercise together takes the emphasis off simply completing the task by filling in the gaps or ringing the right answer and moves it towards a more reasoned and principled approach. When doing this, it is not even necessary for the teacher to input the answers on the board or projector. Just as in the previous technique, your students will come to learn that if they are paying attention, those answers are in the air.

3. **Including the answers as part of your initial teaching.** If you are going to front grammar exercises with a board presentation, you might try to include as many of the answers from the most difficult questions as examples in that presentation. Again, this will provide additional exposure and something for struggling students to refer back to.

Checking corrections

I would like to ask you a question here. What is the sum total of worthless things? Put another way: what is the combined value of a number of worthless endeavours? What is 0 + 0? Or 0 + 0 + 0?

A group of 17-year-old upper-intermediate students had completed an exercise on indirect questions. Unbeknown to me, the three girls on my left had the majority of the answers wrong. So far that lesson they had done one thing and they had got zero value from it – they had learnt nothing. Next, we corrected the exercise. Maybe we had gone too fast. Maybe that warm afternoon in June was overwhelming. In any case, none of the three managed to correct their initial mistakes in this phase so now we had done two things, neither of which had benefitted those students. Finally, I asked the class to test each other in pairs – one as 'the teacher' with their book open, and the other working from memory. Without the correct answers, the girls were unable to do so and it was at this point, as they embarked upon a third round of fruitless activity, that I became aware and was able to set things right.

My message to teachers of teens is this: when it comes to going over exercises, never assume that your students are getting the correct answers down. You may be horrified what they are actually settling on, even during whole class correction. The occasional spot check can be extremely educational here, especially for the teacher. If getting the right answers down on the page matters then we might also give students a chance to double check each other's corrections, or to do so by referring to a projection, screen or printed sheet containing the solutions.

Blank exercises and consolidation

If a student has done an exercise, and if they understand it, then my thinking is that they should be able to do it a second time more easily. As mentioned in Chapter 12, I therefore make considerable use of blank exercises. Students can come up and try to complete those with the teacher or they can test each other. The essential message for the students is that our work does not stop when the exercise is filled in on the page.

Top-down grammar

For some students, bottom-up ways of doing exercises just do not seem to work. What I mean by 'bottom-up' is the sort of staged process by which you turn an active sentence into a passive one for example, or a piece of direct speech into reported speech. I still teach the procedures because I think it is the way the majority of students tackle these things, but I also give learners repeated exposure to a number of ready prepared examples and let them learn these whole sentences in the hope that they will start to get more of an instinct for the rules.

Here are some PowerPoint slides that I used with a Pre-B1 class looking at reported speech.

Direct I like shopping. (Marina)	Direct I am going to spend my money on parties. (Hugo)
Direct I like shopping. (Marina) Reported Speech Marina said that she liked shopping.	Direct I am going to spend my money on parties. (Hugo) Reported speech Hugo said (that) he was going to spend his money on parties.
Direct I must go. (Juanito)	Direct Your videos are weird. (Fabio to Hugo)
Direct I must go. Reported Speech Juanito said that he had to go.	Direct Your videos are weird. (Fabio to Hugo) Reported Speech Fabio told Hugo that his videos were weird.

Figure 46: On the second and subsequent showings, students try to recall the indirect sentences as an act of memory rather than bit-by-bit construction or transformation

At no point did the learners have to construct anything or work anything out. In the first lesson I showed them the slides. In the second, I showed them the first in each set and asked them if they could remember the second. We looked at them in the third, fourth and fifth lessons and by the sixth they could all remember the second sentences. This is more of a top-down *just-tell-me-what-to-say* shortcut for students that have had the grammar rules explained to them many times and still do not get it.

You can make one of these for more or less any structure (passives, indirect questions, negative adverbials with inversion, or even contrasting tenses such as present to past) and use them as supplementary practice after you have taught the rules. Alternatively, you could start with something like this then do retrospective analysis taking each sentence and asking: *"What have we done here? What has changed? Who can make a similar sentence?"*

Another way of saying it…

Grammar summary pages can feel dry and hard to access. You might wonder, *"How can I get my students to even look at this?"* My solution is to target the example sentences given rather than the explanations themselves. I ask students to adapt each of the examples by changing one or two of the details (but leaving the target structure intact) so that it means something different and/or something more personal to them. The following sentence comes from a grammar box on adverbs of frequency:

I usually drink coffee in the morning.

- S1: *"I **usually** drink Cola Cao [a chocolate drink] in the morning."*
- S2: *"I **never** drink coffee in the morning." [S2 has changed the adverb of frequency]*

Or from this grammar example illustrating the present perfect continuous:

Alex **has been digging** in the garden all afternoon.

S1: "*I **have been studying** in my house [at home] all afternoon.*"

S2: "*Alex **has not been digging** in the garden all afternoon.*"

T: "*Come on, a bit more…*"

S2: "*Alex doesn't have a garden.*" *[laughter]*

T: "*With the structure.*"

S2: "*Alex… **has**… **been**… playing PS4.*"

Asking students to actually *do* something with the sentences provides them with a much more tangible entry point. I use this technique in open class and also as homework, asking them to send their sentences to me as audio or a list.

Which answer is right, teacher?

When students have problems accepting that there might be several grammatically correct answers to the same question, I sometimes put a chair on my teacher's table and explain:

> "*Chair + table. You see? The chair is on the table. Present simple. If it is on the table, something strange is happening. Zero conditional. It has been on the table for… 30 seconds. Present perfect. It was on the table 10 seconds ago. Past simple. In 10 more seconds it will have been on the table for… a minute. Future perfect. It won't be on the table much longer. Future negative.*
>
> "*Which sentence was correct? They all were. It's all chair + table but it depends on the message I want to send, and that depends on my intentions for speaking. I use the present if I want you to turn around and look at it now. I use the conditional to make a connection between two things – the table being there and something weird going on. The present perfect for counting time up to now… etc.*"

In a similar way, when we look at sentences in grammar summaries or exercises, we might ask them: *why did the speaker choose that particular tense?* For an excellent look at teaching the rationale for grammar in a way that helps students makes sense out of it – and one that goes beyond our discussion here – please see Danny Norrington-Davies' *From Rules to Reasons*, also published in the Pavilion Publishing *Teaching English* series.

Holding back

Here is my final piece of advice regarding those moments when a student does not quite 'get it'. When a student does not understand something, the best thing we can do is to ask them *what* it is they do not understand and then give them the space to explain. This requires us to enter into the thinking of the student and we cannot do that if we rush in with additional explanations and reiterations of what we have already been saying. In the following example, adapted from one of my own classes, we see one such confusion:

T: *"She's out of breath, she has been running."*

S1: *"Why 'been' teacher?"*

T: *"It's the auxiliary."*

S1: *"Auxiliary, yes but been? Not been?"*

T: *"Yes, been. There are two auxiliaries here: has and been."*

S1*: "But… been or been?"*

S2: [Mutters something to S1]

S1: *"Oh okay."*

T: *"Yeah? You good on that one?"*

Had I not jumped in with both feet here, I might have figured out that S1 understood that the verb *to be* was being used as an auxiliary but was actually momentarily confused between the forms *been* and *being*, which she was pronouncing very lightly so as to appear to have been saying *been* all the time. With less haste to clear up the doubt, I might have heard the student and cleared up the confusion myself, rather than another student having to do it.

Mid-class writing score

Some students struggle to complete in-class writings. Michael has written 30 words of a B1 task that is supposed to be about a 100.

"Is this enough, teacher?"

We could say to him, *"No, write more"*. We could say, *"Another eight sentences"*. We could ask him to count the words himself then figure out how many more he needs. We could also, however, shift the focus to what he can expect to get in return for his offering.

"At the moment, Michael... for what you have written here... you would get about three out of ten."

This makes it more real. After another five minutes, Michael offers us his writing once more.

"And now, teacher?"

"Let me see...I think you would get a five out of ten now. More or less. If you tell the reader a little bit more about your plans for the weekend and if you finish this sentence up here then you could get more. Maybe even a seven."

I have found this method to be the most effective to coax reticent writers to push themselves to produce a little more.

Conveying the value of rewrites

Conveying to our students that the act of redrafting text has value is an important step in drawing them into the process of improving the quality of their written work. One possible line to take is:

"If you've never written a word correctly with me then you will probably not be able to write it correctly on the day of your exam or when you write an important application, or want to help a friend with their project."

Another line of reasoning goes:

"If you write a word and the teacher corrects it, who has written the word badly?"

"We have, teacher."

"And who has written the word correctly?"

"You, teacher."

"And how does that help you?"

"It doesn't. We need to get you writing the words correctly. That's why we do rewrites."

Deep down, I think our teenage students already understand this but, like so much of what we have looked at, holding our classroom rationale up to the light so students can see it now and then restores a sense of purpose. I explain the protocol for rewrites as follows:

"I'm going to give you your writing back. If you have a piece of paper stapled to the back of your writing, that means I'd like you to do a rewrite, incorporating my annotations to your original content… (yes, making the changes). And just to prove that I value these rewrites, I will give you a second mark out of ten for these and your final score will be the average of both your first and second versions."

Enriching input

Where a student has clearly tried hard on a writing but not had at their command much language specific to the topic, we can print off an article or short online piece about the content area. For example, if the assignment was a letter of application to an adventure campsite, we might print off a page of a brochure from a real adventure campsite and staple that to their corrected piece with the following comment:

"Well done. I can see you have tried hard. Please have a look at the attached article. See if you can identify any useful words in it for writing about the topic and try to include a few of them in your rewrite."

This is one way to make the redrafting process one that develops students' repertoires positively, and it is an especially useful technique for pushing more advanced learners and keeping them progressing relative to themselves.

Back and forth noticing

Ramón emails his teacher a short writing homework. The teacher attaches a correction to the reply together with the following note:

"Hi there! Here's your corrected letter. Please have a look at it and identify the changes. On Thursday, when you come to class, I am going to give you a print out of your original submission (the first version) and, without looking at anything else, we will see if you can correct the mistakes by yourself."

This means that Ramón now has to process the corrections and try to assimilate them. For me, back and forth noticing exercises like this are the very stuff of learning. It actually involves no more work for the teacher, who still only corrects the original homework once. It just requires the teacher to make a little more time for Ramón's own learning in the class.

One-to-one correcting

We often feel we have to mark students' writing at home and then present that to them as a *fait accompli*. This is fine and it does have that element of 'the gift' that we mentioned in Chapter 7 (p94). However, there is also a great deal of merit in a student sitting with their teacher and watching as you read through their work making sense and nonsense out of their sentences, acknowledging correct word choice, pointing out errors and offering alternative constructions. These are corrections happening in real time and will be the ones students are most likely to recall. Whenever one-to-one correction in class is feasible, I would suggest that it is preferable to any other form of feedback.

Audio corrections

One of the most useful articles that I have ever read was by Ken Hyland in the *ELT Journal* (1990). In it, he explained how a teacher can record themselves working through a student's writing and commenting upon it, marking up the assignment itself only minimally – with numbers that correspond to the spoken points they are making. The writing is then returned to the student complete with the recording. This has the dual benefit of allowing the marker to go into more detail about a particular language point and also of providing the student with additional listening practice. When the article was written, we were using tape recorders. With digital recording equipment and email, such a feedback mode is now exceptionally easy. I have found it hardly takes any more time than conventional marking and is an excellent option where one-to-one feedback in class is not possible.

Sun, moon, heart, flower

In addition to Queens and Clowns (see Chapter 12, p148) my other favourite game is Sun, Moon, Heart, Flower, and while this is not a manual of activities and games, it has worked for me so many hundreds of times that I feel the need to detail it here.

First, the teacher notes down errors from a set of class writing assignments, trying to include common systematic errors, and at least two from each student but no more than four or five from any one person's work. Twenty to 30 errors is enough, be they single word spelling issues or grammar in phrases, or even full sentences.

We then divide the board into a grid of 20, 25 or 30 squares, numbering the squares discreetly and copying an error into each square. Some examples from the last time I played this game with my own intermediate students are: *the teacher said us, I made a photo, policemans, confortable, in internet* and *I'm writting*. Next the class divides into teams. I use sun, moon, heart and flower (with additional tree or fish if needed) because I find these symbols easy to draw quickly.

Before commencing play, we give students five minutes to confer quietly with their teammates about what might be wrong in each square. This is a very important stage and not one to be skipped.

Then, in turn, teams choose a square and have three chances to correct the error in it, getting their symbol drawn into the square if they manage to do so. Each time a team gets three of their symbols in a row – horizontally, vertically or diagonally – we draw a line through those and they get one point. Adding another of their symbols to a previously scoring line of three earns them another point and the line is drawn starting from the freshly added symbol. Gameplay continues until nobody is able to make another line.

This game is another channel by which to feedback errors and can be used with all levels and is extremely popular with teens. On one intensive B2 summer course we played the game daily for four weeks and, together with daily writing assignments and rewrites, managed to reduce common errors dramatically.

Questions for reflection

- Do you ever do follow up work after completing exercises, such as student-to-student testing with blank exercises?
- How do you feel about the just-tell-me-the-answer philosophy of some of the suggestions in this chapter?
- How good are you at letting students explain what they do not understand rather than jumping in with additional explanations?

Things to try

1. Conduct a spot check once you have corrected a grammar exercise with a class in order to see how accurately your students have recorded their final answers.
2. Identify a grammar structure your students struggle with. Construct a top-down presentation like the one we looked at to help them get a feel for the structure.
3. Think about your own rationale for setting writing and how to explain it in terms your students will appreciate.

Things to share

Trial a selection of the strategies for writing in this chapter (rewrites to raise marks, enriching input, back and forth noticing, audio corrections, one-to-one correction).

- Record your thoughts on the user friendliness of each system.
- Record how effective you thought it was with any tweaks you made.
- Collect an example of student learning from each.

Put these together as a 30 or 45-minute workshop for colleagues. Include time for your audience to discuss the ideas and to share other strategies that they use.

References

Hyland K (1990) Providing productive feedback. *ELT Journal* **44** (41) 279–285.

Norrington-Davies D (2016) *Teaching Grammar: From rules to reasons*. Hove: Pavilion Publishing.

18. Using video clips in the classroom

Discussion

Dealing with requests

The slowest, most painful moments for me in classes with teenagers have been when it is getting close to the end of the lesson and I decide to put a few clips on to amuse and interest everyone. The problem is that the moment students realise you are just showing them a few clips that you have chosen, they start to wonder why you could not be showing them a few clips that *they* have chosen. However, giving teens freedom of choice in this area can have its own issues:

>S: *"El gato volador! El gato volador!"* [translated as 'The Flying Cat'] *Please, teacher!"*
>
>T: *"What is it?"*
>
>S: *"It's funny."*
>
>T: *"Has it got sex or nudity?"*
>
>S: *"No, teacher."*
>
>T: *"How will we learn English from it?"*
>
>S: *"I'll translate teacher"* [offered Mario].

He did not.

It was a young man shouting *"El gato volador!"* then throwing a real cat off a balcony. I explained to the class that I did not like it.

S: *"Salchipapa, teacher! Salchipapa!"*

T: *"What is it? It sounds like it might not have a lot of English in it."*

"Please, teacher" [the whole class].

Again the clip, though inoffensive, was nothing more than 40 seconds of a boy singing about how he had eaten sausages and chips and that they were very tasty. (The clip can be viewed online with details in the references section at the end of this chapter.)

For this reason, I do not do on-the-spot requests. Instead, if students want me to show a clip in class that they have recommended, they have to send me a completed request form as shown below (see **Downloadable resource 9**).

Clip request form

My name is:	
My class is:	

The name of the clip I would like you to show the rest of the class is:

The URL or link to the clip is:

The clip is about:

The reason I like this clip is:

Five questions that you could ask the class after they have watched the clip are:

1.

2.

3.

4.

5.

The answers are:

1.

2.

3.

4.

5.

The clip is connected to what we have looked at in the book because:

There is nothing inappropriate for the classroom in this clip ☐

Write ups

We can use nearly any clip as the basis for later language work by asking students to speak or write about what they have seen. Despite my reservations, even the *salchipapa* clip could be followed up with a task like this:

"Write a short description of what you have just seen. Include an English version of the Salchipapa song and explain what type of food it is."

Have an ace up your sleeve

Each student will, understandably, have their own personal reaction to a clip. Sometimes it will be negative. If you have shown a clip that you think is fun and then asked students to do a write up, one reaction might be: *"Teacher, the clip's just silly. I don't like it."*

My response is usually: *"Yes, the clip is a bit silly but the writing task is serious and the practice you will get from it is real."*

On other occasions students might say: *"Teacher, I don't know what to write about the clip."*

My recommended solution is that before using any clip in class, you write yourself a short paragraph describing it. Even if you never share this with your students it will put you in the shoes you are going to put them in later by helping you realise what there is to say about the clip. It will give you an idea what vocabulary they may ask for. If necessary, you will also be able to use it as an example:

"Teacher, I don't know what to write about the clip."
"What about this?" [Teacher then reads out their own description]
"Can I have that to look at?"
"No. But have you got an idea about what you can write now?"
"Yes, teacher."

Salchipapa can be given this treatment:

> There's a boy in a room. There are some curtains behind him and a door to his right. The boy's wearing white shorts which are pulled up over his tummy. He's got no shirt on and his hair is shaved short. From his Spanish accent, he might be from Latin America. He's singing about something he ate. He sings: *"I ate a salchipapa and what a tasty thing it was!"* Salchipapas are chips with slices of Frankfurter style sausages on them and lots of ketchup and mustard. I have never had salchipapas myself but they look okay. If you're hungry.

Practical applications

Practicalities

On a purely practical level it is difficult to watch a clip and to answer questions or take notes at the same time. Having already watched the clip ourselves before class, we might sometimes overlook this fact. The following, I think, is a perfectly acceptable task:

"We are going to see the clip twice. The first time, just watch it. Take in as much information and as many details as possible."

Again, in terms of practicalities, I find it useful to have the links to any clips on a word document, with the title of the lesson at the top. This saves you having to search directly in YouTube and reduces the amount of other interesting clips students might spot displayed at the side of the screen and consequently ask for. It also sends out the message that the clips you are showing have been decided on beforehand and are part of a planned lesson.

Zone of L1

Three short animated clips that feature perennially in my teens' classes are Christopher Kezelos' *The Maker*, Andreas Hykade's *Nuggets* and Santiago 'Bou' Grasso's *Work*, originally entitled *El Empleo*. Each deals with an existential issue – the cycle of life and death, addiction and exploitation. In the *The Maker* an otherworldly puppet races against an hourglass to make a copy of himself and animate her. In *Nuggets*, a wingless bird type creature stumbles upon a glowing substance that makes it feel fantastic – for a while. In *Work* we see how human industry underlies the functions of the everyday objects around us. I would strongly recommend taking 15 minutes to watch these clips if you have not seen them.

You will notice that none of the three have any English in the audio. They are, however, all perfect for paragraph-length write ups explaining what happens. One approach is, on the second viewing, to give your students this:

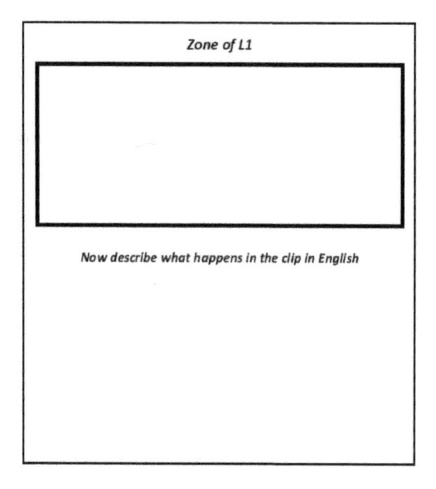

```
                    Zone of L1
    ┌─────────────────────────────────────┐
    │                                     │
    │                                     │
    │                                     │
    └─────────────────────────────────────┘
      Now describe what happens in the clip in English
```

Figure 47: Students can use L1 inside the box as they watch

At the top there is a box where students can record in their L1 what happens in the clip as they watch it. I say: *"Inside the box, your mother tongue is safe!"*

What then tends to happen, freed of L2 limitations, is that students write down what they actually see in the clip. If we ask them to make their notes in English straight off they will be more likely to play it safe and write only words that they know or get bogged down because they cannot produce the language quickly enough. Now, when they come to the actual write up in English afterwards, the completeness of their initial notes prompts them to be more ambitious in English by conveying some of the concepts in the L1 box.

Clip review

The clip resulting in the most productive follow-up work from my students ever was Alan Becker's *Animator vs Animation IV*. This was first recommended to me by a 14-year-old student a year after its release. In it, a young man who is trying to teach himself digital animation unwittingly reawakens a virus on his computer through a stick figure which he has drawn. The stick figure comes to life, running rampage through the computer, finding friends such as emoticons and other stick figures from a simple flash game on file there. A duel then ensues between the animator, using mouse and keyboard controls, and the stick figure who begins to draw its own cartoon-style allies. Finally, the animator and the stick figure reach an agreement and team up – the stick figure helping its new human friend to create better cartoon illustrations.

The reason this clip works so well from a teaching perspective is that, as well as the topic being of particular interest to teenagers, it contains all the elements that we normally ask students to consider when writing a film review. There is an obvious plot with a clear beginning, middle and end so that students can write about setting, conflict and the happy ending. There is artwork and there are a number of very different characters, special effects and choreographed fight scenes as well as some music towards the end. In addition, the technical details such as title, director and duration are clearly displayed on the YouTube clip.

Using 'fail' videos

I was asked recently how I felt about teaching phrasal verbs to intermediate level students (for any new teachers, where a verb is given an idiomatic meaning by the addition of a preposition as in *'give up'* or *'take over'*). I do think phrasal verbs are a central feature of English and I do teach them, normally in full sentences to help learners with the fact that their meaning is not obvious but the context in which they are used is often very specific.

However, there is an often overlooked but very useful structure that lies in between simple single word verbs and the opaque nature of phrasal verbs. I am referring to prepositional verbs. These are similar at first glance to phrasal verbs but the preposition, rather than generating an idiomatic meaning, provides a greater clarity and focus to the verb itself. *"I fell **over** the chair"* is not the same as *"I fell **off** the chair"*. In the first case, we imagine the chair might have been in the speaker's way while in the second the speaker was sitting or standing upon it. Similarly, *"She fell **on** the glass"* suggests there might have been broken pieces of it on the ground already, whereas *"She fell **through** the glass"* conjures up images of her falling through a large window pane.

Movement lies at the very heart of human existence. Life is movement, and language is a codification of that movement – a way of reporting it. The close but transparent relationship that these prepositions have with their verbs allows us to capture the direction of that movement and the richness of it. It allows our students to explain something that they saw, something that happened to them, or any sequence of action or interaction of people with people, and people with things in the world.

In the examples above, *fell* is very much *fell* throughout. Its basic meaning remains intact. To help you differentiate between a prepositional verb and a phrasal verb, you can try giving it the 'Yoda test'[4]. If you can put the preposition at the front of the sentence and it still reads coherently (though perhaps a little poetically) then there is minimal idiomaticity and you have a prepositional verb, as in: *"Over the chair I fell."*

If it makes no sense as in: *"Up red meat I gave"* then you are dealing with a full idiomatic phrasal verb.

This is not a distinction that I have found has much value for my students and the following activity includes only the odd full phrasal verb – the majority of input will be the easier literal constructions.

The perfect vehicle for a cohort of action phrases are 'fail' video compilations. These are the ones that show people tripping over, landing on their bottoms, walking into doorframes and a myriad of other amusing minor catastrophes. At the time of writing, I have spent a term using these extensively to teach a wide range of prepositional verbs.

To begin with, I provide students with a sheet of paper in two columns. One column is headed 'Prepositional verbs' and the second 'Other'. I have included a couple of links to specific videos I have used. The only thing to look out for with fail compilations is expletive ridden reactions from the people starring in such videos. Our students have all heard swearing in English but we might not want to encourage them or to send out the wrong message about the sort of language we are teaching for anyone overhearing our classes from outside.

---

[4] The Jedi Master from George Lucas' Star Wars saga, who often speaks with inverted word order.

Typically, the gaffes last for a few seconds only. I position myself near to the board and pause the footage regularly to provide an input phrase. If the first clip is a girl being knocked over by a wave for example, I shall say, and put on the side of the board, "knocks her over".

T: *"Prepositional verb or other?"*
S: *"Prepositional verb."*

If the next clip shows somebody dropping a water balloon from a balcony and it landing in someone's face I shall provide *"hits her in the face"* or even *"waterbomb"* for the 'other' column. If the next clip shows somebody trying to pull a tree stump out of the ground using a rope tied to the tow bar of their car, with the tree stump coming loose, arcing up and then smashing through the back windscreen of the car I might provide *"goes through the window"*.

I decide which phrases I am going to input as we go; for me that spontaneity makes this activity fun. On the other hand, you could very easily draft up a list of input phrases in your pre-lesson preparation. I do not usually stop the video for every single fail. Even so, five minutes of fails is more than enough to provide dozens of items. Also, there is some inevitable repetition. When there is, we do not record the word again but I do see if I can prompt students to produce the phrase as revision.

The beauty of using fails is that they do not get less funny with a second or a third viewing. They sometimes even get funnier when you know what is about to happen. This means we can revisit them in subsequent lessons and see if students can remember the language.

Finally, I take screenshots of the fails we have covered and make a reference worksheet with them where students need to match thumbnail pictures to the input language – which I provide beneath the images in sentence-length descriptions of each accident. Here we are entering into the realm of invested materials development, as a worksheet like this takes half an hour or so to make. If you are going to put that extra time and effort in, my advice is to make sure you have downloaded the clip, so that regardless of whether it is removed from the YouTube channel where you originally found it, you will always have it, and your linked materials, to use as a resource.

Questions for reflection

- Do you like the idea of a clips request form?
- Would you ever consider using clips that have no English in them at all?
- What do you think about the idea of a worksheet with an L1 zone on it for students to make their initial notes in?

Things to try

1. Look at the three clips mentioned in the chapter and if you like one of them, trial it with a class.
2. Try preparing your own descriptions to any clips you use to serve as input, model or to help you predict your students' language needs.
3. Follow up on the additional resources mentioned after the references section.

Things to share

Work with a fails compilation video in class.

- Preview the sequence.
- Download the clip so you have it for later use.
- Trial it and record the language you cover.
- Follow up with a worksheet using thumbnail images.

If you see positive results for your learners, then share with colleagues.

References

Alan Becker (2014) *Animator v's Animation IV* [online]. Available at: www.youtube.com/watch?v=VufDd-QL1c0 (accessed July 2018).

Fail Army (2016) *The Best Fails of All Time* (so far) [online]. Available at: www.youtube.com/watch?v=imHUmZeAaqQ&t=445s (accessed July 2018).

Mastiner (2015) *Me comí unas Salchipapas* [online]. Available at: www.youtube.com/watch?v=OyUhIGPUQRM (accessed July 2018).

opusBou (2011) El empleo/The employment [online]. Available at: www.youtube.com/watch?v=cxUuU1jwMgM (accessed July 2018).

Andreas Hykade (2014) *Nuggets* [online]. Available at: https://www.youtube.com/watch?v=HUngLgGRJpo&t=2s (accessed July 2018).

Christopher Kezelos (2012) *The Maker* [online]. Zealous Creative. Available at: https://www.youtube.com/watch?v=YDXOioU_OKM (accessed July 2018).

Additional references

Kieran Donaghy has worked extensively to select and license short films for the ELT classroom. He provides both films and recommended lesson plans around them on his website: http://film-english.com/

His book is:
Donaghy, K (2015) *Film in Action*. Surrey: Delta Teacher Development

Jamie Keddie has developed a technique which he terms Videotelling. It involves fronting clips with a teacher led scenario. This blend of online footage and more traditional storytelling is outlined in:
Keddie, J (2017) *Videotelling*. United Kingdom: Lessonstream Books

19. Personalisation

Discussion

Why personalise?

Personalisation involves tailoring language practice and input around our students' own lived experience, both in the past as biography, stories and histories and in the present as their daily lives unfold, which includes what they do, what they feel and what they think.

There are two massive advantages to this. First, any language covered will be immediately more relevant and memorable to them. Second, in a world where many of our teenagers experience teacher after teacher trying to push whole groups through a curriculum, personalising the content of a lesson at any stage tells your teens that you see them. It tells each one that their presence as an *individual* also counts and thus that they are valued. We all know from our own adult lives that people who feel valued are much easier to work with and our adolescent students are no exception.

Grabbing onto student narratives

Please imagine two versions of the same event.

Version 1

Antonio is 15 years old. He rocks up to class short of breath and 17 minutes late.

> *"Yeah, yeah, come on in. Sit down, open up your book to Unit 7A Grammar Summary on page 155. We're doing the present perfect vs present perfect continuous."*

Antonio sits down and starts to match pictures of people who have been digging in their garden on a hot day or baking cakes all morning and so forth to various sentences.

Version 2

Antonio rocks up to class short of breath and 17 minutes late. The teacher stops the class and asks them:

"What has Antonio been doing?"
"He has run, teacher."
"He has been….?"
"Running, teacher."
"Yes! Well… Have you been running?"
[Antonio nods]
[Teacher boards] *"Antonio has been running."*

Antonio can now see that the teacher is interested in the story itself and that, rather than being asked to provide a more detailed excuse, he is being given an opportunity to practise his English and that the story has a place in the lesson. He explains that he has just had to run back to the doctor's to get the bag he left in the waiting room. The teacher boards a few more reformulated sentences as Antonio recounts his exploits. The boarded sentences contain a mixture of present perfect continuous, present perfect simple and past simple tenses.

All of our students have not just a 'life narrative' but a *this morning*, *this afternoon* or *this evening* narrative too. Our lesson forms part of a continuum for them. That continuum is an endless source of material and an inexhaustible vehicle for language. Why would we want to brush over Antonio's experience and go straight to page 155 when we can tap into this event, make it common property, and use it as a vehicle for our target structure?

The coursebook is what we use to create a common narrative when we do not have Antonio standing at the door panting.

Practical applications

Student centred reviews

In Chapter 14 we tied language to a recent experience – playing ping pong. The event was a novelty and in some ways artificial in that it was an add-on created specifically for our language practice. We can also tie language to experience that forms a far more integral part of our students' daily lives.

Students are often asked to review a film, as in Chapter 19. They are sometimes asked to review a book or a play.

> Student: *"I haven't read a book, teacher. I can't remember seeing a play."*
>
> Teacher: *"Okay. Then… review one of your school text books. I know you have those."*

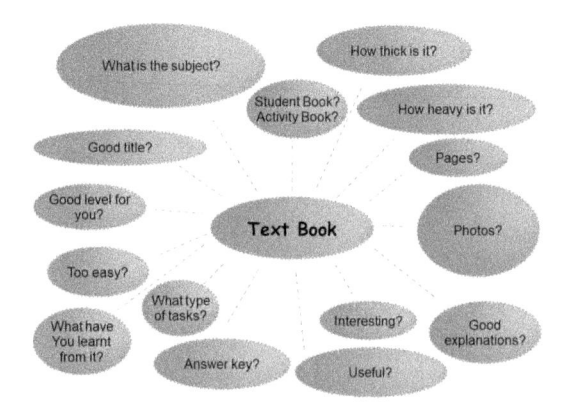

Figure 48: Things to think about when we are reviewing a text book

(See **Downloadable resource 10** for the template with each parameter fully explained.)

Each bubble represents a criterion by which the student might critically appraise the book in question.

PE is a popular subject with many students. We can ask them to outline a PE lesson they particularly enjoyed.

19. Personalisation

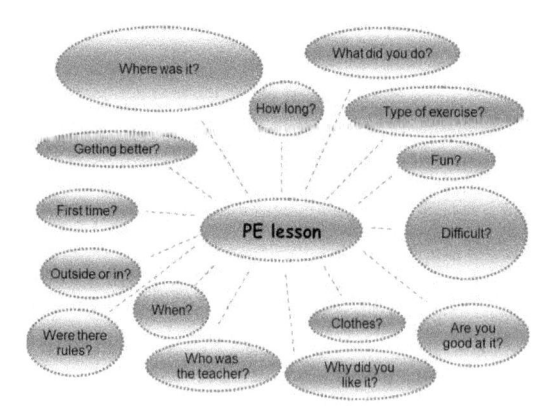

Figure 49: Things to think about when we are reviewing a P.E. lesson

(See **Downloadable resource 11** for the template with a full list of corresponding questions.)

Most of our students study mathematics as an obligatory subject up to a certain age. They could therefore review a maths function.

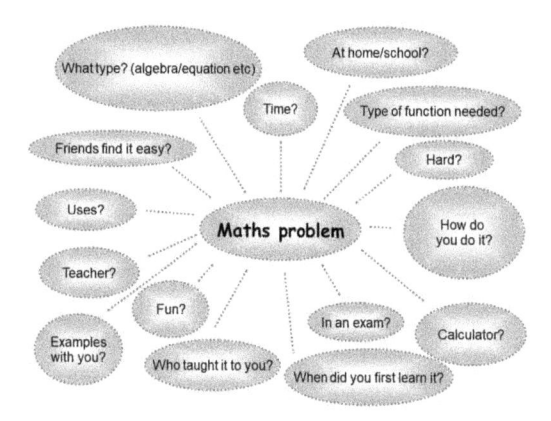

Figure 50: Things to think about when we are reviewing a maths problem

(See **Downloadable resource 12**.)

Another option is to ask them to think and write about a school rule.

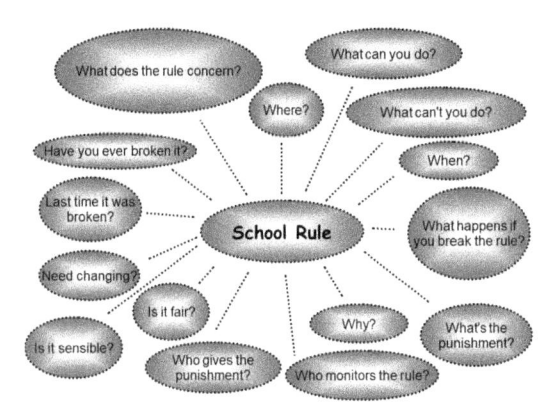

Figure 51: Things to think about when we are reviewing a school rule

(See **Downloadable resource 13**.)

Students could write about their favourite classroom as a space. They could review a break time that they enjoyed recently, a school project or a school day trip. By using their worlds as subject matter and by helping them to articulate their thoughts on these worlds we ensure that the language they practise is personally relevant and will serve as a mode of self-expression. As we saw in Chapter 12, perceived relevance and usefulness are two qualities that propel us to embrace new language far more readily.

Do I know you?

We were reaching the end of an academic year in my language centre. We had done the exams and reports had been given out with final grades, but there were still a couple of classes left. Unsurprisingly, not all the students came. In fact, in one upper intermediate class only one student turned up. We sat and chatted and as we did so, I realised that I knew very little about her at all. I discovered one of her hobbies was making chipboards with Arduino sets and she was into a drama programme called *Glee!* and various spin off shows and tours, which she told me all about. She had been a good student and I had appreciated her participation and attention in class, but she had never appeared truly enthusiastic – not like she did when she was telling me all about *Glee!*. I thought to myself: *This student might have enjoyed my classes much more if she had felt I'd been teaching* **her**.

From time to time I catch myself working through a book and giving students what they need to know for the exam without actually getting to know much about them. So I came up with this figure:

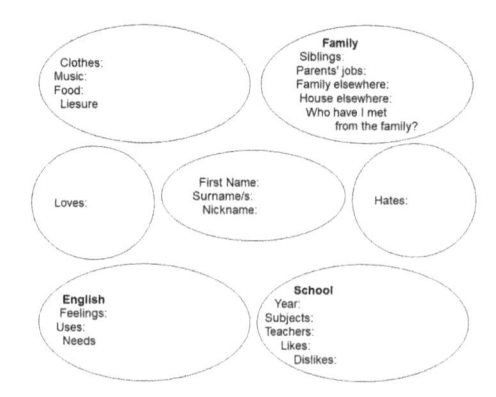

```
        Clothes:              Family
        Music:                Siblings:
        Food:                 Parents' jobs:
        Liesure               Family elsewhere:
                              House elsewhere:
                              Who have I met
                              from the family?

                    First Name:
        Loves:      Surname/s:         Hates:
                    Nickname:

        English              School
        Feelings:            Year:
        Uses:                Subjects:
        Needs                Teachers:
                             Likes:
                             Dislikes:
```

Figure 52: Things we might learn about our students

(see **Downloadable resource 14**.)

This is not for the students. This is for me. What I try to do is to fill out one of these for each student before the end of the year, asking them the odd question from lesson to lesson and week to week. My template varies each year. These ovals may not be the most efficient format for data collection but I have used this exact model successfully.

It told me, for example, that one class of 15-year-olds I was teaching at the time were all born in the Chinese year of the snake (2001). It told me that if I wanted to include as a discussion question: *Have you ever been to...?*, then Paula had family in the Canary Islands so she would spring to life if I included that. It told me that Celia in another class liked Justin Bieber's 'Purpose', so I put that on our class Spotify playlist. Three people in her class liked horses too, so I knew that was a topic for a reading text. It told me that María wanted to design flamenco dresses, Javier played the oboe and liked BMX, and Alberto kept yellow canaries – things that I had no idea about before and things I was able to work into conversation questions very easily indeed.

Tailoring grammar teaching to our learners

Personalisation does not have to mean an in-depth knowledge of the emotional lives of our students. It can mean simply teaching the people in the room. The grammar we teach normally mirrors the progress of the coursebook, which is generally a discrete item syllabus integrated with skills and vocabulary work. Another option is to mold our grammar teaching around our students. We can do this easily by taking the last batch of writing assignments we corrected and identifying the three most serious issues with grammar that our students had in them. We can then think about how best to direct students' attention to these areas, what explanations we might need, how to get them practising, what supplementary materials to use or which sections of our own coursebooks to revisit.

The power of names

In Chapter 17 we saw some PowerPoint slides with direct and reported speech on them. You may have noticed that I also strategically included the names of each class member in the presentation. It may look like token involvement but when it is *your* name, it feels very real. Between slide transitions students remained attentive because they were waiting to see if I had made a sentence about them – and what I might have said. If you think they are not looking out for their own name, wait until you forget one of them: "*And me, teacher?!*"

One-to-one friendly?

Shifting from personalisation to personal attention, I would like to ask you a question: how one-to-one friendly is your classroom?

By this I mean how often do your teenage students get to talk to you on a person-to-person basis, while the others are doing something else? How often do they get to come and show you something or read you something?

I appreciate that most classes are made up of many students and a single teacher, and that we must of necessity speak to a collective much of the time. But I also believe that this one-to-one interaction is essential if each of our students is going to respond to us on a human level. The progress made during one-to-one interaction carries over to when we are addressing the collective. It lays the groundwork for collective cooperation.

19. Personalisation

And the answer?

I believe I have found a way to identify a one-to-one friendly class just by a glance. Let us look at this classroom set up.

Figure 53: Classroom set up 1

We can see here where the students sit. We can see where the teacher sits. This is not very one-to-one friendly. Let's look at another set up.

Figure 54: Classroom set up 2

Can you spot the difference? That is right: there are two teacher-type chairs. With the first set up, if the teacher asks a student to come and read something, we enter into an uncomfortable situation because there is nowhere for the student to put themselves. If they try to sit down, they will find only thin air under them and end up on the floor. In the second set up there is a designated place for the student and the message is clear: *Sometimes you will sit there with the other students and sometimes you will sit here with me, and you have a legitimate place in both locations*.

Having that second chair there is a statement of intent and an indication of the teacher's philosophy. It also gives students the chance to transition from their regular seat to the guest chair, which affords them a brief change of perspective and an opportunity to stretch their legs. The chair, as artefact, is not a new technology but this is progressive practice nevertheless.

Reduced groups

Please imagine that you are at a teachers' conference. At the start of the day you are given a little bag with a lanyard, some free pens and a timetable. You work through the timetable circling the breakout sessions that you are interested in. The day goes by and finally you get to the last parallel talk of the day, find a seat and make yourself comfortable. The speaker arrives and sets up but seems a tad unsettled. They keep leaving and re-entering the room, muttering with their fellow speakers just inside or outside the door. Finally, the speaker explains, because only a small audience has turned up for their talk you are to be put in with people from the session next door. It will be with a different speaker and the talk content might not be quite the same but it will mean that the speaker you originally wanted to see will get to go home early.

How would you feel? Please hold that feeling for a while.

Heatwaves, snowstorms, flu epidemics, local holidays where your institution mysteriously opts to stay open, school outings, sports tournaments and the end of term are all reasons why you might have only one or two students turn up to a class. True, some of those students might have had the decision to attend made for them, but what does not always occur to teachers is that some of those students, like the imagined 'you' in my scenario above, may have chosen to come themselves because they are invested in the class or they are invested in you as a teacher. They might have come to say goodbye to you on the last day – not to your colleague who teaches another group of the same level at the same time.

We might want to rethink the message we send to students if teachers are flitting in and out of classrooms whispering to colleagues things like: *How many have you got? I've only got two.* If I were a student, that would make me regret my decision to come to class or to resent that the decision was made for me.

When a reduced number of students attends, that is the time when we can engage them most fully in conversation and the time when they get to practise what they have been working on all month, term or year. Rather than throwing word searches or crosswords at those students, we can prepare some meaningful discussion questions, pull up a chair, and see if we can get them chatting – giving them the time to actually *answer* our questions.

Volunteering information: what and when

The moment that matters most to a teenage student, in terms of English in the English class, is normally when they want to say something about themselves. HOWEVER (and it is a massive however), that does not mean they want to say something about themselves at any or every given moment.

Teenage students want to tell you about themselves when they want to tell you about themselves. You can go in with a list of well-intentioned questions about a topic you are sure they will find relevant and get relatively little, whereas they might start to volunteer information at a completely unforeseen moment. The question for us is: *how flexible are we to respond to that in the moment and draw our students into a conversation while drawing language out of them?*

When trying to get students to open up, sometimes less is more. If we swamp them with questions or they see we have hundreds written down they might economise with answers. Wait time and minimal follow up prompts can be more effective. If personalised contributions surge during normal class time we can make space for those by sitting down, hearing the speaker out and making the topic common property by throwing it out to the others. We can also refer back to a comment we did not have room to react to earlier: *"So Helena, what was it you were saying before about a phobia for…"*. In all cases we need not be scared of stopping a speaker, backtracking and reformulating: *"This is interesting but it is an English lesson so I've got to help you say it before we continue chatting about this.."*

Resistance vs investment

Within the broad bracket of personalisation we might also treat moments when students express a strong personal preference. For example, when Anna does not want to sit in a certain place; when Sarah *does* want to sit next to Laura; when Damian thinks that it is not fair that another group got a point because he had already given the answer; when Paula does not want someone else to tell a player on the other team the answer or when Adrian has just got something right and wants to say "I'm the best student in the world" but cannot remember 'best'. These expressions of preference, however, might come when the teacher is trying to take the class in a different direction.

Even a very informative and reasonable observation, such as a student pointing out that we have skipped from five to seven on a numbered list we have made on the board, becomes a pain when we are in the middle of trying to respond to another student's query or to stage instructions. These unexpected articulations can sometimes feel as much an obstacle as misbehaviour does. However, it strikes me that although these student contributions might be inconvenient, they might also be good moments to capitalise on language, because right there and then their speakers *do* care about something. Moments of resistance, moments of objection, protest or petition can also be backtracked to, 'Englishified' and supported:

> Teacher: *"Wait! Wait! Wait! I hear you but first we need to make that sentence in English. I need to hear you say it. Then I will respond to your point. Look, this is what you say…"*

Questions for reflection

- Could you integrate more student narratives into your lessons (like the episode with Antonio at the doctor's)?
- How much do you know about your students?
- How much one-to-one time do your students get with their teacher?

Things to try

1. Ask your students to review a feature of their daily lives such as the PE lesson, maths function, school text book or rule that we looked at.
2. Try using your students' day-to-day articulations as subject matter, or allowing spontaneous contributions to be aired and given some class time.
3. If possible, experiment with a two chair set up at the front. Does it feel different? Does it improve the dynamic?

Things to share

Talk to other teachers about classes where few students turned up and/or observe when this happens in your centre:

- How do teachers react?
- What does this suggest about their underlying philosophy of teaching?
- Are opportunities being grasped or lost?
- What do you imagine the student experience is like?

References

Glee! Murphy R, Falchuk B, Brennan I (20th Century Fox Television 2009-2015)

20. Testing, exams and report writing

Discussion

Why evaluate and when?

Imagine you start the year with a group of 13 year olds. One of them is called Fadi. He is a happy, smiley boy. He sits near the back but he is often the first to have his hand up and answer a question.

After three weeks of term, your director asks you:
"How's Fadi doing?"
And you say:
"He's doing fine. He's a happy, smiley boy and he often has his hand up."
"Mmm okay," says your director.

After seven weeks of term Fadi's mother pops by your classroom. She strikes you as a pleasant person, a little bit more serious than Fadi but very polite.
"How's Fadi doing?" she asks.
And you say:
"He's doing fine. He's a happy, smiley boy and he often has his hand up."
"Mmm okay," says Fadi's mother.

After 10 weeks, you give that class their first exam. You check to see that nobody is cheating and that nobody is stuck. Everyone completes the exam in the time allowed and you scan the papers quickly to make sure everyone has answered all the questions.

At the weekend, you sit down to mark the papers. Everything is going fine until you come to Fadi's paper. You look at it with horror. Your blood runs cold and your head starts to spin. He has not got one single answer correct.

We evaluate our students so that we know how, and how much, to help them and we evaluate them right from the beginning of the first class of the year.

You see, if we had looked a little closer, we would have seen that at the front of Fadi's coursebook, there was another name crossed out which said *Mazen*. Mazen is Fadi's older brother and even though Mazen had written the answers in pencil in his workbook, and rubbed them out after, you can still see them a little bit – which is why Fadi could answer questions in open class and looked better than he was.

Again, if we had looked more closely, we might have seen that Fadi normally puts his hand up right at the start of an exercise and answers the easy question – or the one that is given as example – and so looks as if he understands more than he does.

We might also have noticed that when Fadi does grammar exercises, he tends not to read the question very closely and puts down the first answer that comes into his head. He does not connect the question to what he really knows. He does not even spend very long thinking about what the sentence in the question actually means. There is a whole load of things we might have seen, if we had looked more closely.

And that is what evaluation is. It is the act of looking more closely at what our students can do and how they do it. It is about what we learn about their ability. Evaluation takes many forms. It can be monitoring, informal tests or ones taken under strict exam conditions. The success of our evaluation lies not in the difficulty or density of the test but in the quality of our attention and our ability to observe and remember. We can learn as much from watching a student complete a grammar exercise for two minutes in regular class time as we can from correcting a two-hour exam they have done.

In this chapter we shall take a brief look at more informal testing, exams, how to follow up both to ensure better learning, and then finally look at report writing.

Practical applications

Testing and exams

Getting a quick idea
Anyone who has acted as a tutor in one-to-one support classes will appreciate that watching a student complete an exercise or a section of a test gives you a very definite insight into the underlying thought processes going on. You can see what is not recognised as their pen hovers over the paper hesitantly and you can see what they do recognise when the ink flows.

Uncompromised class testing
Back in the early 2000s I conducted a battery of four one-to-one tests with each student in a 30-strong class of 15 year olds at a semi-private school where I was the regular English teacher. The tests took place over a four-week period in normal class time. We took a two column irregular verbs chart and divided it up into half columns so that the students were tested on some 20 verbs each time. Each student came and sat next to me – one on my right and one on my left – and had two minutes to write the past and participle forms of 10 verbs taken randomly from the section they had studied. No two tests were completely the same, so conferring with colleagues that had already been tested would not put a student at any advantage.

As a communicative language teacher, this was not my finest moment – the items were decontextualised and the exercise was pure focus on form. As a tester and a facilitator, I was pleased with the exercise though. By safeguarding the integrity of the tests and witnessing performance first hand (on what was a reasonable and manageable task) I left students with nowhere to hide. *"Thankyou. This is the first time I realised that I can actually **learn** something,"* said Alejandro, a student who had struggled but succeeded in learning the lists.

This example illustrates that some level of one-to-one testing is possible even in medium to large classes.

Deliberately compromised tests
At the other end of the scale we have tests into which we might allow an element of 'help' to creep so that they become more of a learning exercise.

One example of this is the 'Test in 10 minutes'.

> *"Okay class, we're going to start the end of unit review in a little while."* [Deliberate wait time]
>
> *"Teacher, can we have 10 minutes to revise?"*
>
> *"Erm…* [Deliberate pause] *yeah okay but as soon as I see people are chatting and not revising then we start the test".*

If everyone were to revise properly during this time, we could give them the whole lesson. We would not even need the test. Another option is to conduct an open test, which students do not expect in an English language class:

> Teacher: *"Here are your test papers. You can start when you get yours."*
>
> Student 1: *"Teacher, can we use our books?"*
>
> Teacher: *"Yes."*
>
> Student 1: *"Yes?!"*
>
> Teacher: *"Yes, you can use your books. Just today."*
>
> Student 2: *"Can we use the books?!"*

Other paradigms

Obviously we do not want to compromise systematically all of our class testing. As a teacher of teens, it is important to be able to move from the playful to the serious – or indeed to be playfully serious. I tell my classes that the rules may change from one test to another, depending on my rationale. For example:

> *"Today's test is to see how much you can get right on your own. I will record the scores but they will not contribute to your end of term grade."*

Or:

> *"Tuesday's test is a practice for the end of term exam. It will tell me who is able to take a test in a responsible manner. As well as your test score, I will award you a mark out of 10 for professional conduct. Points will be given for bringing a pencil and rubber or pen and Tipex, for sitting straight, focusing on your own paper and not drawing attention to yourself either during the test or while others are still finishing."*

Marking tests in class

Having students mark each other's tests is one way to lighten our own work loads. One way to encourage them to mark it thoroughly is to introduce an element of accountability by asking them to use a different coloured pen and to put on the front of whichever classmate's test they have: *Corrected by…* and their name.

Constructive retakes

Another classic default blueprint is that if a student gets more than 50% or 60% total on a test then they pass, everything is fine and we do not think any more about it. If they get less than that they fail. Again, we can challenge the blueprint and also analyse performance a little more closely. For each student we can note down which exercises they scored less than 50% on – even if their total exam score was a pass. They then go away and learn the correct answers, or familiarise themselves with the sentences in that exercise, and next class show the teacher what they have remembered.

Maintaining exam integrity

Sometimes students have a hard time adjusting to our shift in role on real exam day. One solution is to prime them for it with something along these lines:

> *"You know me as a helper. In day-to-day classes you ask me for a word and I give it to you. When you don't behave well I give you second chances and when you don't take them I'm still your friend. That's my job. But when we have a mid-course or an end of course exam, my job changes. My job is then to make sure that the exam is administered and conducted under exam conditions with no communication between students and no teacher help. I take this job very seriously as well. You may wonder where the love has gone on exam day. It will still be there, but do not look for it, not on exam day."*

Attrition tactics

I have had groups who would bombard me with queries at the start of an exam about quite obvious things, getting me to move around the classroom – up and down the aisles if it were a larger set up. Sometimes it seemed that students had come to an unspoken accord to try to wear me down:

"Teacher, can you come here please?"

"Yes?"

"Do I put my name here or here?"

Or:

"I don't have enough room to put the answer here."

Or:

"Pen or pencil, teacher?"

At other times a student might ask me out loud for a word, without putting their hand up, in the full knowledge that I would refuse to tell them:

"Teacher, what does _____ mean?"

On occasions like this, however, the SOS has already been put out there and at a suitable moment a helpful colleague is free to mutter the meaning of that word to them.

I explain this to my current students with a smile and they normally laugh. I then explain the system I now use to avoid all those games.

"If you want to ask me a question during the exam – any question – then the price of asking it is 1 point from your exam score."
"You take a point off us?!"

"No. You pay me a point for the privilege of asking a question. It's not quite the same."

"And then, for example, would you tell us the meaning of a word?"

"No, I will never do that (and it will still cost you a point). However, if it is a reasonable question about the instructions to a whole exercise then it might be worth paying one point to save yourself numerous."

The first time you explain this students may tell you it is a little harsh, but they soon adapt. The logic of the system is very clear and so far it has never failed to act as an effective guide for my own classes.

Going over the answers

Once the exams are done and marked, you may wish to go over the papers with your students. Using blank copies of the exam or targeting one exercise per day and doing it with students on the board may help focus students' attention on content rather than on looking for extra half marks and querying the teacher's ability to add up scores.

Exam follow up: big moments

Writing exams will also contain valuable errors that can be drip-fed back to your students as a regular slot in post-exam lessons. One simple approach is to take one student's written exam a day and put the errors they made on the board as below:

Lucía's Big moment!

I hate play instruments.
I really love listen music.
I listen every type of music.
We can do some photos.
beautifull
It doesn't really mean.

Figure 55: *Lucía's* big moment

I do this in conjunction with the Wheel of Fortune described in Chapter 2 (see p34). Whoever's day it is gets to try to correct a handful of errors from their exam composition. If it is Lucía's day, I say: *"Lucía, it's your day and it's your big moment!"* Then as a class we correct each of her errors. Lucía always gets first chance. Then with each error she cannot correct, she is allowed to ask a friend. The fact that she gets to go first and gets to nominate referrals helps compensate, in terms of ownership, for the fact that we are looking at her mistakes. Next time it is another student's *Big moment*. Part of our role is to promote a classroom culture whereby students can participate in this sort of activity without feeling the need to be defensive. I have done this across many teenage classes without anyone laughing at each other.

Ultimately, we are taking what the exam flagged up and acting upon it, telling our students what each one needs to know in order to write better. It is systematic, it is regular and the message is clear: *Errors are valuable and one student's errors will be useful to others*.

What I learnt from my exam

Another way to turn grammar and writing exams into a learning experience is to return corrected scripts to students and allow them to cut out sections where they had problems. They can glue these onto coloured paper to make a jigsaw collage and write in additional comments at the sides of the snippets explaining what the errors were, what they wanted to put and what it has taught them.

Report writing

We might ask ourselves who reports are actually for. We often address them to parents, writing about a student in the third person. However, those comments ultimately need to filter back to the individual whose performance we are appraising. When we sit down to write our report, we are opening up another form of dialogue with our students. The strategies below provide alternative entry points into this dialogue and are each systems I have trialled with success over various academic years.

How do *you* think you have done?

Imagine that you have a student who has done very little all term. If that students thinks everything is fine and their efforts are enough, then your report comments need to redress that discrepancy in perspectives and help the student realise they need to shift gear. On the other hand, where a student has underperformed but acknowledges this and has expressed an intention to work harder, then maybe your comments can document those intentions – and also the fact that the two of you have already been in negotiations about this, thus demonstrating a certain level of initiative and proactivity on your part as teacher. In both these situations, it is easier to know where the student's head is at if you have asked them.

To this end, before report writing, you might copy and cut out a supply of the cards below, put them in stacks on your table and ask students to look at each comment in turn, picking the one that they feel most fairly applies to them and adding any additional comments.

Comment 1

Name:

I honestly think I have studied a lot this term. I am very happy with my progress and I hope the teacher is too.

_____
_____
_____

Comment 2

Name:

I think that I have done quite well this term. I think that if I maintain this level of work I will pass. I think that the teacher is satisfied with my work.

_____
_____
_____

Comment 3

Name:

I think that I have done the required work this term but from the teacher's point of view, perhaps I haven't done much to help the class function well either.

_____
_____
_____

Comment 4

Name:

I realise that I haven't tried hard enough this term but I shall make more of an effort next term.

_____
_____
_____

Comment 5 Name: I haven't worked very hard this term, maybe because I haven't had the time or the interest. I don't think that I will be able to do any more next term either. _____ _____ _____	Comment 6 Name: I realise that I didn't do very well in the first half of this term but more recently I have been trying harder. I understand that my report/grades must reflect the whole of the term and so probably won't be very good but I would like the teacher to remember my recent improvements, which I will try to maintain. _____ _____
Comment 7 Name: I have paid attention in class and I have done the required homework but I have realised I have a problem in one or more areas of my English. I would like the teacher to make some recommendations for me. _____ _____	Comment 8 Name: I don't think that any of the other comments apply to me. I'm a special case and will explain why below: _____ _____

Self-evaluation comments for students to choose from

(First published in Roland, 2010) (See **Downloadable resource 15**)

Having some input like this from your students will give your own report comments an extra dimension and perhaps help you decide whether to swing one way or the other when it comes to some of the trickier cases.

Showing students what their reports look like

If your reports are in digital format, on templates where they can be written bit by bit, saved and modified, then you have the option of allowing students to see how their grades and your comments are shaping up. Last term, one of my 13-year-old students was whispering four letter expletives and making sexually explicit moaning sounds once in a while. I showed him the comments section of his report, due very soon, which was in PDF file, on which I had described his immature behaviour stating quite specifically what the problem was.

> *"This doesn't have to be the final version that gets printed out, but that's how it's looking now. Would you like to work with me so that we can change this?"*
>
> *"Yes."*
>
> *"Okay, if you can give me four classes that are perfect, I can remove those comments and if you can give me another four after that without the sounds or the swearing, I can move your behaviour from unsatisfactory to satisfactory."*

He did give me those perfect classes and I did remove the comments.

This can also be used to keep students motivated, showing them that they already have high scores for participation or have received comments on how much homework they have been doing.

Their reaction to their report

Whenever my teenagers receive their reports in class, I have noticed that first they scan the paper for their own scores then they turn to have a look what their nearest classmate has got. If a student feels that their scores are not fair, a little fire can start to burn inside them. A little wounded voice might say: *Hmmmm, maybe the teacher doesn't like me. Maybe I'll start not liking the teacher too!*

One technique that serves to release some of these feelings is a form like this one:

20. Testing, exams and report writing

Your reaction to your report
Are there any scores on your report that you think are <u>not</u> an accurate reflection of your performance or ability? For example, did you look at any of the scores and think: *"Only a ....?!"* (If so, which areas were they and how can you show me that you should get a higher score next time?)
Are there any scores you think you can improve on for next time? (If so, what are they? What scores do you think you can get and how?)
Which area of English do you think is your strongest? Is this the area you got the highest score on?
Are there any scores that have made you happy on your report?

A form like this will help tell us how our students feel about their grades

(See **Downloadable resource 16**.)

Just like a hotel or a restaurant might have a complaints book, this gives them the chance to answer back. There are four questions, but the most important one is probably the first. One student wrote, and these are her exact words:

I think PARTICIPATION and SPEAKING are not correct. Because I participate a lot in class and I think I speak well when I want. Some people of the class has tell me that I participate more than them and they have more or the same note like.

On this occasion, she was right. *"Most of the time"*, I tell my students, *"when it comes to a difference in perspectives, you will be wrong and I will be right. That's to be expected. You are 14 and I am 44. But, when you are right, I will tell you so. Helen, I think you might be right. Here's what we'll do. I shall watch you working more closely this week and if everything's good, I shall change your grades on the report card in time for parents' evening."*

Now I had Helen on side. She had got something to prove and something to work for. I had turned what could have been an angry 14 year old into an ally.

Parents and reports

If a student has underperformed, one very positive step to take before parents' evening is to work out an action plan with that student. One way to do this is to print off a blank calendar for the next several months and to identify where they can fit an extra 20 minutes of extensive reading or listening practice – pencilling that in once, twice or three times a week or at weekends.

It is also very helpful to have something to tell each parent that is personal to their child. To this end, in the weeks prior to parents' evening, one of my colleagues at ELI Triana, Nadia Slienger, makes an effort to write down an observation about each student on her register. Yes, we are looking at our students all the time but such an endeavour encourages us to actually notice things – and I thank her for allowing me to share the idea here.

Questions for reflection

- How much one-to-one testing do you or can you do in your classes?
- What do you think about the idea of compromised tests as described in the chapter?
- Do you ever give students a pre-exam pep talk? If so, what does it consist of?
- When was the last time you thought a student was doing fine until they bombed in an exam? Retrospectively, is there any way you might have spotted it earlier?

Things to try

1. Trial a system that allows you to drip feed exam content back to your students.
2. Similarly, see if you can put the emphasis on them learning from their exams.
3. Where your students have had speaking exams with a colleague, use their feedback as the basis for speaking activities in class for the next several weeks.

Things to share

When you write your next set of reports, try sharing the process with your students, opening up a dialogue which centres on their progress. You might:

- Ask for their thoughts on their performance prior to writing.
- Let them see how their grades and your comments are shaping up throughout term time.
- Collect some sort of reaction from students on their reports.
- Work out individual action plans when grades have been low.

I recommend trying one or two of these strategies but not all of them with the same group at the same time.

References

Roland C (2010) Report Writing in 3D. *English Teaching Professional* **67** 22–24.

21. Techniques for teaching low-level teens

Discussion

A road map

It was our first extra-curricular fluency class of the year and a 16-year-old girl called Maria came up to me at the start of the lesson and said the equivalent of: *"Teacher, I don't know anything in English, what do I do?"* Now the timetables were fixed. It was an intermediate group and she was in it for the year. There was definitely no changing that and yet there she was standing in front of me explaining, admitting, confessing even, that she did not know a word of English and asking what was to be done.

We have all had or will have students like Maria in our classes. However good the school or institution, in nearly every teens class you teach there is a student who you will look at and wonder: *How did they get into this class? How have they managed for so long on so little?*

What the problem entails is teaching elementary English to Maria through the medium of an intermediate class, but first I think we should be able to give Maria some sort of answer. Having thought about this in the years since she posed her question, my answer now would be something like:

"Don't worry. By the end of this course you will know some verbs in the present and the past and the present perfect which I will give to you in example sentences that you can learn. You'll know some key vocabulary and you'll know some basic questions and answers for speaking exams."

That would have been a useful road map in the context that we shared at the time – it was something that I would have been able to deliver. Classes, groups and timetables are all different so what you are able to offer your low-level students will not necessarily be the same, but I think it is worth formulating, as baseline reference, an answer to the following question (after all, we are paid to teach people words):

What will my least able student learn in terms of specific words and sentences this term or year?

A lot of the time, I suspect that posing this question will throw back at us the answer: *I don't know what he or she will learn because I don't really know what he or she knows now*. But it is a place to start nonetheless. The gap between where we are at and knowing the answer to this question may also be one indicator of how good a job we are doing.

Rethinking low levels

Before we go on, let us restore some dignity to our low-level teenage students with the following maxim:

All our students, including the ones with a very low level, are exactly as good at English as they should be. (Adapted from Roland, 2013.)

By this I mean that things are the way they are because of the way that they have been. Our low-level students probably do not enjoy studying English very much. They probably do not hear English very often at home and they probably have not had much opportunity to use it in their lives so far. They probably do not have a choice about coming to classes. They might not like English as a language itself – and there is no particular reason why they should.

We are all walking demonstrations of ourselves – like mathematical operations with their workings displayed. Those workings are the interactions we have had with the world. They are narratives. Our low-level students are simply demonstrations of a storyline in which an individual and the English language have not had much reason to come together – like two people who have not hit it off. If we can play a role in helping the two of them get along, then marvellous. That is all. Once we have cast aside the view of our low-level students as something-gone-wrong then we can start to get the language moving through them.

Practical applications

Help with meaning

Lower-level students will never feel as lost as when they are being asked to make decisions about tense choice or other grammatical constructions in a sentence they do not understand. Have a look at the following sentence:

David is two hours blaghedy-bla. He _____ be blaghedy-bla.

That is what the sentence below looks like to a student who *does* not know the meaning of *late* or *lost*.

David is two hours late. He _____ be lost.

The question is designed to practise modals of speculation. Ideally, we would be expecting *must* or at a push *might* in the space, but our low-level student is stuck at a much more fundamental stage of processing. If all you have is: *David is two hours. He be* then it is much harder to glean the meaning of the sentence to know which modal to use. For the rest of the class this exercise is a question of choosing modals. For this student the most pressing question is basic vocabulary. To help them, we need to drop down to a more basic function. This will take us to a place where the actual answer to the original question as designed is less important. We can therefore provide the answer:

"Look, here's the answer: it's 'must', but do you understand what the two sentences mean?"

The important thing is that this student has 'late' and 'lost' (as well as must) at the end of it. We can come back to them five minutes later:

"What was that word that means you are not at a place at the right time? What was the word that means you don't know where you are? Can you read those two sentences again? That's good. Now can you do it without looking at them?"

We can ask them again at the end of the class and even at the start of the next one. That is how we help a low-level student to learn something from an exercise that they are struggling with.

Priming students for questions

Another thing we can do if we want to make our lower-level students' lives more bearable is to stop asking them for answers they do not have. Repeatedly asking students for the answers to questions they do not understand is like poking an injured animal with a stick. Instead, while students are completing the task in the first place, we can check our lower-level students' answers so when it comes to going over the exercise we already know they have the correct answers (or that they have the correct answers to at least the first three questions of an exercise) and can ask them for those. In this way, they can start to enjoy the dynamic of positive teacher-student-teacher exchanges that end in: *"That's correct. Well done."*

Shielded roles that encourage engagement

In trying to kickstart our lower-level students' relationship with English we can put them in roles where they are required to engage with the language, but which take them out of the direct line of fire in terms of needing to get things right. We can ask Maria to be the one who asks questions to her classmates and who times their answers. This way she is positioned right at the centre of the activity, is still processing the language in the questions, and will also pick up some of her colleagues' answers as she waits for each to finish.

In vocabulary dictations we can allow her to read out the words to the rest of the class so that she is again seeing and processing the word items without the frustration of having to write them. If the opportunity is there, we can even run through the pronunciation of the words with her first so that she can later dictate the words to the others with more confidence. When checking answers to an exercise from an audio we can put her in control of the mouse to play and pause the recording, sentence by sentence. She is much more likely to listen to sentences that she is controlling than sentences she is not.

Support on vocabulary dictations

Whether we are giving the class words in their L1 and asking them to write the equivalent in English, or giving them definitions in English as prompts, or simply reading the words out themselves (as a straight spelling test), we can take the strain off students who might struggle by providing them with partial word prompts. During a dictation of words connected to nature and animals, we might give a student who struggles heavily with spelling something like this:

anim_l
aut_mn
be_ach
b_e
b_rd
b_tterfl_
co_ntrys_de
c_mel
c_mpsite
d_lphin

Now they can participate in the activity and interact with the words. The level of difficulty and exact function of our support can be tailored. In the example below we are providing the start of each word as a prompt. This would be suitable for a student who struggles more with remembering and retaining vocabulary than with spelling per se:

ani___
aut___
bea__
be_
bi__
but_____
cou_____
ca___
cam____
dol____

When it comes to differentiating tasks like this, sometimes teachers express reservations. *What if the others think this is unfair? What if Maria feels belittled by being given a simpler task?*

In my experience, students are normally much more aware of each other's language abilities than the teacher. They will be painfully conscious that a classmate is struggling. I have never had a teenage student object because I was helping a classmate. Of course, if a struggling student wishes to try the task without additional support, they are always free to do so.

Support on longer dictations

If you are giving the class a longer dictation, then lower-level students can be given a template with the first letter and a space for each word. This will help them count and place words within a framework. Below is one such template for this paragraph.

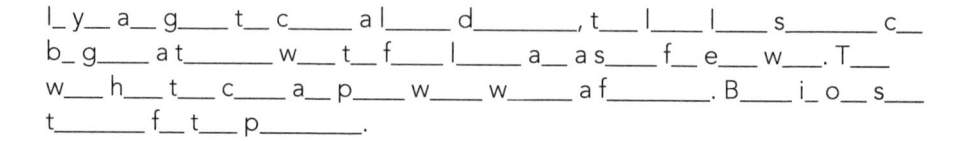

I_ y__ a_ g____ t__ c_____ a l_____ d_____, t__ l____ l____ s_____ c__ b_ g____ a t_____ w___ t_ f____ l____ a_ a s____ f_ e__ w___. T___ w__ h___ t__ c____ a_ p____ w____ w_____ a f_____. B____ i_ o__ s__ t_____ f__ t___ p_____.

This gives them something to work from and a sense of task completion as they see the spaces gradually being filled in. With something like this, they are much more likely to ask you to read out the text again or play whatever audio you are using for the dictation another time – and the more times they listen to it, the more likely they are to pick it up.

Support with writing

The beauty of text is that it can be drafted, redrafted, changed and added to innumerable times. A piece of writing might pass back and forth between student and teacher any number of times. Imagine that most of the class have produced three paragraphs but one student has only been able to manage three sentences.

"That's no problem. I'll take this from you now. I'll correct what you have done so far and I'll give it a mark. It might be two out of 10 but don't worry. That will not be the final mark. I will give it back to you. You can then copy it out again with the corrections and add another two or three sentences. Then I will correct it again and give it back to you with a new mark and we will continue like that until we are both happy. Okay?"

I call this slow process writing. My rationale here is that as long as a student is still working on a piece of writing, they are still learning from it. The mark that a piece of work receives reflects the work put in. With lower-level students, perhaps it does not matter whether that work is put in all at once or is put in little by little over the course of various weeks.

Support on speaking exercises

If you ask a student to talk about a topic or to discuss something with a partner and they do not have at least the minimum words and phrases they need, then the speaking activity will not work. It is not rocket science – It is a very simple equation. Knowing what language students have and do not have, and predicting what language they will want or need, are more complicated matters. You certainly will not get it right all the time, but providing a few sentence stems as reference will allow very low-level speakers to participate much more than if you try to provide all the language they require at the point of need in a busy class.

Below we have five conversation questions and a corresponding number of language stems:

Is there any food you are particularly fond of?
Is there any food you can't stand?
Are you allergic to any foods?
What food do you go for when you eat at a restaurant?
What's your all-time favourite dish?

I'm particularly fond of…
I can't stand…
I'm allergic to…
I often go for…
My all-time favourite is…

(The corresponding language stems to a hundred conversation questions are available as **Downloadable resource 17**.)

Sentence stems like these can be prepared for any speaking activity, and while students at higher levels might find them unnecessarily prescriptive, they will be welcomed by those that struggle. A lot of the time they might just echo the question but they will help low-level speakers get started.

Use of L1 as a way into texts

If you have low-level students on the one hand and a difficult text on the other, perhaps the most sensible thing is not to put the two together. If you do not have a choice, and if you can also communicate in your students' L1, then providing a quick spoken translation of the piece will help orientate them conceptually so that they can start to work with the English actually knowing what it means. Language is no fun when you do not understand it.

In addition to the techniques here, the following are also appropriate for accommodating a range of levels: audio homework (Chapter 7, p93), troubleshooting guide for helping students who are stuck (Chapter 11, p136), Priming the students with answers (Chapter 17, p204) and top down grammar (Chapter 17, p206).

Questions for reflection

- Did you enjoy my defense of low-level students?
- What will your least able students learn in terms of specific language this month?
- Do you like the idea of slow process writing with assignments going back and forth between teacher and student?

Things to try

1. Prime low-level students for going over answers by checking they have at least the first few questions correct.
2. Try giving low-level students the answers to questions they cannot do then shifting emphasis to understanding the whole sentence.
3. Use a brief spoken translation of a text into L1 to help low-level students grasp the overall context.
4. Trial the sentence stems shown in this chapter or make your own.

> **Things to share**
>
> Trial a range of the strategies shown in this chapter as well as any other techniques appropriate for accommodating differences in level, such as the audio homework in Chapters 7 and 10; helping stuck students in Chapter 11 and top-down grammar and just-tell-me-the-answer techniques in Chapter 17.
>
> - Record your thoughts on each technique and adjustments that you made.
> - Decide how effective each was in assisting learning.
> - Save or note down any examples of student-generated language.
>
> Put this together as a workshop and present it to teachers in your centre.

References

Roland C (2013) Some considerations for teaching low-level teens. *Teaching with Technology and the Human Touch*. Ed Rebecca Place, Olga Fdez. Vicente. TESOL Spain.

22. Awareness and reasoning with teenagers

Discussion

To improve the class dynamic we have looked at highlighting each student's relationship to their teacher's evaluations via one-to-one interactions and feedback (Chapters 5 and 19). We have also looked at the role that positive regard plays (Chapter 6) as well as providing students with some release from a world in which they may feel trapped (Chapters 1 and 14). Throughout this book, in the many examples of student-teacher exchanges, I have tried to show how we might make our rationale explicit. The book is called *Understanding Teenagers in the ELT classroom*. It might easily have been called *Talking to teenagers in the ELT classroom*. This chapter takes that talk further, exploring how we might share our 'teacher logic' so that students better understand the systems and procedures around them.

If you know why you are doing something, you can do it with purpose, commitment and conviction. I have developed a number of short anecdotes with a central line of reasoning, couched in terms and images that students will understand. We looked earlier at class currency in terms of words, rules and dynamic. Here my aim is to create a conceptual currency – a point of reference – to act as a vehicle for reasoning.

I was inspired by two schools of thought that are slightly 'outside the box', as it were, with regards to mainstream ELT. First, writers on *tagmemic theory* (Young *et al*, 1970) emphasise the importance of perspective. They describe the act of transcending one's own vectors of experience and looking for common ground with others – in everyday communication as well as in more structured rhetoric. We might achieve this common ground by referring to a familiar instance that serves as a demonstration of an idea we wish to convey.

My second influence was an idea found in a book on the German *Didaktik* tradition – that the concepts used in education should not be above the comprehension level of the children (Westbury *et al*, 2000), again reinforcing the importance of dealing in phenomena that our students can see or easily imagine.

After examining how to do this, we will shift perspective to look briefly at student logic as well.

Practical applications

Sharing our rationale

The anecdotes in italics below appear as I would recount them to my students. They are meant as examples of sharing teacher logic. You are welcome to adapt and retell them according to your context and purposes.

Teacher logic #1: Decisions

Two students, Fatima and Maxi, are sitting in class. They are talking to each other about something that isn't the English class. They are not talking in English, either. Now the teacher wants to talk to the class. The teacher wants to explain something important. The teacher signals this to the class by holding up a hand. Fatima and Maxi both stop talking and look at the teacher for a fraction of a second.

They now have two choices.

Choice A is to keep looking at the teacher and hear what the teacher has to say. Choice B is to continue again with their conversation and ignore the teacher's signal.

In both cases it is a conscious decision. It might be a very quick decision: [finger click] 'I'm going to do that', but it is still a decision.

The moment we can get students to accept the fact that everything they do is a decision, we open the door to further discussions and reflection on the sort of accountability that comes from that. That is, they become responsible for their behaviour in a proactive way (this idea was shared in Roland, 2012; 2013).

Teacher logic #2: The rubber

I was at a primate sanctuary in a little village outside of Barcelona. It is called the Mona Foundation. It's not a zoo. It's more like a safe house for chimpanzees that have been mistreated – kept in cages. They have space and peace there and can live out the rest of their lives.

It was there I learnt about self-fighting syndrome. There are also some macaque monkeys at Mona. In the wild macaques have natural enemies like eagles and snakes and big cats. In the wild, they are always on the lookout for these dangers. When you put a macaque in a cage, it gets bored. It doesn't know what to do with its instincts. So it invents enemies. It pretends, for example, that its leg is a snake. I have seen with my own eyes a macaque monkey bite its own leg then run off screaming. And because it was doing that all day long, the leg was injured. It was bleeding. This is a real condition and there are articles written about it (Allyn et al, 1976) which I can show you.

The thing is though, I've realised it's not just macaques that suffer this syndrome. Paco was a student of mine. Paco had a rubber. It was a good rubber he could use to get rid of mistakes and make his work better quality. Then Paco made an enemy of his rubber. He sawed into it with his ruler. He stabbed pencils into it. He drew on it with blue ink and black ink and green ink. Now he can't use it anymore because it leaves a dirty mark on his paper. Now he has to ask his classmates or his teacher for a rubber and they don't always have one. Paco has made his own life more difficult.

Figure 56: Paco's rubber

I know that sometimes it is hard being in a classroom, but try to remember that the objects around you are not your enemies. If you squeeze the ink out of a biro pen and drip it onto your text book, you make the pages more difficult to read for yourself. If you take the screws out of the chair you are sitting on then you make your own seat a less comfortable place to be in. Your own life might be difficult, but why make it more difficult than it needs to be?

Teacher Logic #3: Survivor

"Do you know who this is?" [teacher shows a picture of Bear Grylls or another popular survivalist presenter]

"Yes, he's on…" [Discovery Max channel for example]

"So this guy can survive anywhere, yeah? He can catch food and he can light fires and build little houses – shelters to sleep in, even in the rain."

"Yes."

*"But you know, before he goes, he thinks about what he's going to need. He takes a really good knife. I think you can even buy his knives. And he has a waterproof bag and some special boots. He can be effective **because** he's prepared. If he was in this class, he would never ever have to ask somebody else for a pencil. So next class, before you leave home, I want you to think about what you are going to do in English class and what you are going to need. Be like him."*

Teacher Logic #4: Daniel's moment

"Let's imagine that you have a classmate called Daniel. Daniel's done some writing. He takes that writing to the teacher. He has to wait in a line because there are some other students waiting to see the teacher – but that's okay. Daniel doesn't mind. Finally, he gets to the front of the queue and the teacher looks at his work. When is the moment in the class that Daniel can learn the most?"

"When he's with the teacher."

"Exactly. But what happens if you make a lot of noise while the teacher is trying to look at Daniel's work?"

"The teacher tells us to be quiet."

"Well, yes. Why?"

"Because the teacher can't concentrate."

"That's right, because teachers can get distracted very easily as well. So, basically, what you have done is to rob Daniel of his most important moment in the lesson. Is that generous or selfish?"

"Selfish."

"And is it what you want Daniel to do when the teacher is trying to look at your work?"

When I tell students this anecdote, it is normally because the exact case has just happened, so I often use the student whose work I am trying to look at as the example.

Teacher logic #5: The hunter

"Imagine a golden eagle. Have you got that image in your heads?"

"Yes, teacher."

"It's an excellent hunter. It can snatch food from in the air, like other birds. It can snatch fish from the water. It can dive down and kill small mammals on land. It gets what it needs from the world around it. Now imagine a nest with some chicks in it. Are you imagining that?"

"Uh huh."

"They are small, helpless. They need to be fed. That's why they sit there all day chirping for food. What do you need from this class?"

"English."

"Yep. And the English that you need is all around you. It's in your coursebooks, in your notebooks, on the board. It's even in the air when you ask me for a word or when your classmates are talking about the answers. Can you take it, like the eagle, or are you helpless like the chicks?"

Teacher logic #6: Your Life

Your life can be measured in minutes and hours and days and years – and there's a limited supply of them. Imagine it like the life bar on a computer game that is slowly going down. When somebody else is stopping the class because of their behaviour, they are using up their minutes but they are also using up your minutes too. They are using up your life. If you encourage them, if you laugh when they act like a clown or if you join in, then you are saying: "Hey, it's okay to use up my life". But is it really okay? If it isn't, you don't need to be rude, but you are allowed to ask them, politely: "Excuse me, please, I'm trying to listen to what the teacher's got to say". Or "Excuse me please, I'm trying to improve my English here, will you practise with me like we've been asked to?" That doesn't mean you are a suck, a swot, a creep or a teacher's pet. It just means that you value your life and you value your time.

Teacher logic #7: Pop star

"Do you know who this is?" [Teacher shows a picture of Shakira.]

"Of course, teacher."

"Okay. Well, you're used to seeing her on stage, in concerts. She dances, she sings, and she's confident, fun and a little bit crazy. But before she does any of that she has to practise all the moves with her dancers. They practise for days and days and days. And then she has to practise with her band. They practise for hours and hours and hours. Then she has to put the dancers and the musicians together and they practise for one last time. It's called rehearsing. So when you see her looking good and sounding good, she's done it all before, lots of times. It's the same with speaking English. If you want to speak with people in English and if you want to sound good and speak with confidence then you need to have practised every single sentence before, in this classroom."

The above anecdotes on their own will not make a difficult class behave. They are simply nudges in the right direction designed to appeal to our teenage students' emerging sense of citizenship. I maintain that reasoning with your students is a worthwhile endeavor. It is after all reason that guides behaviour.

Being flexible

Moving on, I would like to ask the reader to imagine two versions of another event.

Version 1

It is almost the end of the week. Student 1 is sitting in her language class. The teacher is talking to the class. Student 2 enters the classroom. He is late. He sits down near to Student 1. They start talking to each other. The teacher tells them both to be quiet. The class continues.

Version 2

It is almost the end of the week. Student 1 is sitting in her language class. The teacher is talking to the class. Student 2 enters the classroom. He is late. Student 1 knows that he has just come back from receiving the results of a scan at the hospital. He is fighting a losing battle with a very serious illness.

> *"How did it go?"* she whispers to him when he has sat down.

> *"I'm screwed,"* he replies.

At that point the teacher tells them to be quiet and their conversation comes to an end. Student 2 is too ill to come to school the next week. In fact, he does not come to school again. His condition deteriorates rapidly and some weeks later he loses the battle. It turns out that these were to be the last words these students ever exchanged.

Now in her 30s, Student 1 remembers the exchange vividly, right down to the colour of the clothes Student 2 was wearing.

Though it may jar with the cheerful tone and general optimism of this book, I have included this very poignant story, told to me by a dear friend and colleague (and printed with her permission), to make the very important point that *we never quite know*. As teachers we need to move forward with confidence and certainty but there will always be things going on in our classrooms that we are unaware of. We mentioned vectors of experience before. No two versions of any event will ever be completely the same. It is inevitable that there will be times when we unwittingly trample over our students' feelings, but if we remain sensitive to the fact that there *will* always be other versions we can make this a much less common occurrence.

We will not always be told if there is a serious illness affecting another member of a student's family. We will not always know if they have lost a grandparent or a close uncle, aunt or cousin. This is especially true in extra-curricular language academies where there is a lower level of pastoral care. On a more everyday basis, a student might come to class having just had a monumental argument with their parents. It might have been a necessary argument, a significant renegotiation of roles, and who knows, our student might even have been right. They may still not be able to concentrate for the first 20 minutes of class though.

So while we move forward with our own versions of events, and our own teaching agendas, perhaps we could do so not with 100% certainty, but with 75% certainty. A margin of flexibility will allow us to accommodate the unknown. Extending to our teenage students the courtesy of being allowed to finish the odd private conversation, or allowing them to not have the correct answer (or any answer), will not compromise our teaching very much, but it may preserve their sense of personal dignity.

Reinterpreting [mis]behaviour

Moving one step further, I would like to propose a radical shift of perspective with regard to unwanted behaviours and everyday tensions. Though the reader may feel this borders on the absurd, it is only for a moment and may provide useful insight.

As suggested already, we tend to judge student misbehaviour from our own paradigms. We might view them slumping in their chairs as negative because we would prefer them to be sitting up straight. We might view them huffing when we set an exercise because we would prefer an enthusiastic response. But let us try for a moment to see everything they do as completely and utterly legitimate. Let us imagine that their version of events is absolutely the correct one. Everything our students do is what makes most sense under the current situation. So, for example, they are talking in L1 to each other. Why would they not? That is the language they share. It makes sense. They do not want to read a text on the invention of the weaving machine. Understandable. Neither perhaps does the teacher.

There is always an internal logic. What our students do makes sense to them. Acknowledging the logic behind a student's behaviour does not mean we have to supplant our own perspective, but dipping into that logic once in a while does mean that we will be able to see them better. It is the flip side to our teacher logic.

Questions for reflection

- Do you tell your students anecdotes about previous classroom incidents?
- Do you ever share your thoughts on and philosophy of teaching with them?
- Do you ever engage your students in exchanges of rhetoric or critical thinking?
- Can you remember a time when you misinterpreted a student's behaviour?

Things to try

1. Take an issue relevant to one of your groups.
2. Work out your own stance on the matter.
3. Reduce your rationale to the clearest logic possible.
4. Couch that in concepts you share with your students or find a simple analogy.
5. Present that to your students as an awareness-raising technique.

Things to share

Identify an issue, strain or obstacle that teachers in your centre/school face with regards to student performance or behaviour.

- Rethink the issue using what you imagine to be your students' logic system.
- Staying within that logic system, look for a solution to the issue.
- When you find one, reappraise that solution from a teacher's perspective.

If you find a solution that works for both the teacher's and student's logic, share that with colleagues.

References

Allyn G, Deyme A & Bègue I (1976) Self-fighting syndrome in macaques. *Primates* **17** (1)

Roland (2012) Talking about discipline at APAC. *Proceedings APAC Convention*. 84–87.

Roland C (2013) Let's talk about discipline. *English Teaching professional* **89** 4–6.

Westbury I, Hopmann S & Riquarts K (2000) *Teaching as a Reflective Practice: The German Didaktik tradition*. New Jersey: Lawrence Erlbaum Associates.

Young R, Becker A & Pike KL (1970) *Rhetoric: Discovery and change*. New York: Harcourt.

23. Control of the class

Discussion

Why are classes difficult?

The strain on a teacher in a roomful of teenage students comes from a number of tensions. There is the discrepancy between the students' logic systems or behaviours and the teacher's rationale and agenda. There is also a constant tension between the interests of the individual student and the interests of the collective. There is the students' battle with themselves and there is the ratio of one teacher to many students, which is inherently repressive in some respects because it requires that students be less than themselves while the teacher amplifies their own self, in order for the set up to work.

How much control?

For me, good discipline is the minimum amount of order and control required for a class to work productively. It is where there is just enough self-control on the part of the students and just enough self-projection on the part of the teacher for learning to take place and everyone to be happy. That is not always an easy balance to find though, and we sometimes might try to compensate with the latter for lack of the former.

Default system 1

There are two particular default systems we might be tempted to use as props but which I think, ultimately, are blind alleys. The first is the conceptual blueprint left over by our notions of the traditional classroom. I refer to the tyrannical figure of the teacher generating fear simply in and because of itself, or exploiting the worry that students have of being shouted at. It is easy to reach for these when challenged, but this sort of coercion is a soft form of something we have inherited from more violent times. For *Star Wars* fans, I liken running your classes on this sort of negative energy to using the dark side of 'The Force'.

Incidentally, I believe the ratio of one teacher to many students is also a hierarchical throwback to an authoritarian paradigm, as is the assertion: *You'll do it because I say so*. Perhaps we stand at a crossroads in education, perhaps not. Some of these features still seem reasonable to us while others less so. It will be interesting to see which of them continue to seem reasonable in the future and which do not.

Default system 2

The other default system is more primal. It is how the teacher assumes and maintains leadership on an animal level. It is about the teacher staying top dog through charisma, charm, non-verbal communication, persona, pack politics, conscious voice tone or unconscious voice cadence. It is how new teachers sometimes manage to survive on personality and positive energy alone, or conversely why some classes automatically pay more respect to an older teacher. It is why some students will compete with one teacher but not with another.

It is nice to feel liked. It is nice to feel popular, and while the above factors do undeniably play a part in teaching they are not the most reliable foundations upon which to base your teaching practice and your professional development, week after week, term after term and year after year.

Where does your control come from?

The most solid footing for a teacher of teens is a genuine interest in and genuine awareness of each student's language abilities, coupled with a solid understanding of their institution's systems and objectives.

If you are in an ELT classroom, it follows that you belong to an institution – be it a regular school, language academy or a one-person initiative that you have set up yourself. How did the class come about? What were the implicit understandings and the explicit agreements between the institution and the student, and the student's parents, at the time of enrolment? It is these that determine both your obligations and your remit for action. Furthermore, the control you have in class will be determined directly by the strength of your relationship with that institution and the amount of support it gives you to carry out your work as its representative. How you ask for that support can also be key – something we shall touch on below.

Punishment vs classroom management

There is a difference between a punishment and a classroom management technique. A punishment is designed to cause some sort of psychological discomfort in response to a broken rule, whereas a classroom management technique is designed to get things running smoothly with the minimum of discomfort. It is meant to reconcile the student to the system or to limit their disruption of others. This latter approach represents a desire to work *with* our teenagers rather than in spite of them, and there will be more ideas specifically on this in the next chapter.

Practical applications

Cloud hammer

I invented 'cloud hammer' as an analogy – only. I use it to represent the growing discontent that a teacher may feel from moment to moment as a class does not do what it is supposed to. Can you see it?

Figure 57: The cloud hammer

Yes? That is because you are a teacher. Students cannot see it. Students in a class might be having a really good time, splitting their sides with laughter at a private joke. Another one of them says something else funny and then *everything* is funny. They have forgotten the teacher at the front who is still trying to talk to them. They have forgotten the instructions to the task they were on. The teacher can see they have forgotten. There is no way they will finish the work today. Cloud hammer begins to take shape. It is formed of frustration in the ether above their heads. It hovers over them. The teacher feels personally affronted by what is going on. How can they not know this is unacceptable? Cloud hammer is big now. They should know. They WILL know. Then they will behave. Yes. When the hammer has fallen upon one of them, the others will behave. WALLOP! The hammer falls. One student gets singled out, told off, docked points or sent out. The other students suddenly all have their heads down working and there is an unpleasant, hushed and subjugated silence in the room.

The problem is that teenage students can be astoundingly unaware of the emotional state of their teacher, sometimes. It is nothing personal. They have teachers standing in front of them all day. Nor do they always see the impending negative reaction to their behaviours.

Fronting discipline

Much more effective is to lay out the structure of the lesson or task right at the very start.

"I want you to do this…, this… and this. That is what I want to happen and if it all goes to plan then we're going to be fine. There are a couple of things I really don't want to you to do and they are this…, this… and this. If you do do them, I'll still like you, but the consequences will be this…, this… and this. Anyway, I'm sure you won't 'cos you are far too clever for that."

The above can even be delivered with a smile because we are still right at the start of the lesson when nobody has done anything wrong. The students are aware that the teacher has expanded their game plan to accommodate and re-channel extraneous activity, but they are not defensive. Fronting classroom management in this way is transparent and friendly. I have noticed that whenever one of my own lessons has derailed it tends to coincide with me not having fronted the lesson structure in this way.

Resetting jelly

I had asked a class of pre-teens to write six sentences and illustrate them with simple sketches. The activity had collapsed. I had lost them. One had worked himself up into a state of super excitability. Another was giggling catatonically and a third was curled up in her seat hugging her knees and rocking back and forth. Zero work was getting done. Several worksheets had been snatched from their owners by classmates and either scribbled on or thrown to the floor. I watched on. My first thought was to let cloud hammer fall by really telling one of them off, but no one student was any more at fault than the others.

I'm going to have to find another way to reset this, I thought. Then another analogy occurred to me. It is like making jelly. If your jelly does not turn out right – if it does not hold its shape – you do not apply more force. You do not shake it. You do not hit it with a hammer. No, you put it back in the saucepan, melt it down again, repour it into the mould and let it set – slowly and gently.

I now use the hitting-soft-jelly-with-a-hammer image to represent the pointlessness of further destabilising an already unstable situation by adding teacher agitation to it. I liked the imagery so much that I went home and made a couple of concept photos, much to the bemusement of my family – but reproduced here for your entertainment.

Figure 58: The consequences of hitting a jelly with a hammer

So, back in the class of pre-teens I let the silliness come to a close. This gave me time to formulate my next move. I said:

"Guys, if I told you that what you've just done was going to be one of the pieces of work that I show to your parents on parents' night, would you be happy with that?"

Fernando's hand shot up into the air:

"I couldn't do it very well because I only had this really short pencil."
"Seriously? Well, yeah, that pencil doesn't look very good. I tell you what, I'll lend you my pencil. This one does good pieces of work. I've tested it."

The class asked for more time and there truly was no comparison between their first attempts and their second. While only one way to reset an activity, I still use the idea that I am collecting samples of work for parents' night now and again.

Sending students out: the journey

There will be occasions when a single student's behaviour is sabotaging a lesson or that you feel they are unfairly robbing the others of their teacher's time – and decide they need a while outside. Having mandate to move students about and to exploit space beyond the classroom is a useful tool but we need to manage the student's journey as well.

There is the practical consideration that the universe does not stop when a student gets outside our door. If we send a student out, where are they going to go? What are they going to do? How long do they stay? When do they come back and who decides? How do we reintegrate them when they return? We need to be thinking it terms of a return journey – like a figure of eight, which is why I sometimes refer to it as *8ing out*. What is it going to be like from start to finish?

Our message to the student needs to be twofold. First, we need to convey: *I'm not afraid of leading you through this journey. It doesn't harm me in any way, but it might not be so good for you.*

And second: *You're still welcome and wanted in the class. You just need to leave that behaviour out there.*

Sending students out: the steps

Obviously we would prefer not to get upset or angry in the classroom, but there will inevitably be times when we do get wound up, sometimes greatly so. Even if we are shaking inside, if our peripheral vision has gone a bit misty and the students can see that – it is all okay. It is an honest show of emotion. Even in an altered state, we can stick to principled procedure.

Standing at the board and pointing to the door saying: *"Get out!"* only really increases confusion. The student will not know what to do and is most likely to try to appeal the decision. If you need a student to leave the room, go over to them, ask for the material they are working with (such as their coursebook) and then, with that in your hand, request that the student follow you. Leading a student out of the class is infinitely more effective than sending them out. Before you do so, think ahead. What are you going to ask them to do outside and will they need any additional materials, books or pens?

Take the student to where you want them to sit. Tell them what they need to do and when to come back in. Finally, reassure them it is nothing personal: *"I like you, but I think you can see I'm not happy with your actions right now. We'll talk when I'm a little bit calmer."*

Sending students out: support systems

If there is a secretary, customer service person, member of admin, or director of studies who is responsible for supervising the space where we have taken our student, then we can explain the situation to them, starting with a smile:

"Hi. This is _____. He/She is a wonderful person, but just needs 10 minutes think about some of the decisions they are making in class. I've given them some exercises to do while they're here and have asked them to come back into class once they've finished."

That makes you a much nicer person to work with. The fact that you are smiling, albeit perhaps a strained smile, and the fact you are articulating positive statements about the student will help reassure your colleagues that you are working to a plan. The student will also be taking note of how you manage these out of class interactions with the rest of your institution's representatives.

Working with the director

If we foresee a problematic situation, we can also prepare the ground by letting our senior teacher, supervisor or director of studies know what we might be doing.

"If you see Pepe sitting outside later, don't be surprised."

Or:

"I might send this student to have a word with you during this next class, if that's okay. The problem is this… this… and this…, and I think a little chat from you might work wonders at this point."

Negotiating these things with your institution beforehand saves doing so at the crucial moment when the student is with you. If your director can see that your classroom management measures are thought out and coherent with house rules, they will come to trust your judgement and support you all the more.

The after-class chat

Whether you have sent a student out or just kept them behind to have a word, the after-class chat is something that can degenerate into something of a pantomime. The teacher wants the student to be repentant. The student tries to comply by looking so. The teacher vents a little but forgets where they are going with the complaint and ends up coming out with something that sounds like their own teachers when they were at school. The student continues to look apologetic and promises to be good next time. The teacher lets them go. The student manages to keep their sorry face on almost all the way to the corner of the corridor where their friends are waiting – before smiling.

The system I recommend does not rely on anyone feeling sorry. It does not require apologies, concessions or confessions. First, you make brief notes about the incident before the end of class about what is unsatisfactory and needs to change. This helps maintain focus when the student is in front of you. Then, after the class, you state the problem clearly and accurately. You tell the student exactly what it is that you want to see them doing differently from now on and you keep it simple. This is their way out, their second chance. You are highlighting areas of poor decision making and giving that student the opportunity to make better decisions. You then provide a timescale – for example, you need to see change by the end of next week, or they need to act better over the next four classes. You establish how you will let them know such as: "We'll have another chat next week". Then finally you explain to them the next step in your institution's disciplinary procedures if there is no satisfactory change.

Games you do not want to play: Punch and Judy

Punch and Judy is a traditional Italian puppet show. Punch is quite nasty. He goes around hitting the other characters, sometimes killing them. Then at the end he argues with the Devil (and the audience).

– *I didn't do it.*
– *Oh yes you did.*
– *Oh no I didn't.*
– *Oh yes you did.*

This back and forth exchange is not what we want to get involved in with students in an after-class chat. Once we have stated the behaviour we do not like, the student may insist: *"But I didn't do it"*. Rather than play *Punch and Judy* we can simply move on to state the behaviour we do want to see.

Games you do not want to play: CSI

A similar game is to protest with:

"What did I do? What did I do?"

My usual reply is something along the lines of:

"It's not my job to prove to you that you've been doing something wrong. You're confusing me with someone else. I'm not Horatio Caine from CSI Miami, or Grissom from CSI Vegas and I'm definitely not Agent Hotchner from Criminal Minds. I'm a teacher and I'm not happy with you. That's all."
"But what did I do wrong?"
"I've already told you."

"But I didn't do that."
"I'm not playing that game."
"But what did I do wrong?"
"That's not the question, my friend. The question is: what did you do right? What did you do to help the class?"

Observation

One practical thing that you can do to try to understand a difficult student is to observe them. Watch them. Make notes. Who do they prefer to sit with? Which individuals do they interact with in the group? What currencies do those interactions run on? Who do they not speak to? Who do they look to for support? Where are their pay offs? Who laughs at their jokes? When do they act defensively? When do they challenge you? What kind of flow of energy do you perceive there? What is their world like? What makes them tick? By observing a student's behaviour, you will better understand the underlying needs that drive that behaviour and you will be more able to predict how they might try to satisfy those needs within the dynamics of your English class.

Questions for reflection

- Where does the strain on you in lessons primarily come from?
- What do you think of the cloud hammer and resetting jelly analogies?
- What patterns do your after-class chats usually follow?
- Do you ever find yourself playing games you do not want to play?

Things to try

1. Explain the consequences of misbehaviour at the start of a class or complex task.
2. Try following the steps for an after-class chat detailed in this chapter.
3. Observe a challenging student's behaviour, as objectively as you can, over time.

Things to share

Reconsider the people who provide additional support systems to your class.
- Talk to admin staff. Seek a deeper understanding of each other's roles and productive mutual assistance. Make them feel part of the teaching team.
- Open up a non-defensive, non-competitive dialogue about classroom management with colleagues.
- Learn about your director's mindset when it comes to behaviour codes, school rules and individual students.

24. Classroom management strategies

Discussion

This final chapter looks principally at various classroom management techniques that involve framing a request that students change their behaviour and then providing them with both the space and structure in which to do it. I would first like to address the conceptual space that you as a teacher move around in by continuing with the theme of teacher and institution from the previous chapter.

Mission vs condition

I use the phrase 'mission vs condition' to talk about how your purpose as a teacher, as you see it, sits within your institution's modus operandi. Your purpose is the *mission* part of the equation. The actual circumstances that have brought the class together and under which the teaching takes place is the *condition* part. The complete phrase represents the synthesis of these two positions: of your beliefs about your job, about education in general or about language acquisition and the reality of the set up that you practise in.

If you have a passion for project work, arts and craft, but are tied to a very strict discrete item grammar syllabus then you probably will not be happy. Or, if you see your role as promoting your students' personal growth through drama, roleplay and deep end communicative language tasks but your school has hired you to prepare them for their B2 exam on a six-week intensive course, then again there is a mismatch between your mission and condition. How you see yourself affects what you try to do in your lessons. How that fits with the wider context in which your lessons take place has a bearing on how much success you can expect. For this reason, it is worth picking your institution with care and reappraising its philosophy and direction once in a while.

24. Classroom management strategies

Mission VS **Condition**
Teacher's self-perceptions and motivations | The reality of his/her teaching context and institution's rationale

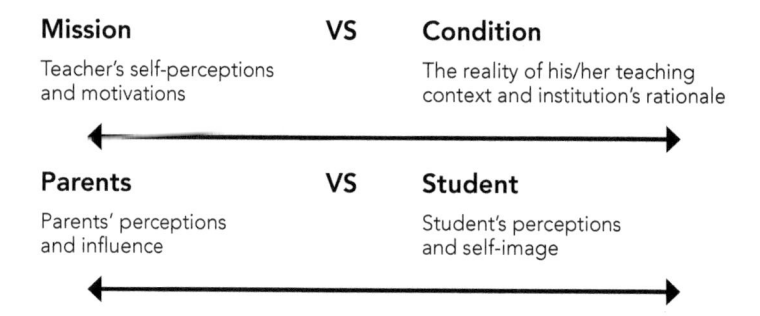

Parents VS **Student**
Parents' perceptions and influence | Student's perceptions and self-image

Figure 59: Our teaching can be seen from a number of perspectives

The relationship between teacher and institution is echoed to some extent by a parallel dialectic, which is how your students see themselves compared to what their parents expect of them. This may equate to what the 15-year-old boy giggling in the corner is actually doing right now and what his mother imagines he is doing in class.

Mission VS **Condition**
Teacher's self-perceptions and motivations | The reality of his/her teaching context and institution's rationale

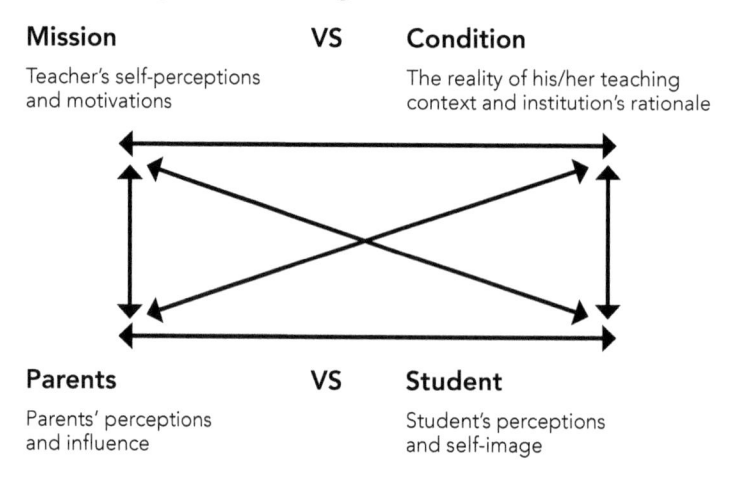

Parents VS **Student**
Parents' perceptions and influence | Student's perceptions and self-image

Figure 60: What goes on in our classroom is a nexus of these positions

Any one of these positions can be factored into the others. The sum total of all of these tensions is what will give you your whole. The human mind tends to want to reduce things and to simplify them. The whole may be a very complicated mass of tensions. Notice though, that my schematic diagrams at least simplify considerably when a) the teacher's positioning is aligned with their institution and b) a student's perspective is aligned with their parents'. If the parent understands the institution, we could even join these up for a continuous loop.

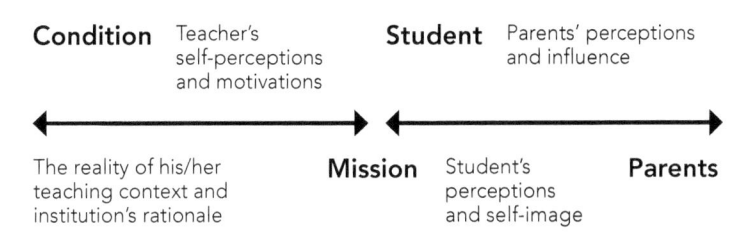

Condition Teacher's self-perceptions and motivations   **Student** Parents' perceptions and influence

The reality of his/her teaching context and institution's rationale   **Mission** Student's perceptions and self-image   **Parents**

Figure 61: Basic harmony and agreement between all parties

If there is relatively little discrepancy between your own vision and the operating model of your centre (that is, if what you are doing is what you are *meant* to be doing) then you are going to feel more comfortable implementing your institution's rules and asking your students to follow them too, which is what we shall look at now.

Practical applications

Pre-class meeting

If we are not happy with a student's performance, we might speak to them at the end of a lesson but by the start of the next lesson they have often forgotten what was said, especially if there has been a weekend in between. Just a little reminder at the start of the lesson can serve to reactivate a previous conversation and any agreements made.

"Can you remember what we talked about at the end of last class?"
"Ah! Yes, teacher."

Or:

"So, can you remember what I said that I needed you to show me in today's class?"
"I remember, teacher."

I would even go so far as to say that one pre-class chat is worth two after-class chats.

You choose

It was one October several years ago. One of my intermediate teens came to our first class of the year wearing a studded dog collar. We shall call him Leonard. Another student in that class arrived two minutes late and proceeded to arrive two minutes late for the rest of the month, which was something of a mystery because he was always the first student to arrive at the centre. We shall call him Morris. For the first three weeks or so there was a constant banter between these two. They were fairly low-level exchanges spiced up with the odd muttered gangster-style expletive. It used to set the others off and made the class hard work.

By the fourth week, I had prepared something. Leonard came in at the start of class:

"Ah Leonard! I've got something for you."
"What?"
"Just sit down over here at my desk a second and choose which one of these you want."

Draft Report Comments	
Option 1	Option 2
Leonard works well but sometimes displays an attitude that is not entirely appropriate for the classroom.	Leonard works well and his attitude and level of participation are very good, contributing to our class dynamic.

He looked at the two options but was not sure what to do yet. The comments were actually in Spanish, my students' L1.

"Tick the one you want and I'll give it to you. Well, you tick it and if you do it, I'll give it to you on your report card. Just like it is there."

He ticked the more favourable comment, gave it to me and sat down.

"What's that?" Asked Mercedes, Leonard's classmate and neighbour for the lesson.

"What's 'What that?'?" I replied, and she went back to her exercise.

Two minutes later Morris came in and I asked him to choose, too.

Draft Report Comments	
Option 1	Option 2
Morris works well but his behaviour at the moment is a little immature.	Morris works well. His attitude and level of participation are very good and he always tries to speak in English.

He could see the truth in the writing but he could also see the way out.

"Why this, teacher?"

I cupped my hands around my mouth and replied in a Darth Vader style voice:

"Because you can choose your own destiny, son."

He smiled, but to be sure, we had just turned things around.

Now, at no point had there been any confrontation and I think that is the part that most of us English teachers find uncomfortable. At no point had I needed to play the serious teacher. The only tension here was between the students' knowledge of the truth and the implications of my articulations.

For the rest of the class, Leonard and Morris were as good as gold. For the first time I felt I had the whole class's attention when I spoke and I was able to be genuinely nice to Leonard and Morris and to listen to what they had to say. Left alone in the classroom when the students had filed out, it made me smile. It made me smile again as I was walking home at the end of the night, thinking to myself: *That, Chrissy-boy, was perhaps the single most effective classroom management technique you've tried in years. I have to tell people about that one.*

By parents evening in February, that class had become one of my favourites of all time and I have since shared some great conversations with the two boys – but it all started there.

Every discipline strategy needs to be context sensitive, but every discipline strategy is also a gamble. My gamble here was that these were basically 'good boys' who did care about their report comments. It worked precisely because they *were* good boys, and I managed to convey that on the one hand I was capable and willing to articulate the issues but on the other that nothing had been decided.

Receipts and bills

In another class a student who we shall call Malcom was off task much of the time. With him, I tried a different tack. At the beginning of one class I said:

"Malc, Malc, I've got something for you."
"Yeah?"

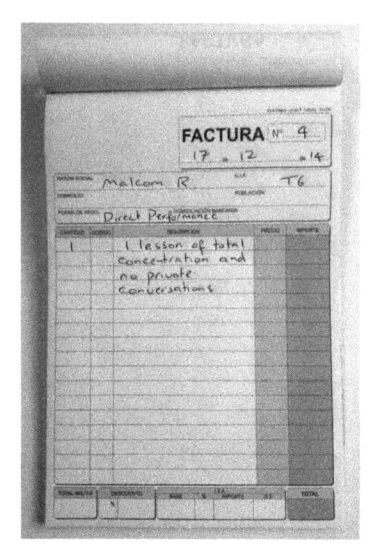

Figure 62: Malcolm's bill

"Here you are, it's a bill."
"What for?"
"It says you owe me one lesson with total concentration and no private conversations. Here you go, this copy's for you. This carbon copy's for me."
"But what do I do with this?"
"You gotta pay it."
"When?"
"Now, this lesson. You pay it by doing it."
"And if not this lesson, teacher?"
"Then you owe me another time, but you don't want the bills to accumulate, that's when you start to owe more than you can pay back which can lead to economic crisis and bankruptcy."

Malcom is at a complete loss. He does not have an answer. He shows the bill to a classmate. Here we are playing outside of his conceptual horizons. He still does not completely understand what the bottom line is with this bill thing, if you will pardon the pun, but he knows he does not want it (it looks like something the secretary uses outside – grown up, real world stuff). He does not speak in L1 that class and at the end he says:

"And this, teacher?"
"Yep, beautiful. You've paid it. Let me write you a receipt to show you've done it."

And I take out my little receipt book.

Figure 63: Malcolm's receipt

Mid class scores

The easiest way to let students know how you are feeling about their performance is to tell them. If you tell them in the middle of the class, they still have time to change what they are doing.

"So everyone, if I were going to give you a grade out of ten for this class up to now, roughly speaking it would be like this: Marina, 8/10, you're working well. Mary 7 and Bill 7 because you guys are chatting a bit. Juan you'd get a 4/10 at the moment – I like you but I don't like that sound you keep making: Whoop whoop! Scabadab scabadab! Whoop whoop! None of us need that in our lives, Juan. I mean… that's in my head now and I'm going to have to take it home with me. Hugo, a 5/10 for calling Juan a… well, you know what you called him. I don't care if he is. It's not your call…"

Juan puts up his hand.
"And if I don't make the silly sounds for the rest of the class?"
"Then your score would go up."
"By how much, teacher?"
"Don't know. Do you want to try it and we'll see?"
"Yes, teacher."

What we are doing with all these strategies is finding ways to frame a request that a student change their behaviour in some way – some more novel and some more familiar. Above all, we are finding ways to do this while smiling.

Targeting specific behaviours

With particularly challenging groups, one strategy I find very helpful is to identify target behaviours at the beginning of the class, put these at the top of the board and refer to them during the lesson. For example, in a class of overly enthusiastic pre-teens I wrote four behaviours along the top of the board: *speaking nicely to each other; putting your hand up to answer questions without saying 'me me me me me'; not huffing when I ask somebody else to give me the answer; saying 'Okay, teacher' when I ask you to do something.*

If the behaviours have already been talked about and are still up there during the course of the lesson, you will be able to remind students by pointing to them and also praise people when you see they have made an effort to check their own behaviour and modify it.

Being reticent to call parents

A teacher might spend time debating with themselves as to whether to call the parents of a student or not. Will the parents be on the teacher's side? Does having to ring them constitute failure in managing the student or negotiating with them? Is it fair? Is it really warranted? Will it damage relations with that student irreparably?

I try to see the calling of teenagers' parents not as an aggressive move. In fact, I like meeting them. We might view the parent-teacher dialogue as a continuation of our out of class game (the top part of the *8* in *8ing out*). As with any other classroom management measure, our wider aim is to reconcile the student to the system. We are doing this by taking an intermediate step towards reconciling what the parent believes their child is doing to the child's actual performance. You might see it as a case of putting these two in a dialogue with each other. You might also see it as opening up a closer working relationship with those parents to help provide the student with more consistent guidance and a more coherent message in the different ambits of their life.

Most people in this world are fine. Most students are fine – though they may not be doing quite what you want. Most parents are fine as well. That is worth repeating. *Most parents are fine*. Here I am only reminding you of something you already know. In most cases phoning a parent and setting up a meeting goes very smoothly. You may get the help you wanted or you may get slightly less, but in very few cases does calling up a student's parents go very badly – and even if it does, that does not mean you were wrong to do it. Some tensions are unavoidable. If you are thinking of calling a student's parents for the first time, you probably should have already done it.

Working with parents

It is worth remembering that we are not declaring war on a student when we meet their parents. Starting off the conversation with a list of accusations and charges in the style of a prosecution lawyer will most likely result in that parent standing in front of you with crossed arms. Instead we might try:

"I was hoping you could help me."

Or:

"This is what's happening at the moment… and this is what I'd like to happen…. What do you think the best approach to take with your daughter/son would be?"

Once this concession to their knowledge of their child has been made, they will often throw the prerogative back to you, along with their support.

Daily report

Some satisfactory outcomes of meeting with parents are: the parent saying they will talk to the student and inviting you to contact them whenever necessary, establishing email contact or arranging another meeting. With one student who had a whole host of issues, I even agreed with his mum that I would complete this tailor-made daily report after every class and send it home with him for her to sign.

Daily report

Date _____

Sit properly and not use feet to distract classmates	
Limit use of L1	
Start and finish exercises with care	
Demonstrate a more mature attitude	
Pay attention to the teacher	
Have done the homework set in the previous class	

Signed (teacher): _____

Signed (mum): _____

Again, for this student we were fronting classroom management by making it a theme right from the beginning of each class when nobody was angry. This form was how we helped this particular student. It was not the first strategy I had tried with him but it was the one that worked and consequently it was the last. Whenever using this strategy, I recommend making the behaviours called for specific to the student in question – that is one of the strengths of this particular technique. If possible, I also would also suggest writing those behaviour descriptors directly in the student's L1 for maximum clarity on the part of the student and their parent/s. As **Downloadable resource 18**, you have a blank template to start working with.

Something nice

We can use telephones to deliver good news as well. Imagine you are a teenage student and you get home from school to find out that the secretary or the director has called your parents to let them know how well you have done in a recent class activity. Imagine how positively that would impact on your day. I might do this once or twice a year when a student has really earned it by making a super effort and performing exceptionally relative to their ability. It is a motivating strategy worth bearing in mind.

Over to you

At some point in the future there is a good chance that you will be standing in front of a class and the noise level will have gone through the roof and nobody is taking any notice of you. You may think to yourself:

I'm better than this. The students don't realise what they've got here. All that effort to do my job better, the training, the reading, the conferences – for this: to be stuck in a room with a bunch of rude, rowdy kids who won't even listen to me. I'm not getting to use even 2% of my expertise here.

Yes, it is humbling, indeed such experiences can take us *past* the point of humility into humiliation and indignation. But there is one certain way out. The way out is to do workshops, lead sessions, give talks, pen articles or chapters, do something like this, like you are reading here. I am absolutely sure that classroom management in my lessons will be no better than in the reader's, but I am also fairly sure that when things do go badly I feel less upset by it. Why? It is not because I do not care. It is because I get a voice. I get to answer back. So, my final suggestion is that all teachers should speak or write in some form or other, on classroom management in their classes.

The fact that you are going to share your experiences later gives you the feeling that you are not alone in those moments of frustration and difficulty. The fact that you are going to use that misbehaviour and chaos as a case study, as material, as fuel for ideas or discussion, gives those otherwise negative experiences a sense of utility and makes them interesting – still tricky, but interesting. It gives a sense of higher purpose to your place in that room with 10, 20, 30 or more people who may not seem to appreciate you in the moment.

You might be thinking: *Chris, the very idea of that makes me nervous.*

You do not have to pitch for large audiences or extensive readership. You can set up a work group with a few colleagues where each person takes it in turn to lead just one session over the course of the term or year. You can contact local teaching associations and contribute a small piece to their magazine or website.

But Chris, I don't have the answers.

That is fine, too. Nobody does. Do not even try to. Why not aim to lead a 30 or 45-minute session? Nobody will complain that it is not an hour. You could call it something like: *My Teens this Term: Highs and lows*. You could tell your colleagues about four things you did that seemed to work and share two situations that you have still yet to resolve, inviting their opinions. That will give you a motive to get scribbling down some ideas during the term and it will turn any classroom nightmares into mini-projects.

Questions for reflection
- Does the mission vs condition concept make sense to you?
- How does your own practice sit within your institution's philosophy?
- How well do you draw on your institution's rules for support?
- How do you normally approach conversations with the parents of challenging students?

Things to try
1. For a challenging student, try the **You choose** technique described on p290.
2. For a challenging class, try listing desired behaviours at the top of the board.
3. Consider putting together your own talk on classroom management, as recommended above.

Things to share
If you have worked through the book and if you have followed up on even just one or two of the end-of-chapter reflections or suggestions each time, then I believe that getting here will constitute the end of a significant journey.

This box normally invites you to share something with your students, colleagues or profession. Here I would like to share my thanks with you, the reader, for having chosen this title and for having worked through it to the end. I very much hope you feel the rewards of that in the months and years to come.

Why teach teens?

I am going to offer a short answer and then a slightly longer one. I think the short answer to the question has to be: *to see them getting better*. With this end purpose underlying your work you will see the evidence of your efforts and you will see yourself flourish as a practitioner.

The slightly longer answer is that along the way you will see the work you do coming back to you and I shall try to demonstrate this with three final anecdotes.

One September afternoon in 2005 as I was preparing to leave Seville to take up a position with the British Council in Damascus, a moped pulled up on the stretch of pavement I was on. A tall young man in a Kashmir type V-neck sweater got off, removed his helmet and gave me a hug. It took me a second to recognise him. It was Álvaro, a student who I had taught in his last two years of obligatory secondary school. He told me that he was now at university doing a degree in economics.

"I didn't like school much," he said, *"but you were my favourite teacher."*

Of course, we cannot be every student's favourite teacher and I recommend not trying to be anyone's – but the fact that someone stopped their vehicle because they wanted to say hello, tell me how they were doing and comment on the teaching they had received *did* mean something. That was my work coming back to me after five years.

A few years after teaching Álvaro, I taught Sabina, an upper-intermediate student, in after-school academy classes. Over a decade later we crossed paths again at an exam centre where she was taking her Cambridge Proficiency. I was not able to chat at the time, which was a shame – I was the interlocutor in the exam – but by chance we ran into each other again just a few days later, in the centre of the city, jam packed with pre-Christmas shoppers. She explained that one of the factors that had motivated her to continue studying English and even to begin teaching it, were those academy classes. That was my work coming back to me after more than ten years.

My final anecdote took place this academic year, at the time of writing. All the teachers at my current institution had our photo taken together at the beginning of the course. At least 70 of us appeared in the picture, which made its way onto Facebook, and from there one of those teachers, Katie, showed it to her husband, Genaro, to see if he could recognise or remember a number of her colleagues.

'I remember him', said Genaro, pointing at me in the picture, *'He was my English teacher'*.
'You've never had classes with him,' Katie replied, thinking of the English classes she knew he had taken with the academy.
'No, he was my English teacher at school when I was a kid.'

That one made me laugh.
'I didn't realise you were even that old,' she later told me. *'He said he liked you though.'*

Being recognised, remembered and having played a positive part in someone's life is quite special – this was my work coming back to me after 15 years.

Russell Crowe's character, the Roman general Maximus in Ridley Scott's film *Gladiator*, tells his troops: *"What we do in life, echoes in eternity"*. I am not sure it does, but what we do in our teenagers' English classes certainly echoes for a while.

Enjoy your teaching!

List of downloadable resources

These resources are available at www.pavpub.com/understanding-teenagers-resources/

1. 'Bare Bones' alternative first lesson of the year
2. Individual vs Collective: sliding scales for reflection
3. Example and record of a keyboard mediated class
4. Differentiation: sliding scale to increase challenge
5. Ink blot irregular verbs (PowerPoint)
6. Template for gapped irregular verbs (PowerPoint)
7. 100 questions to ask your students at the door
8. 300 conversation questions for teens
9. Video clip request form (template)
10. School text book review (parameters/template)
11. PE lesson review (parameters/template)
12. Maths problem/function review (parameters/template)
13. School rule review (parameters/template)
14. Do I know you? (template)
15. 3D Report cards
16. Your reaction to your report form
17. 100 language stems
18. Blank daily report (template)